FREE Test Taking Tips Video/DVD Offer

To better serve you, we created videos covering test taking tips that we want to give you for FREE. **These videos cover world-class tips that will help you succeed on your test.**

We just ask that you send us feedback about this product. Please let us know what you thought about it—whether good, bad, or indifferent.

To get your **FREE videos**, you can use the QR code below or email freevideos@studyguideteam.com with "Free Videos" in the subject line and the following information in the body of the email:

    a. The title of your product

    b. Your product rating on a scale of 1-5, with 5 being the highest

    c. Your feedback about the product

If you have any questions or concerns, please don't hesitate to contact us at info@studyguideteam.com.

Thank you!

SSAT and ISEE Middle Level Prep Book 2025-2026

Study Guide and Practice Test for Both Exams
[3rd Edition]

Lydia Morrison

Interested in buying more than 10 copies of our product? Contact us about bulk discounts:
bulkorders@studyguideteam.com

ISBN 13: 9781637759837

Table of Contents

Welcome

Dear Reader,

Welcome to your new Test Prep Books study guide! We are pleased that you chose us to help you prepare for your exam. There are many study options to choose from, and we appreciate you choosing us. Studying can be a daunting task, but we have designed a smart, effective study guide to help prepare you for what lies ahead.

Whether you're a parent helping your child learn and grow, a high school student working hard to get into your dream college, or a nursing student studying for a complex exam, we want to help give you the tools you need to succeed. We hope this study guide gives you the skills and the confidence to thrive, and we can't thank you enough for allowing us to be part of your journey.

In an effort to continue to improve our products, we welcome feedback from our customers. We look forward to hearing from you. Suggestions, success stories, and criticisms can all be communicated by emailing us at info@studyguideteam.com.

Sincerely,
Test Prep Books Team

FREE Videos/DVD OFFER

Doing well on your exam requires both knowing the test content and understanding how to use that knowledge to do well on the test. We offer completely FREE test taking tip videos. **These videos cover world-class tips that you can use to succeed on your test.**

To get your **FREE videos**, you can use the QR code below or email freevideos@studyguideteam.com with "Free Videos" in the subject line and the following information in the body of the email:

    a. The title of your product
    b. Your product rating on a scale of 1-5, with 5 being the highest
    c. Your feedback about the product

If you have any questions or concerns, please don't hesitate to contact us at info@studyguideteam.com.

This material is provided for exam preparation purposes only and does not indicate an endorsement of any specific scientific, political, or religious point of view. © TPB Publishing. You have been licensed one copy of this document for personal use only. Any other reproduction or redistribution is strictly prohibited. All rights reserved.

Quick Overview

As you draw closer to taking your exam, effective preparation becomes more and more important. Thankfully, you have this study guide to help you get ready. Use this guide to help keep your studying on track and refer to it often.

This study guide contains several key sections that will help you be successful on your exam. The guide contains tips for what you should do the night before and the day of the test. Also included are test-taking tips. Knowing the right information is not always enough. Many well-prepared test takers struggle with exams. These tips will help equip you to accurately read, assess, and answer test questions.

A large part of the guide is devoted to showing you what content to expect on the exam and to helping you better understand that content. In this guide are practice test questions so that you can see how well you have grasped the content. Then, answer explanations are provided so that you can understand why you missed certain questions.

Don't try to cram the night before you take your exam. This is not a wise strategy for a few reasons. First, your retention of the information will be low. Your time would be better used by reviewing information you already know rather than trying to learn a lot of new information. Second, you will likely become stressed as you try to gain a large amount of knowledge in a short amount of time. Third, you will be depriving yourself of sleep. So be sure to go to bed at a reasonable time the night before. Being well-rested helps you focus and remain calm.

Be sure to eat a substantial breakfast the morning of the exam. If you are taking the exam in the afternoon, be sure to have a good lunch as well. Being hungry is distracting and can make it difficult to focus. You have hopefully spent lots of time preparing for the exam. Don't let an empty stomach get in the way of success!

When travelling to the testing center, leave earlier than needed. That way, you have a buffer in case you experience any delays. This will help you remain calm and will keep you from missing your appointment time at the testing center.

Be sure to pace yourself during the exam. Don't try to rush through the exam. There is no need to risk performing poorly on the exam just so you can leave the testing center early. Allow yourself to use all of the allotted time if needed.

Remain positive while taking the exam even if you feel like you are performing poorly. Thinking about the content you should have mastered will not help you perform better on the exam.

Once the exam is complete, take some time to relax. Even if you feel that you need to take the exam again, you will be well served by some down time before you begin studying again. It's often easier to convince yourself to study if you know that it will come with a reward!

Test-Taking Strategies

1. Predicting the Answer

When you feel confident in your preparation for a multiple-choice test, try predicting the answer before reading the answer choices. This is especially useful on questions that test objective factual knowledge. By predicting the answer before reading the available choices, you eliminate the possibility that you will be distracted or led astray by an incorrect answer choice. You will feel more confident in your selection if you read the question, predict the answer, and then find your prediction among the answer choices. After using this strategy, be sure to still read all of the answer choices carefully and completely. If you feel unprepared, you should not attempt to predict the answers. This would be a waste of time and an opportunity for your mind to wander in the wrong direction.

2. Reading the Whole Question

Too often, test takers scan a multiple-choice question, recognize a few familiar words, and immediately jump to the answer choices. Test authors are aware of this common impatience, and they will sometimes prey upon it. For instance, a test author might subtly turn the question into a negative, or he or she might redirect the focus of the question right at the end. The only way to avoid falling into these traps is to read the entirety of the question carefully before reading the answer choices.

3. Looking for Wrong Answers

Long and complicated multiple-choice questions can be intimidating. One way to simplify a difficult multiple-choice question is to eliminate all of the answer choices that are clearly wrong. In most sets of answers, there will be at least one selection that can be dismissed right away. If the test is administered on paper, the test taker could draw a line through it to indicate that it may be ignored; otherwise, the test taker will have to perform this operation mentally or on scratch paper. In either case, once the obviously incorrect answers have been eliminated, the remaining choices may be considered. Sometimes identifying the clearly wrong answers will give the test taker some information about the correct answer. For instance, if one of the remaining answer choices is a direct opposite of one of the eliminated answer choices, it may well be the correct answer. The opposite of obviously wrong is obviously right! Of course, this is not always the case. Some answers are obviously incorrect simply because they are irrelevant to the question being asked. Still, identifying and eliminating some incorrect answer choices is a good way to simplify a multiple-choice question.

4. Don't Overanalyze

Anxious test takers often overanalyze questions. When you are nervous, your brain will often run wild, causing you to make associations and discover clues that don't actually exist. If you feel that this may be a problem for you, do whatever you can to slow down during the test. Try taking a deep breath or counting to ten. As you read and consider the question, restrict yourself to the particular words used by the author. Avoid thought tangents about what the author *really* meant, or what he or she was *trying* to say. The only things that matter on a multiple-choice test are the words that are actually in the question. You must avoid reading too much into a multiple-choice question, or supposing that the writer meant something other than what he or she wrote.

5. No Need for Panic

It is wise to learn as many strategies as possible before taking a multiple-choice test, but it is likely that you will come across a few questions for which you simply don't know the answer. In this situation, avoid panicking. Because

3

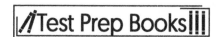
most multiple-choice tests include dozens of questions, the relative value of a single wrong answer is small. As much as possible, you should compartmentalize each question on a multiple-choice test. In other words, you should not allow your feelings about one question to affect your success on the others. When you find a question that you either don't understand or don't know how to answer, just take a deep breath and do your best. Read the entire question slowly and carefully. Try rephrasing the question a couple of different ways. Then, read all of the answer choices carefully. After eliminating obviously wrong answers, make a selection and move on to the next question.

6. Confusing Answer Choices

When working on a difficult multiple-choice question, there may be a tendency to focus on the answer choices that are the easiest to understand. Many people, whether consciously or not, gravitate to the answer choices that require the least concentration, knowledge, and memory. This is a mistake. When you come across an answer

 choice that is confusing, you should give it extra attention. A question might be confusing because you do not know the subject matter to which it refers. If this is the case, don't eliminate the answer before you have affirmatively settled on another. When you come across an answer choice of this type, set it aside as you look at the remaining choices. If you can confidently assert that one of the other choices is correct, you can leave the confusing answer aside. Otherwise, you will need to take a moment to try to better understand the confusing answer choice. Rephrasing is one way to tease out the sense of a confusing answer choice.

7. Your First Instinct

Many people struggle with multiple-choice tests because they overthink the questions. If you have studied sufficiently for the test, you should be prepared to trust your first instinct once you have carefully and completely read the question and all of the answer choices. There is a great deal of research suggesting that the mind can come to the correct conclusion very quickly once it has obtained all of the relevant information. At times, it may seem to you as if your intuition is working faster even than your reasoning mind. This may in fact be true. The knowledge you obtain while studying may be retrieved from your subconscious before you have a chance to work out the associations that support it. Verify your instinct by working out the reasons that it should be trusted.

8. Key Words

Many test takers struggle with multiple-choice questions because they have poor reading comprehension skills. Quickly reading and understanding a multiple-choice question requires a mixture of skill and experience. To help with this, try jotting down a few key words and phrases on a piece of scrap paper. Doing this concentrates the process of reading and forces the mind to weigh the relative importance of the question's parts. In selecting words and phrases to write down, the test taker thinks about the question more deeply and carefully. This is especially true for multiple-choice questions that are preceded by a long prompt.

4

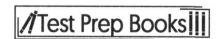

9. Subtle Negatives

One of the oldest tricks in the multiple-choice test writer's book is to subtly reverse the meaning of a question with a word like *not* or *except*. If you are not paying attention to each word in the question, you can easily be led astray by this trick. For instance, a common question format is, "Which of the following is…?" Obviously, if the question instead is, "Which of the following is not…?," then the answer will be quite different. Even worse, the test makers are aware of the potential for this mistake and will include one answer choice that would be correct if the question were not negated or reversed. A test taker who misses the reversal will find what he or she believes to be a correct answer and will be so confident that he or she will fail to reread the question and discover the original error. The only way to avoid this is to practice a wide variety of multiple-choice questions and to pay close attention to each and every word.

10. Reading Every Answer Choice

It may seem obvious, but you should always read every one of the answer choices! Too many test takers fall into the habit of scanning the question and assuming that they understand the question because they recognize a few key words. From there, they pick the first answer choice that answers the question they believe they have read. Test takers who read all of the answer choices might discover that one of the latter answer choices is actually *more* correct. Moreover, reading all of the answer choices can remind you of facts related to the question that can help you arrive at the correct answer. Sometimes, a misstatement or incorrect detail in one of the latter answer choices will trigger your memory of the subject and will enable you to find the right answer. Failing to read all of the answer choices is like not reading all of the items on a restaurant menu: you might miss out on the perfect choice.

11. Spot the Hedges

One of the keys to success on multiple-choice tests is paying close attention to every word. This is never truer than with words like *almost*, *most*, *some*, and *sometimes*. These words are called "hedges" because they indicate that a statement is not totally true or not true in every place and time. An absolute statement will contain no hedges, but in many subjects, the answers are not always straightforward or absolute. There are always exceptions to the rules

in these subjects. For this reason, you should favor those multiple-choice questions that contain hedging language. The presence of qualifying words indicates that the author is taking special care with his or her words, which is certainly important when composing the right answer. After all, there are many ways to be wrong, but there is only one way to be right! For this reason, it is wise to avoid answers that are absolute when taking a multiple-choice test. An absolute answer is one that says things are either all one way or all another. They often include words like *every*, *always*, *best*, and *never*. If you are taking a multiple-choice test in a subject that doesn't lend itself to absolute answers, be on your guard if you see any of these words.

12. Long Answers

In many subject areas, the answers are not simple. As already mentioned, the right answer often requires hedges. Another common feature of the answers to a complex or subjective question are qualifying clauses, which are groups of words that subtly modify the meaning of the sentence. If the question or answer choice describes a rule to which there are exceptions or the subject matter is complicated, ambiguous, or confusing, the correct answer will require many words in order to be expressed clearly and accurately. In essence, you should not be deterred by answer choices that seem excessively long. Oftentimes, the author of the text will not be able to write the correct answer without offering some qualifications and modifications. Your job is to read the answer choices thoroughly and completely and to select the one that most accurately and precisely answers the question.

13. Restating to Understand

Sometimes, a question on a multiple-choice test is difficult not because of what it asks but because of how it is written. If this is the case, restate the question or answer choice in different words. This process serves a couple of important purposes. First, it forces you to concentrate on the core of the question. In order to rephrase the question accurately, you have to understand it well. Rephrasing the question will concentrate your mind on the key words and ideas. Second, it will present the information to your mind in a fresh way. This process may trigger your memory and render some useful scrap of information picked up while studying.

14. True Statements

Sometimes an answer choice will be true in itself, but it does not answer the question. This is one of the main reasons why it is essential to read the question carefully and completely before proceeding to the answer choices. Too often, test takers skip ahead to the answer choices and look for true statements. Having found one of these, they are content to select it without reference to the question above. The savvy test taker will always read the entire question before turning to the answer choices. Then, having settled on a correct answer choice, he or she will refer to the original question and ensure that the selected answer is relevant. The mistake of choosing a correct-but-irrelevant answer choice is especially common on questions related to specific pieces of objective knowledge.

15. No Patterns

One of the more dangerous ideas that circulates about multiple-choice tests is that the correct answers tend to fall into patterns. These erroneous ideas range from a belief that B and C are the most common right answers, to the idea that an unprepared test-taker should answer "A-B-A-C-A-D-A-B-A." It cannot be emphasized enough that pattern-seeking of this type is exactly the WRONG way to approach a multiple-choice test. To begin with, it is highly unlikely that the test maker will plot the correct answers according to some predetermined pattern. The questions are scrambled and delivered in a random order. Furthermore, even if the test maker was following a pattern in the assignation of correct answers, there is no reason why the test taker would know which pattern he or she was using. Any attempt to discern a pattern in the answer choices is a waste of time and a distraction from the real work of taking the test. A test taker would be much better served by extra preparation before the test than by reliance on a pattern in the answers.

Introduction to This Book

Thank you for choosing this book for preparation. The contents of this book cover both the SSAT Middle Level and ISEE Middle Level exams. This format works well because much of the material on the exams overlap. However, there are some differences between the two exams When a section of this book only applies to one exam that is noted with [SSAT] or [ISEE] following the section header. If you are preparing for the ISEE then you can skip the sections that say "[SSAT]". Likewise, if you are preparing for the SSAT then you can skip the sections that say "[ISEE]".

Information about the SSAT Middle Level Exam

Function of the Test

The Secondary School Admission Test (SSAT) is a standardized test used for students that are applying to an independent or private school. The Middle Level SSAT is administered to students currently in grades 5 through 7, and it evaluates writing, math, reading, and verbal skills. The test is used in the United States and is also available in several other countries throughout the world to determine if students have the necessary skills for success in a college preparatory program.

Test Administration

The standard SSAT is administered in groups and offered on six Saturdays throughout the year. The standard test is available at hundreds of testing centers in the US and locations throughout the world.

Closed Standard Test

If you are testing with a member school that is not open to the public, you will take a "closed" Standard test, which requires an access code obtained directly from the school for registration.

Open Standard Test

An open Standard test is an administration that is open to the general public. No access code is required for an Open Standard test.

Limited Standard Test

Sunday testing is available to those who observe religious events on Saturdays, but must be approved before registration.

Prometric Test

Middle Level SSAT test-takers can opt to take the Prometric Test. This is a computer-based SSAT administered at a Prometric Test Center.

At-Home SSAT

Middle Level SSAT test-takers may also opt take a SSAT at Home. This is also a computer-based SSAT that is administered online and taken at a student's home or other suitable location.

The SSAT Flex Test

A Flex test is an in-person paper exam that can be taken any day except when the Standard test is administered. The Flex test may be provided in an open or closed format. Same as the Standard test, Open Flex tests are open to the general public and do not require an access code. The Closed Flex test requires an access code.

Students may repeat the standard test without penalty. Students must create an account on the SSAT website in order to register. This account also allows students to print their admission tickets and receive their test scores. Registration opens about 10 weeks prior to a testing date. Late registration begins 3 weeks before the test date and rush registration starts 10 days before the test date. Late and rush registrations incur additional fees.

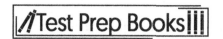

Testing accommodations are available for students with disabilities. Students requiring accommodations must apply and be approved before registering for the test. Approval is only required once in an academic year. The official guidelines for accommodations can be accessed on the SSAT.org website.

Test Format

The Middle Level SSAT consists of multiple-choice questions in Quantitative (Math), Verbal, Reading Comprehension, and Experimental sections, and a writing sample. The writing sample is not scored, but is sent to prospective schools to demonstrate a student's writing ability.

The writing sample asks the student to choose between two writing prompts—a traditional essay or a creative writing stimulus—and to write an original essay or story based on the prompt. The Quantitative section is broken down into two parts, each with 25 questions in the areas of number concepts, geometry, algebra, and probability. A calculator is not permitted. The Verbal section includes 60 questions: 30 synonyms and 30 analogies. The Reading Comprehension section includes a total of 40 questions relating to several short passages that range from approximately 250-350 words. The passages may be pulled from literary fiction, social sciences, humanities, and sciences and the questions focus mainly on reading comprehension skills, including inferences, identifying the main idea, and determining the author's purpose. The Experimental section includes 16 questions (6 Verbal, 5 Reading, and 5 Quantitative) in order to test their reliability for SSAT forms to be used in the future. The Experimental section is not scored. The testing period and sections are broken down as follows:

Section	Number of Questions	Question Type	Time Allotted
Writing Sample	1	Written Response	25 minutes
Break			10 minutes
Quantitative (Part 1)	25	Multiple Choice	30 minutes
Reading	40	Multiple Choice	40 minutes
Break			10 minutes
Verbal	60	Multiple Choice	30 minutes
Quantitative (Part 2)	25	Multiple Choice	30 minutes
Experimental	16	Multiple Choice	15 minutes

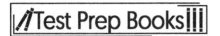

Scoring

In the Middle Level SSAT, students are given one point for each correct answer, and they lose a quarter of a point for each incorrect answer. Unanswered questions do not affect the score either way.

A free scoring report is available online through a student's SSAT account roughly 2 weeks after the test date. The report includes a narrative explanation of the scores, along with a raw score, a scaled score, percentile rank, and total scaled score. The possible scaled score ranges from 440 – 710 per section, and the percentile rank is from 1 – 99. The total scaled score range is 1320 – 2130, with a mid-point of 1725.

The SSAT is a norm-referenced test, meaning that the score is compared to a norm group of test takers' scores from the last 3 years. The score report includes the student's scores, as well as the average norm scores in each section for comparison. The percentile rank shows how a student performed relative to the norm group. For example, if a student's percentile is 80, it means he or she scored the same or better than 80% of those in the norm group. Schools use many factors to select students for admission, so a "good score" or passing score is difficult to determine.

Information about the ISEE Middle Level Exam

Function of the Test

The Independent School Entrance Exam (ISEE) middle level is an entrance exam for grades 7 and 8 for independent schools across the U.S and abroad, developed and facilitated by the Educational Records Bureau (ERB). Complete scores are sent to the school of choice for application review. Although schools take the score into consideration, the score is not the only indication for acceptance.

Test Administration

The ISEE is offered in three separate testing seasons throughout the year through Prometric testing centers, approved ERB member school test sites, or ERB's New York City office. Testing seasons are Fall (August through November), Winter (December through March), and Spring/Summer (April through July). Students must register well before the test date, as registration closes two weeks before the test is given. For retesting, students may retake the ISEE up to 3 times in a 12-month admission period, but only once per testing season.

Test Format

Students must arrive at the testing center well before the test begins. Those who arrive late are not permitted into the testing room and must reschedule their exam. Personal items are not allowed in the exam room, including cell phones, paper, rulers, watches, compasses, etc. Paper testing permits students to bring four #2 pencils and two pens with either blue or black ink. Two ten-minute breaks are given during the exam. The first break is after the Quantitative Reasoning section. The second break is after the Mathematics Achievement section.

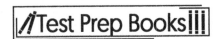

The ISEE middle level is for students entering seventh or eighth grade, and includes Verbal Reasoning, Quantitative Reasoning, Reading Comprehension, Mathematics Achievement, and an essay, in that order. Below is a table with more details on each section:

Section	Questions	Time
Verbal Reasoning	40	20 minutes
Quantitative Reasoning	37	35 minutes
Reading Comprehension	36	35 minutes
Mathematics Achievement	47	40 minutes
Essay	1 prompt	
Total		**160 minutes**

Scoring

Students should try to narrow down correct answers, as scores are determined by the number of questions answered correctly. There is no score difference between an omitted answer and an incorrect answer, and therefore no guessing penalty. Students are compared to fellow students by grade within the previous three years by a percentile ranking on the score report. For paper tests, scores are sent to the Individual Student Report (ISR) and an email will be sent when scores are ready. For online tests, score reports will post 3 to 5 days after the test. Essays are released only to ERB schools and are not scored.

Scoring comes with a raw score and a scaled score. Raw scores might be something like 35/40 for the Verbal Reasoning section, showing the amount of questions guessed correctly. Scaled scores have been converted to a higher number and show a range from 760 to 940.

Study Prep Plan for the SSAT Middle Level

1   **Schedule -** Use one of our study schedules below or come up with one of your own.

2   **Relax -** Test anxiety can hurt even the best students. There are many ways to reduce stress. Find the one that works best for you.

3   **Execute -** Once you have a good plan in place, be sure to stick to it.

One Week Study Schedule

Day	Topic
Day 1	Writing Sample [SSAT]
Day 2	Fractions
Day 3	Geometry/Measurement
Day 4	Reading Comprehension
Day 5	Verbal Section
Day 6	SSAT Practice Test
Day 7	Take Your Exam!

Two Week Study Schedule

Day	Topic	Day	Topic
Day 1	Writing Sample [SSAT]	Day 8	Reading Comprehension
Day 2	Estimation	Day 9	Tone/Style/Figurative Language
Day 3	Decimals	Day 10	Verbal Section
Day 4	Algebra	Day 11	Vocabulary
Day 5	Geometry/ Measurement	Day 12	SSAT Practice Test
Day 6	Surface Area and Volume of Geometric...	Day 13	SSAT Answer Explanations
Day 7	Data Analysis/ Probability	Day 14	Take Your Exam!

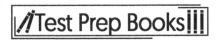

	One Month Study Schedule				
Day 1	Writing Sample [SSAT]	Day 11	Geometry/Measurement	Day 21	Tone/Style/Figurative Language
Day 2	Practice Writing Sample [SSAT]	Day 12	Surface Area and Volume of Geometric Shapes	Day 22	Practice Questions
Day 3	Quantitative Reasoning	Day 13	Cone	Day 23	Verbal Section
Day 4	Ratio Reasoning	Day 14	Measuring Lengths of Objects	Day 24	Verbal Analogies [SSAT]
Day 5	Estimation	Day 15	Locating Ordered Pairs in All Four Quadrants...	Day 25	Vocabulary
Day 6	Decimals	Day 16	Data Analysis/Probability	Day 26	Practice Questions
Day 7	Converting Fractions, Decimals, and...	Day 17	Interpreting Displays of Data	Day 27	Essay [ISEE]
Day 8	Representing Fractions, Decimals...	Day 18	Practice Questions	Day 28	SSAT Practice Test
Day 9	Algebra	Day 19	Reading Comprehension	Day 29	SSAT Answer Explanations
Day 10	Multi-step One-Variable Linear Equations...	Day 20	Deriving the Meaning of a Word or Phrase from its Context	Day 30	Take Your Exam!

Build your own prep plan by visiting:
testprepbooks.com/prep

14

Study Prep Plan for the ISEE Middle Level

1 **Schedule -** Use one of our study schedules below or come up with one of your own.

2 **Relax -** Test anxiety can hurt even the best students. There are many ways to reduce stress. Find the one that works best for you.

3 **Execute -** Once you have a good plan in place, be sure to stick to it.

One Week Study Schedule

Day 1	Quantitative Reasoning
Day 2	Basic Concepts of Number Theory [ISEE]
Day 3	Geometry/Measurement
Day 4	Reading Comprehension
Day 5	Verbal Section
Day 6	ISEE Practice Test
Day 7	Take Your Exam!

Two Week Study Schedule

Day 1	Quantitative Reasoning	Day 8	Reading Comprehension
Day 2	Determining the Reasonableness of...	Day 9	Tone/Style/Figurative Language
Day 3	Fractions	Day 10	Verbal Section
Day 4	Algebra	Day 11	Practice Questions
Day 5	Geometry/Measurement	Day 12	ISEE Practice Test
Day 6	Surface Area and Volume of Geometric...	Day 13	ISEE Answer Explanations
Day 7	Data Analysis/Probability	Day 14	Take Your Exam!

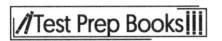

One Month Study Schedule					
Day 1	Quantitative Reasoning	Day 11	Measuring Lengths of Objects	Day 21	Practice Questions
Day 2	Basic Concepts of Addition, Subtraction...	Day 12	Locating Ordered Pairs in All Four Quadrants...	Day 22	Verbal Section
Day 3	Determining the Reasonableness of...	Day 13	Data Analysis/ Probability	Day 23	Vocabulary
Day 4	Fractions	Day 14	Graphical Representation of Data	Day 24	Practice Questions
Day 5	Converting Fractions, Decimals, and...	Day 15	Practice Questions	Day 25	Essay [ISEE]
Day 6	Representing Fractions, Decimals...	Day 16	Reading Comprehension	Day 26	Developing a Well-Organized Paragraph
Day 7	Algebra	Day 17	Deriving the Meaning of a Word or Phrase...	Day 27	Practice Essay [ISEE]
Day 8	Geometry/ Measurement	Day 18	Organization/Logic [ISEE]	Day 28	ISEE Practice Test
Day 9	Perimeter and Area of Geometric Shapes	Day 19	Opinions, Facts, and Fallacies	Day 29	ISEE Answer Explanations
Day 10	Surface Area and Volume of Geometric Shapes	Day 20	Tone/Style/Figurative Language	Day 30	Take Your Exam!

Build your own prep plan by visiting:

testprepbooks.com/prep

16

As you study for your test, we'd like to take the opportunity to remind you that you are capable of great things! With the right tools and dedication, you truly can do anything you set your mind to. The fact that you are holding this book right now shows how committed you are. In case no one has told you lately, you've got this! Our intention behind including this coloring page is to give you the chance to take some time to engage your creative side when you need a little brain-break from studying. As a company, we want to encourage people like you to achieve their dreams by providing good quality study materials for the tests and certifications that improve careers and change lives. As individuals, many of us have taken such tests in our careers, and we know how challenging this process can be. While we can't come alongside you and cheer you on personally, we can offer you the space to recall your purpose, reconnect with your passion, and refresh your brain through an artistic practice. We wish you every success, and happy studying!

Math Reference Sheet

Symbol	Phrase
+	added to, increased by, sum of, more than
-	decreased by, difference between, less than, take away
×	multiplied by, 3 (4, 5 . . .) times as large, product of
÷	divided by, quotient of, half (third, etc.) of
=	is, the same as, results in, as much as
x, t, n, etc.	a variable which is an unknown value or quantity
<	is under, is below, smaller than, beneath
>	is above, is over, bigger than, exceeds
≤	no more than, at most, maximum; less than or equal to
≥	no less than, at least, minimum; greater than or equal to
√	square root of, exponent divided by 2

Geometry	Description
$P = 2l + 2w$	for perimeter of a rectangle
$P = 4 \times s$	for perimeter of a square
$P = a + b + c$	for perimeter of a triangle
$A = \frac{1}{2} \times b \times h = \frac{bh}{2}$	for area of a triangle
$A = b \times h$	for area of a parallelogram
$A = \frac{1}{2} \times h(b_1 + b_2)$	for area of a trapezoid
$A = \frac{1}{2} \times a \times P$	for area of a regular polygon
$C = 2 \times \pi \times r$	for circumference (perimeter) of a circle
$A = \pi \times r^2$	for area of a circle
$c^2 = a^2 + b^2; c = \sqrt{a^2 + b^2}$	for finding the hypotenuse of a right triangle
$SA = 2xy + 2yz + 2xz$	for finding surface area
$V = \frac{1}{3}xyh$	for finding volume of a rectangular pyramid
$V = \frac{4}{3}\pi r^3; \frac{1}{3}\pi r^2 h; \pi r^2 h$	for volume of a sphere; a cone; and a cylinder

Radical Expressions	Description
$\sqrt[n]{a} = a^{\frac{1}{n}}; \sqrt[n]{a^m} = (\sqrt[n]{a})^m = a^{\frac{m}{n}}$	a is the radicand, n is the index, m is the exponent
$\sqrt{x^2} = (x^2)^{\frac{1}{2}} = x$	to convert square root to exponent
$a^m \times a^n = a^{m+n}$	multiplying radicands with exponents
$(a^m)^n = a^{m \times n}$	multiplying exponents
$(a \times b)^m = a^m \times b^m$	parentheses with exponents

Property	Addition	Multiplication
Commutative	$a + b = b + a$	$a \times b = b \times a$
Associative	$(a + b) + c = a + (b + c)$	$(a \times b) \times c = a \times (b \times c)$
Identity	$a + 0 = a; 0 + a = a$	$a \times 1 = a; 1 \times a = a$
Inverse	$a + (-a) = 0$	$a \times \frac{1}{a} = 1; a \neq 0$
Distributive		$a(b + c) = ab + ac$

Data	Description
Mean	equal to the total of the values of a data set, divided by the number of elements in the data set
Median	middle value in an odd number of ordered values of a data set, or the mean of the two middle values in an even number of ordered values in a data set
Mode	the value that appears most often
Range	the difference between the highest and the lowest values in the set

Graphing	Description
(x, y)	ordered pair, plot points in a graph
$y = mx + b$	slope-intercept form; m represents the slope of the line and b represents the y-intercept
$f(x)$	read as f of x, which means it is a function of x
(x_2, y_2) and (x_2, y_2)	two ordered pairs used to determine the slope of a line
$m = \frac{y_2 - y_1}{x_2 - x_1}$	to find the slope of the line, m, for ordered pairs
$Ax + By = C$	standard form of an equation, also for solving a system of equations through the elimination method
$M = (\frac{x_1 + x_2}{2}, \frac{y_1 + y_2}{2})$	for finding the midpoint of an ordered pair
$y = ax^2 + bx + c$	quadratic function for a parabola
$y = a(x - h)^2 + k$	quadratic function for a parabola with vertex
$y = ab^x; y = a \times b^x$	function for exponential curve
$y = ax^2 + bx + c$	standard form of a quadratic function
$x = \frac{-b}{2a}$	for finding axis of symmetry in a parabola; given quadratic formula in standard form
$f = \sqrt{\frac{\Sigma(x - \bar{x})^2}{n - 1}}$	function for standard deviation of the sample; where $\bar{x}$ = sample mean and n = sample size

Proportions and Percentage	Description
$\frac{gallons}{cost} = \frac{gallons}{cost} : \frac{7\ gallons}{\$14.70} = \frac{x}{\$20}$	written as equal ratios with a variable representing the missing quantity
$\frac{y_1}{x_1} = \frac{y_2}{x_2}$	for direct proportions
$(y_1)(x_1) = (y_2)(x_2)$	for indirect proportions
$\frac{change}{original\ value} \times 100 = percent\ change$	for finding percentage change in value
$\frac{new\ quantity - old\ quantity}{old\ quantity} \times 100$	for calculating the increase or decrease in percentage

18

Writing Sample [SSAT]

The Middle Level SSAT begins with a 25-mintue writing sample section where test takers are asked to write a creative story based on one of two prompts to choose from. While this section is not scored, the writing sample can be provided with the score report to each admission's office for an additional fee. This section gives test takers the opportunity to show their writing ability as well as demonstrate creativity and self-expression. Test takers should be sure that their stories have a beginning, middle, and end.

Planning should occur after looking at the picture or reading the prompt but before beginning any writing. This brainstorming stage is when writers consider their purpose and think of ideas that they can use in their writing. Graphic organizers like story webs are excellent tools to use during the planning stage. Graphic organizers can help connect the writing purpose to supporting details, and they can help begin the process of structuring the writing piece.

POWER Strategy for Writing

The POWER strategy helps writers focus and be successful during the writing process.

The POWER strategy stands for the following:

- Prewriting or Planning
- Organizing
- Writing a first draft
- Editing the writing
- Revising and rewriting

Prewriting
During the Prewriting and Planning phase, writers learn to consider their audience and purpose for the writing assignment. Then they compile information they wish to include in the piece of writing from their background knowledge and/or new sources.

Organizing
Next, writers decide on the organizational structure of their writing project. There are many types of organizational structures, but the common ones are: story/narrative, informative, opinion, persuasive, compare and contrast, explanatory, and problem/solution formats.

Writing
The following are characteristics that make writing readable and effective no matter what genre of writing is being used:

- Ideas
- Organization
- Voice
- Word choice
- Sentence fluency
- Proper Writing Conventions
- Presentation

19

Ideas

This refers to the content of the writing. Writers should select an important topic for their writing or focus correctly on the topic depicted in the picture or prompt. They should narrow down and focus their idea, remembering that during the test, they only have fifteen minutes to plan and write, and that time can go quickly! Then they learn to develop and elaborate on the specific idea and choose the information and details that best convey the idea to others.

Organization

Many writers, especially during a test, are inclined to jump into their writing without a clear direction for where it is going. Organization helps plan a successful piece of writing.

Writers must choose an organizational strategy or purpose for the writing and build the details upon that structure. There are many purposes for writing, and they all have slightly different frameworks. Writers can learn to effectively organize their writing so it makes sense to the reader.

- Introduction (beginning): Writers should invite the reader into their work with an effective introduction. They should restate the prompt or topic sentence in their own words so that readers know what they are going to read about.

- Body (middle): The body is where the main thoughts and ideas that were developed during brainstorming are put together. Thoughtful transitions between ideas and key points help keep readers engaged and understanding. Writers should create logical and purposeful sequences of ideas.

- Conclusion (end): Writers should include a powerful conclusion to their piece that summarizes the information but leaves the reader with something to think about.

Voice

This characteristic gives the writing a sense of individuality and connection to the author. It shows that the writing is meaningful and that the author cares about it. It is what makes the writing uniquely the author's own. It is how the reader begins to know the author and what he or she "sounds like."

Word Choice

The right word choice helps an author communicate their ideas in a text that is clear, rich, and enjoyable for readers. If the work is narrative, the words create images in the mind's eye. If the work is descriptive, the words clarify and expand thoughts and ideas. If the work is an opinion piece, the words give new perspective and invite thought. Writers should choose descriptive vocabulary and language that is accurate, concise, precise, and lively.

Sentence Fluency

When sentences are built to fit together and move with one another to create writing that is easy to read aloud, the author has written with fluency. Sentences and paragraphs start and stop in just the right places so that the writing moves well. Sentences should have a variety of structures and lengths.

Proper Writing Conventions

Writers should make their writing clear and understandable through the use of proper grammar, spelling, capitalization, and punctuation.

Presentation

Writers should try to make their work inviting and accessible to the reader of the end product. Writers show they care about their writing when it is neat and readable.

20

Evaluating
In this stage, writers reread the writing and note the segments that are particularly strong or need improvement.

Revising and Rewriting
Finally, the writer incorporates any changes he or she wishes to make based on the evaluating process. Then writers rewrite the piece into a final draft however it best fits the audience and purpose of the writing.

Tips for the Writing Section

- Don't panic! This section isn't scored. It's just a great way to show teachers how smart you are and how well you can tell a story and write. You can do it!

- Use your time well. Fifteen minutes is quick! It is shorter than almost every TV show. Don't spend too much time doing any one thing. Try to brainstorm briefly and then get writing. Leave a few minutes to read it over and correct any spelling mistakes or confusing parts.

- Be yourself! You are smart and interesting and teachers want to get to know you and your unique ideas. Don't feel pressured to use big vocabulary words if you aren't positive what they mean. You will be more understandable if you use the right word, not the fanciest word.

Information for the ISEE essay portion of the test can be found at the end of this guide.

21

Practice Writing Sample [SSAT]

Select one of the following two-story starters and write a creative story in the space provided. Make sure that your story has a beginning, middle, and end and is interesting for readers.

- The snow continued to fall for four full days.

- I waited and waited but my luggage did not make it off the plane.

Quantitative Reasoning

Number Concepts and Operations

Arithmetic Word Problems (Percent, Ratio)

Word problems present the opportunity to relate mathematical concepts learned in the classroom into real-world situations. These types of problems are situations in which some parts of the problem are known and at least one part is unknown.

There are three types of instances in which something can be unknown: the starting point, the modification, or the final result can all be missing from the provided information.

- For an addition problem, the modification is the quantity of a new amount added to the starting point.
- For a subtraction problem, the modification is the quantity taken away from the starting point.

Keywords in the word problems can signal what type of operation needs to be used to solve the problem. Words such as *total, increased, combined*, and *more* indicate that addition is needed. Words such as *difference, decreased*, and *minus* indicate that subtraction is needed.

Regarding addition, the given equation is $3 + 7 = 10$

The number 3 is the starting point. 7 is the modification, and 10 is the result from adding a new amount to the starting point. Different word problems can arise from this same equation, depending on which value is the unknown. For example, here are three problems:

- If a boy had three pencils and was given seven more, how many would he have in total?
- If a boy had three pencils and a girl gave him more so that he had ten in total, how many was he given?
- A boy was given seven pencils so that he had ten in total. How many did he start with?

All three problems involve the same equation, and determining which part of the equation is missing is the key to solving each word problem. The missing answers would be 10, 7, and 3, respectively.

In terms of subtraction, the same three scenarios can occur. The given equation is $6 - 4 = 2$.

The number 6 is the starting point, 4 is the modification, and 2 is the new amount that is the result from taking away an amount from the starting point. Again, different types of word problems can arise from this equation. For example, here are three possible problems:

- If a girl had six quarters and four were taken away, how many would be left over?
- If a girl had six quarters, purchased a pencil, and had two quarters left over, how many did she pay with?
- If a girl paid for a pencil with four quarters and had two quarters left over, how many did she have to start with?

The three question types follow the structure of the addition word problems, and determining whether the starting point, the modification, or the final result is missing is the goal in solving the problem. The missing answers would be 2, 4, and 6, respectively.

The three addition problems and the three subtraction word problems can be solved by using a picture, a number line, or an algebraic equation. If an equation is used, a question mark can be utilized to represent the unknown

23

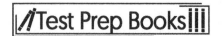

quantity. For example, $6 - 2 =?$ can be written to show that the missing value is the result. Using equation form visually indicates what portion of the addition or subtraction problem is the missing value.

Similar instances can be seen in word problems involving multiplication and division. Key words within a multiplication problem involve *times, product, doubled,* and *tripled.* Key words within a division problem involve *split, quotient, divided, shared, groups,* and *half.* Like addition and subtraction, multiplication and division problems also have three different types of missing values.

Multiplication consists of a specific number of groups having the same size, the quantity of items within each group, and the total quantity within all groups. Therefore, each one of these amounts can be the missing value.

For example, the given equation is $5 \times 3 = 15$.

5 and 3 are interchangeable, so either amount can be the number of groups or the quantity of items within each group. 15 is the total number of items. Again, different types of word problems can arise from this equation. For example, here are three problems:

- If a classroom is serving 5 different types of apples for lunch and has three apples of each type, how many total apples are there to give to the students?
- If a classroom has 15 apples with 5 different types, how many of each type are there?
- If a classroom has 15 apples with 3 of each type, how many types are there to choose from?

Each question involves using the same equation to solve, and it is imperative to decide which part of the equation is the missing value. The answers to the problems are 15, 3, and 5, respectively.

Similar to multiplication, division problems involve a total amount, a number of groups having the same size, and a number of items within each group. The difference between multiplication and division is that the starting point is the total amount, which then gets divided into equal quantities.

For example, the equation is $15 \div 5 = 3$.

15 is the total number of items, which is being divided into 5 different groups. In order to do so, 3 items go into each group. Also, 5 and 3 are interchangeable, so the 15 items could be divided into 3 groups of 5 items each. Therefore, different types of word problems can arise from this equation depending on which value is unknown. For example, here are three types of problems:

- A boy needs 48 pieces of chalk. If there are 8 pieces in each box, how many boxes should he buy?
- A boy has 48 pieces of chalk. If each box has 6 pieces in it, how many boxes did he buy?
- A boy has partitioned all of his chalk into 8 piles, with 6 pieces in each pile. How many pieces does he have in total?

Each one of these questions involves the same equation, and the third question can easily utilize the multiplication equation $8 \times 6 =?$ instead of division. The answers are 6, 8, and 48, respectively.

Word problems can appear daunting, but don't let the verbiage psyche you out. No matter the scenario or specifics, the key to answering them is to translate the words into a math problem. Always keep in mind what the question is asking and what operations could lead to that answer.

Word problems involving elapsed time, money, length, volume, and mass require:

- determining which operations (addition, subtraction, multiplication, and division) should be performed, and
- using and/or converting the proper unit for the scenario.

24

The following table lists key words which can be used to indicate the proper operation:

Addition	Sum, total, in all, combined, increase of, more than, added to
Subtraction	Difference, change, remaining, less than, decreased by
Multiplication	Product, times, twice, triple, each
Division	Quotient, goes into, per, evenly, divided by half, divided by third, split

If a question asks to give words to a mathematical expression and says "equals," then an $=$ sign must be included in the answer. Similarly, "less than or equal to" is expressed by the inequality symbol $\leq$, and "greater than or equal to" is expressed as $\geq$. Furthermore, "less than" is represented by $<$, and "greater than" is expressed by $>$.

Example:

A store is having a spring sale, where everything is 70% off. You have $45.00 to spend. A jacket is regularly priced at $80.00. Do you have enough to buy the jacket and a pair of gloves, regularly priced at $20.00?

There are two ways to approach this.

Method 1:

Set up the equations to find the sale prices: the original price minus the amount discounted.

$$\$80.00 - (\$80.00(0.70)) = sale\ cost\ of\ the\ jacket$$

$$\$20.00 - (\$20.00(0.70)) = sale\ cost\ of\ the\ gloves$$

Solve for the sale cost.

$$\$24.00 = sale\ cost\ of\ the\ jacket$$

$$\$6.00 = sale\ cost\ of\ the\ gloves$$

Determine if you have enough money for both.

$$\$24.00 + \$6.00 = total\ sale\ cost$$

$30.00 is less than $45.00, so you can afford to purchase both.

Method 2:

Determine the percent of the original price that you will pay.

$$100\% - 70\% = 30\%$$

Set up the equations to find the sale prices.

$$\$80.00(0.30) = cost\ of\ the\ jacket$$

$$\$20.00(0.30) = cost\ of\ the\ gloves$$

Solve.

$$\$24.00 = cost\ of\ the\ jacket$$

$$\$6.00 = cost\ of\ the\ gloves$$

Determine if you have enough money for both.

$$\$24.00 + \$6.00 = total\ sale\ cost$$

$30.00 is less than $45.00, so you can afford to purchase both.

Example:

Mary and Dottie team up to mow neighborhood lawns. If Mary mows 2 lawns per hour and the two of them can mow 17.5 lawns in 5 hours, how many lawns does Dottie mow per hour?

Given rate for Mary.

$$Mary = \frac{2\ lawns}{1\ hour}$$

Unknown rate of D for Dottie.

$$Dottie = \frac{D\ lawns}{1\ hour}$$

Given rate for both.

$$Total\ mowed\ together = \frac{17.5\ lawns}{5\ hours}$$

Set up the equation for what is being asked.

$$Mary + Dottie = total\ together$$

Fill in the givens.

$$2 + D = \frac{17.5}{5}$$

Divide.

$$2 + D = 3.5$$

Subtract 2 from both sides to isolate the variable.

$$2 - 2 + D = 3.5 + 2$$

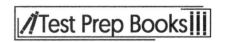

Solve and label Dottie's mowing rate.

$$D = 1.5 \text{ lawns per hour}$$

Identifying and utilizing the proper units for the scenario requires knowing how to apply the conversion rates for money, length, volume, and mass. For example, given a scenario which requires subtracting 8 inches from $2\frac{1}{2}$ feet, both values should first be expressed in the same unit (they could be expressed $\frac{2}{3}$ ft & $2\frac{1}{2}$ ft, or 8in and 30in). The desired unit for the answer may also require converting back to another unit.

Consider the following scenario: A parking area along the river is only wide enough to fit one row of cars and is $\frac{1}{2}$ kilometers long. The average space needed per car is 5 meters. How many cars can be parked along the river? First, all measurements should be converted to similar units: $\frac{1}{2}$ km = 500 m. The operation(s) needed should be identified. Because the problem asks for the number of cars, the total space should be divided by the space per car. Five-hundred meters divided by five meters per car yields a total of 100 cars. Written as an expression, the meters unit cancels and the cars unit is left: $\frac{500 \text{ m}}{5 \text{ m/car}}$ the same as $500 \text{ m} \times \frac{1 \text{ car}}{5 \text{ m}}$ yields 100 cars.

When dealing with problems involving elapsed time, breaking the problem down into workable parts is helpful. For example, suppose the length of time between 1:15pm and 3:45pm must be determined. From 1:15pm to 2:00pm is 45 minutes (knowing there are 60 minutes in an hour). From 2:00pm to 3:00pm is 1 hour. From 3:00pm to 3:45pm is 45 minutes. The total elapsed time is 45 minutes plus 1 hour plus 45 minutes. This sum produces 1 hour and 90 minutes. 90 minutes is over an hour, so this is converted to1 hour (60 minutes) and 30 minutes. The total elapsed time can now be expressed as 2 hours and 30 minutes.

The following word problem resembles one of the question types most frequently encountered on the exam.

Working with Money
Walter's Coffee Shop sells a variety of drinks and breakfast treats.

Price List		Costs	
Hot Coffee	$2.00	Hot Coffee	$0.25
Slow Drip Iced Coffee	$3.00	Slow Drip Iced Coffee	$0.75
Latte	$4.00	Latte	$1.00
Muffins	$2.00	Muffins	$1.00
Crepe	$4.00	Crepe	$2.00
Egg Sandwich	$5.00	Egg Sandwich	$3.00

Walter's utilities, rent, and labor costs him $500 per day. Today, Walter sold 200 hot coffees, 100 slow drip iced coffees, 50 lattes, 75 muffins, 45 crepes, and 60 egg sandwiches. What was Walter's total profit today?

To accurately answer this type of question, determine the total cost of making his drinks and treats, then determine how much revenue he earned from selling those products. After arriving at these two totals, the profit is measured by deducting the total cost from the total revenue.

Walter's costs for today:

Item	Quantity	Cost Per Unit	Total Cost
Hot Coffee	200	$0.25	$50
Slow-Drip Iced Coffee	100	$0.75	$75
Latte	50	$1.00	$50
Muffin	75	$1.00	$75
Crepe	45	$2.00	$90
Egg Sandwich	60	$3.00	$180
Utilities, rent, and labor			$500
Total Costs			$1,020

Walter's revenue for today:

Item	Quantity	Revenue Per Unit	Total Revenue
Hot Coffee	200	$2.00	$400
Slow-Drip Iced Coffee	100	$3.00	$300
Latte	50	$4.00	$200
Muffin	75	$2.00	$150
Crepe	45	$4.00	$180

28

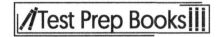

Item	Quantity	Revenue Per Unit	Total Revenue
Egg Sandwich	60	$5.00	$300
Total Revenue			$1,530

$$Walter's\ Profit = Revenue - Costs = \$1,530 - \$1,020 = \$510$$

This strategy is applicable to other question types. For example, calculating salary after deductions, balancing a checkbook, and calculating a dinner bill are common word problems similar to business planning. Just remember to use the correct operations. When a balance is increased, use addition. When a balance is decreased, use subtraction. Common sense and organization are your greatest assets when answering word problems.

This strategy is applicable to other question types. For example, calculating salary after deductions, balancing a checkbook, and calculating a dinner bill are common word problems similar to business planning. Just remember to use the correct operations. When a balance is increased, use addition. When a balance is decreased, use subtraction. Common sense and organization are your greatest assets when answering word problems.

Unit Rate

Unit rate word problems will ask you to calculate the rate or quantity of something in a different value. For example, a problem might tell you that a car drove a certain number of miles in a certain number of minutes and then ask how many miles per hour the car was traveling. These questions involve solving proportions. Consider the following examples:

1) Alexandra made $96 during the first 3 hours of her shift as a temporary worker at a law office. She will continue to earn money at this rate until she finishes in 5 more hours. How much does Alexandra make per hour? How much will Alexandra have made at the end of the day?

This problem can be solved in two ways. The first is to set up a proportion, as the rate of pay is constant. The second is to determine her hourly rate, multiply the 5 hours by that rate, and then add the $96. We'll solve it using both methods.

To set up a proportion, put the money already earned over the hours already worked on one side of an equation. The other side has x over 8 hours (the total hours worked in the day). It looks like this: $\frac{96}{3} = \frac{x}{8}$. Now, cross-multiply to get $768 = 3x$. To get x, we divide by 3, which leaves us with $x = 256$. Thus, Alexandra will make $256 at the end of the day. To calculate her hourly rate, we need to divide the total by 8, which gives us $32 per hour.

Alternatively, we could figure out the hourly rate by dividing $96 by 3 hours to get $32 per hour. Now we can figure out her total pay by multiplying $32 per hour by 8 hours, which comes out to $256.

2) Jonathan is reading a novel. So far, he has read 215 of the 335 total pages. It takes Jonathan 25 minutes to read 10 pages, and the rate is constant. How long does it take Jonathan to read one page? How much longer will it take him to finish the novel? Express the answer in time.

To calculate how long it takes Jonathan to read one page, we need to divide the 25 minutes by 10 pages to determine the page per minute rate. Thus, it takes 2.5 minutes to read one page.

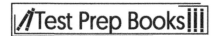

Jonathan must read 120 more pages to complete the novel. (This is calculated by subtracting the pages already read from the total.) Now, we need to multiply his rate per page by the number of pages. Thus, $120 \times 2.5 = 300$. Expressed in time, 300 minutes is equal to 5 hours.

3) At a hotel, $\frac{4}{5}$ of the 120 rooms are booked for Saturday. On Sunday, $\frac{3}{4}$ of the 120 rooms are booked. On which day are more of the rooms booked, and by how much more?

The first step is to calculate the number of rooms booked for each day. We can do this by multiplying the fraction of the rooms booked by the total number of rooms.

$$\text{Saturday: } \frac{4}{5} \times 120 = \frac{4}{5} \times \frac{120}{1} = \frac{480}{5} = 96 \text{ rooms}$$

$$\text{Sunday: } \frac{3}{4} \times 120 = \frac{3}{4} \times \frac{120}{1} = \frac{360}{4} = 90 \text{ rooms}$$

Thus, more rooms were booked on Saturday by 6 rooms.

4) In a veterinary hospital, the veterinarian-to-pet ratio is $1 : 9$. The ratio is always constant. If there are 45 pets in the hospital, how many veterinarians are currently in the veterinary hospital?

We can set up a proportion to solve for the number of veterinarians: $\frac{1}{9} = \frac{x}{45}$

After cross-multiplying, we're left with $9x = 45$, which works out to 5 veterinarians.

Alternatively, as there are always 9 times as many pets as veterinarians, we can divide the number of pets (45) by 9. This also arrives at the correct answer of 5 veterinarians.

5) At a general practice law firm, 30% of the lawyers work solely on tort cases. If 9 lawyers work solely on tort cases, how many lawyers work at the firm?

We need to solve for the total number of lawyers working at the firm, which we will represent with x. We know that 9 lawyers work solely on torts cases, and they make up 30% of the total lawyers at the firm. Thus, 30% multiplied by the total, x, will equal 9. Written as an equation, this is:

$$30\% \times x = 9$$

It's easier to deal with the equation if we convert the percentage to a decimal, leaving us with $0.3x = 9$. Thus, $x = \frac{9}{0.3} = 30$ lawyers working at the firm.

6) Xavier was hospitalized with pneumonia. He was originally given 35mg of antibiotics. Later, after his condition continued to worsen, Xavier's dosage was increased to 60mg. What was the percent increase of the antibiotics? Round the percentage to the nearest tenth.

For questions asking for the increase in percentage, we need to calculate the difference, divide by the original amount, and multiply by 100. Written as an equation, the formula is

$$\frac{new\ quantity - old\ quantity}{old\ quantity} \times 100$$

This formula also works if you are asked for the percentage decrease.

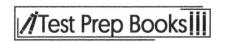

Here, the question tells us that the dosage increased from 35mg to 60mg, so we can plug those numbers into the formula to find the percentage increase.

$$\frac{60-35}{35} \times 100 = \frac{25}{35} \times 100 = .7142 \times 100 = 71.4\%$$

Ratio Reasoning

Using Ratio Reasoning to Convert Rates

Ratios and rates can be used together to convert rates into different units. For example, if someone is driving 50 kilometers per hour, that rate can be converted into miles per hour by using a ratio known as the **conversion factor**. Since the given value contains kilometers and the final answer needs to be in miles, the ratio relating miles to kilometers needs to be used. There are 0.62 miles in 1 kilometer. This, written as a ratio and in fraction form, is:

$$\frac{0.62 \text{ miles}}{1 \text{ km}}$$

To convert 50km/hour into miles per hour, the following conversion needs to be set up:

$$\frac{50 \text{ km}}{\text{hour}} \times \frac{0.62 \text{ miles}}{1 \text{ km}} = 31 \text{ miles per hour}$$

Using Ratios to Describe a Relationship Between Two Quantities

Ratios are used to show the relationship between two quantities. The ratio of oranges to apples in the grocery store may be 3 to 2. That means that for every 3 oranges, there are 2 apples. This comparison can be expanded to represent the actual number of oranges and apples, such as 36 oranges to 24 apples. Another example may be the number of boys to girls in a math class. If the ratio of boys to girls is given as 2 to 5, that means there are 2 boys to every 5 girls in the class. Ratios can also be compared if the units in each ratio are the same. The ratio of boys to girls in the math class can be compared to the ratio of boys to girls in a science class by stating which ratio is higher and which is lower.

Rates are used to compare two quantities with different units. **Unit rates** are the simplest form of rate. With unit rates, the denominator in the comparison of two units is one.

For example, if someone can type at a rate of 1,000 words in 5 minutes, then their unit rate for typing is:

$$\frac{1,000}{5} = 200 \text{ words in one minute}$$

or

$$200 \text{ words per minute}$$

Any rate can be converted into a unit rate by dividing to make the denominator one. 1,000 words in 5 minutes has been converted into the unit rate of 200 words per minute.

Solving Problems Involving Scale Factors

The ratio between two similar geometric figures is called the **scale factor**. For example, a problem may depict two similar triangles, A and B. The scale factor from the smaller triangle A to the larger triangle B is given as 2 because the length of the corresponding side of the larger triangle, 16, is twice the corresponding side on the smaller triangle, 8. This scale factor can also be used to find the value of a missing side, x, in triangle A. Since the scale

31

factor from the smaller triangle (A) to larger one (B) is 2, the larger corresponding side in triangle B (given as 25) can be divided by 2 to find the missing side in A ($x = 12.5$). The scale factor can also be represented in the equation $2A = B$ because two times the lengths of A gives the corresponding lengths of B. This is the idea behind similar triangles.

Basic Concepts of Addition, Subtraction, Multiplication, and Division

The four most basic and fundamental operations are addition, subtraction, multiplication, and division. The operations take a group of numbers and achieve an exact result, according to the operation. When dealing with positive integers greater than 1, addition and multiplication increase the result, while subtraction and division reduce the result.

Addition
Addition is the combination of two numbers so their quantities are added together cumulatively. The sign for an addition operation is the + symbol. For example, $9 + 6 = 15$. The 9 and 6 combine to achieve a cumulative value, called a sum.

Addition holds the Commutative Property, which means that numbers in an addition equation can be switched without altering the result. The formula for the Commutative Property is $a + b = b + a$. Let's look at a few examples to see how the Commutative Property works:

$$3 + 4 = 4 + 3 = 7$$

$$12 + 8 = 8 + 12 = 20$$

Addition also holds the Associative Property, which means that the groups of numbers don't matter in an addition problem. The formula for the Associative Property is $(a + b) + c = a + (b + c)$.

Here are some examples of the Associative Property at work:

$$(6 + 14) + 10 = 6 + (14 + 10) = 30$$

$$8 + (2 + 25) = (8 + 2) + 25 = 35$$

Subtraction
Subtraction is taking away one number from another, so their quantities are reduced. The sign designating a subtraction operation is the − symbol, and the result is called the difference. For example, $9 - 6 = 3$. The second number detracts from the first number in the equation to reach the difference.

Unlike addition, subtraction doesn't follow the Commutative or Associative Properties. The order and grouping in subtraction impact the result.

$$22 - 7 \neq 7 - 22$$

$$(10 - 5) - 2 \neq 10 - (5 - 2)$$

When working through subtraction problems involving larger numbers, it's necessary to regroup the numbers. Let's work through a practice problem using regrouping:

$$\begin{array}{r} 325 \\ -\ 77 \\ \hline \end{array}$$

32

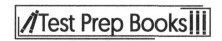

Here, we see that the ones and tens column for 77 is greater than 325. Thus, we need to borrow from the tens and hundreds column to complete the operation.

When borrowing from a column, we subtract one digit from the lender and add ten to the borrower's column:

$$\begin{array}{r} 3\overset{1}{\cancel{2}}5 \\ -\ 77 \\ \hline 8 \end{array}$$

$$\begin{array}{r} \overset{2}{\cancel{3}}\overset{11}{\cancel{2}}\overset{1}{5} \\ -\ 77 \\ \hline 48 \end{array}$$

$$\begin{array}{r} \overset{2}{\cancel{3}}\overset{11}{\cancel{2}}\overset{1}{5} \\ -\ 77 \\ \hline 248 \end{array}$$

After ensuring greater numbers at the top of each column, we subtract as normal and arrive at the answer of 248.

Multiplication

Multiplication involves taking multiple copies of one number. The sign designating a multiplication operation is the $\times$ symbol. The result is called the product. For example, $9 \times 6 = 54$. Multiplication means adding together one number in the equation as many times as the number on the other side of the equation:

$$9 \times 6 = 9 + 9 + 9 + 9 + 9 + 9 = 54$$

$$9 \times 6 = 6 + 6 + 6 + 6 + 6 + 6 + 6 + 6 + 6 = 54$$

Like addition, multiplication holds the Commutative and Associative Properties:

$$2 \times 4 = 4 \times 2$$

$$2 \times 5 = 5 \times 2$$

$$(2 \times 4)10 = 2(4 \times 10)$$

$$3(7 \times 4) = (3 \times 7)4$$

Multiplication also follows the Distributive Property, which allows the multiplication to be distributed through parentheses. The formula for distribution is $a \times (b + c) = ab + ac$. This will become clearer after some examples:

$$5(3 + 6) = (5 \times 3) + (5 \times 6) = 45$$

$$4(10 - 5) = (4 \times 10) - (4 \times 5) = 20$$

Multiplication becomes slightly more complicated when multiplying numbers with decimals. The easiest way to answer these problems is to ignore the decimals and multiply as if they were whole numbers. After multiplying the factors, add a decimal point to the product, and the decimal place should be equal to the total number of decimal places in the problem.

33

Here are two examples to familiarize you with the trick:

1.

$$\begin{array}{r} 0.7 \\ \times \quad 3 \\ \hline 2.1 \end{array}$$

2.

$$\begin{array}{r} 2.6 \\ \times \quad 4.2 \\ \hline 10.92 \end{array}$$

Let's tackle the first example. First, count the decimal places (one). Second, multiply the factors as if they were whole numbers to arrive at a product: 21. Finally, move the decimal place one position to the left, as the factors have only one decimal place. The second problem works the same exact away, except that there are two decimal places in the factors, so the product's decimal is moved two places over.

Division

Division is the opposite of multiplication as addition and subtraction are opposites. The signs designating a division operate are the ÷ or / symbols. In division, the second number divides the first. Like subtraction, it matters which number comes before the division sign. For example, $9 \div 6 \neq 6 \div 9$.

The number before the division sign is called the dividend, or, if expressed as a fraction, then it's the numerator. For example, in $a \div b$, a is the dividend. In $\frac{a}{b}$, a is the numerator.

The number after the division sign is called the **divisor**, or, if expressed as a fraction, then it's the denominator. For example, in $a \div b$, b is the divisor. In $\frac{a}{b}$, b is the denominator.

Division doesn't follow any of the Commutative, Associative, or Distributive Properties.

$$15 \div 3 \neq 3 \div 15$$

$$(30 \div 3) \div 5 \neq 30 \div (3 \div 5)$$

$$100 \div (20 + 10) \neq (100 \div 20) + (100 \div 10)$$

Division with decimals is similar to multiplication with decimals. When dividing a decimal by a whole number, ignore the decimal and divide as if it were a whole number. Once you solve for the answer (also called the **quotient**), then place the decimal at the decimal place equal to that in the dividend.

$$15.75 \div 3 = 5.25$$

When the divisor is a decimal, change it to a whole number by multiplying both the divisor and dividend by the factor of 10 that makes the divisor into a whole number. Then complete the division operation as described above.

$$17.5 \div 2.5 + 175 \div 25 = 7$$

34

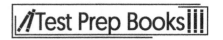

There are a variety of real-world situations in which one or more of the operators is used to solve a problem. The tables below display the most common scenarios.

Addition & Subtraction

	Unknown Result	Unknown Change	Unknown Start
Adding to	5 students were in class. 4 more students arrived. How many students are in class? ?	8 students were in class. More students arrived late. There are now 18 students in class. How many students arrived late? Solved by inverse operations	Some students were in class early. 11 more students arrived. There are now 17 students in class. How many students were in class early? Solved by inverse operations
Taking from	15 students were in class. 5 students left class. How many students are in class now?	12 students were in class. Some students left class. There are now 8 students in class. How many students left class? Solved by inverse operations	Some students were in class. 3 students left class. Then there were 13 students in class. How many students were in class before? Solved by inverse operations

	Unknown Total	Unknown Addends (Both)	Unknown Addends (One)
Putting together/ taking apart	The homework assignment is 10 addition problems and 8 subtraction problems. How many problems are in the homework assignment?	Bobby has $9. How much can Bobby spend on candy and how much can Bobby spend on toys?	Bobby has 12 pairs of pants. 5 pairs of pants are shorts, and the rest are long. How many pairs of long pants does he have? Solved by inverse operations

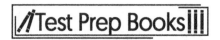

	Unknown Difference	Unknown Larger Value	Unknown Smaller Value
Comparing	Bobby has 5 toys. Tommy has 8 toys. How many more toys does Tommy have than Bobby? Solved by inverse operations Bobby has $6. Tommy has $10. How many fewer dollars does Bobby have than Tommy?	Tommy has 2 more toys than Bobby. Bobby has 4 toys. How many toys does Tommy have? Bobby has 3 fewer dollars than Tommy. Bobby has $8. How many dollars does Tommy have? Solved by inverse operations	Tommy has 6 more toys than Bobby. Tommy has 10 toys. How many toys does Bobby have? Solved by inverse operations Bobby has $5 less than Tommy. Tommy has $9. How many dollars does Bobby have?

Multiplication and Division

	Unknown Product	Unknown Group Size	Unknown Number of Groups
Equal groups	There are 5 students, and each student has 4 pieces of candy. How many pieces of candy are there in all?	14 pieces of candy are shared equally by 7 students. How many pieces of candy does each student have? Solved by inverse operations	If 18 pieces of candy are to be given out 3 to each student, how many students will get candy? Solved by inverse operations

	Unknown Product	Unknown Factor	Unknown Factor
Arrays	There are 5 rows of students with 3 students in each row. How many students are there?	If 16 students are arranged into 4 equal rows, how many students will be in each row? Solved by inverse operations	If 24 students are arranged into an array with 6 columns, how many rows are there? Solved by inverse operations

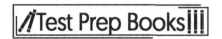

	Larger Unknown	Smaller Unknown	Multiplier Unknown
Comparing	A small popcorn costs $1.50. A large popcorn costs 3 times as much as a small popcorn. How much does a large popcorn cost?	A large soda costs $6 and that is 2 times as much as a small soda costs. How much does a small soda cost? Solved by inverse operations	A large pretzel costs $3 and a small pretzel costs $2. How many times as much does the large pretzel cost as the small pretzel? Solved by inverse operations

Order of Operations

When reviewing calculations consisting of more than one operation, the order in which the operations are performed affects the resulting answer. Consider $5 \times 2 + 7$. Performing multiplication then addition results in an answer of $17 (5 \times 2 = 10; 10 + 7 = 17)$. However, if the problem is written $5 \times (2 + 7)$, the order of operations dictates that the operation inside the parentheses must be performed first. The resulting answer is $45 (2 + 7 = 9,$ then $5 \times 9 = 45)$.

The order in which operations should be performed is remembered using the acronym PEMDAS. PEMDAS stands for parentheses, exponents, multiplication/division, addition/subtraction. Multiplication and division are performed in the same step, working from left to right with whichever comes first. Addition and subtraction are performed in the same step, working from left to right with whichever comes first.

Consider the following example: $8 \div 4 + 8(7 - 7)$. Performing the operation inside the parentheses produces $8 \div 4 + 8(0)$ or $8 \div 4 + 8 \times 0$. There are no exponents, so multiplication and division are performed next from left to right resulting in: $2 + 8 \times 0$, then $2 + 0$. Finally, addition and subtraction are performed to obtain an answer of 2. Now consider the following example: $6 \times 3 + 3^2 - 6$. Parentheses are not applicable. Exponents are evaluated first, which brings us to $6 \times 3 + 9 - 6$. Then multiplication/division forms $18 + 9 - 6$. At last, addition/subtraction leads to the final answer of 21.

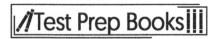
Properties of Operations

Properties of operations exist that make calculations easier and solve problems for missing values. The following table summarizes commonly used properties of real numbers.

Property	Addition	Multiplication
Commutative	$a + b = b + a$	$a \times b = b \times a$
Associative	$(a + b) + c = a + (b + c)$	$(a \times b) \times c = a \times (b \times c)$
Identity	$a + 0 = a;\ 0 + a = a$	$a \times 1 = a;\ 1 \times a = a$
Inverse	$a + (-a) = 0$	$a \times \dfrac{1}{a} = 1;\ a \neq 0$
Distributive	$a(b + c) = ab + ac$	

The commutative property of addition states that the order in which numbers are added does not change the sum. Similarly, the commutative property of multiplication states that the order in which numbers are multiplied does not change the product. The associative property of addition and multiplication state that the grouping of numbers being added or multiplied does not change the sum or product, respectively. The commutative and associative properties are useful for performing calculations. For example, $(47 + 25) + 3$ is equivalent to $(47 + 3) + 25$, which is easier to calculate.

The identity property of addition states that adding zero to any number does not change its value. The identity property of multiplication states that multiplying a number by 1 does not change its value. The inverse property of addition states that the sum of a number and its opposite equals zero. Opposites are numbers that are the same with different signs (ex. 5 and -5; $-\frac{1}{2}$ and $\frac{1}{2}$). The inverse property of multiplication states that the product of a number (other than 0) and its reciprocal equals 1. Reciprocal numbers have numerators and denominators that are inverted (ex. $\frac{2}{5}$ and $\frac{5}{2}$). Inverse properties are useful for canceling quantities to find missing values (see algebra content). For example, $a + 7 = 12$ is solved by adding the inverse of 7 (which is -7) to both sides in order to isolate a.

The distributive property states that multiplying a sum (or difference) by a number produces the same result as multiplying each value in the sum (or difference) by the number and adding (or subtracting) the products. Consider the following scenario: You are buying three tickets for a baseball game. Each ticket costs $18. You are also charged a fee of $2 per ticket for purchasing the tickets online. The cost is calculated: $3 \times 18 + 3 \times 2$. Using the distributive property, the cost can also be calculated: $3(18 + 2)$.

Determining the Reasonableness of Results [ISEE]

The Reasonableness of Results

When solving math word problems, the solution obtained should make sense within the given scenario. The step of checking the solution will reduce the possibility of a calculation error or a solution that may be mathematically correct but not applicable in the real world. Consider the following scenarios:

A problem states that Lisa got 24 out of 32 questions correct on a test and asks to find the percentage of correct answers. To solve the problem, a student divided 32 by 24 to get 1.33, and then multiplied by 100 to get 133 percent. By examining the solution within the context of the problem, the student should recognize that getting all

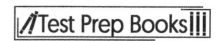

32 questions correct will produce a perfect score of 100 percent. Therefore, a score of 133 percent with 8 incorrect answers does not make sense, and the calculations should be checked.

A problem states that the maximum weight on a bridge cannot exceed 22,000 pounds. The problem asks to find the maximum number of cars that can be on the bridge at one time if each car weighs 4,000 pounds. To solve this problem, a student divided 22,000 by 4,000 to get an answer of 5.5. By examining the solution within the context of the problem, the student should recognize that although the calculations are mathematically correct, the solution does not make sense. Half of a car on a bridge is not possible, so the student should determine that a maximum of 5 cars can be on the bridge at the same time.

Estimation

Estimation is finding a value that is close to a solution but is not the exact answer. For example, if there are values in the thousands to be multiplied, then each value can be estimated to the nearest thousand and the calculation performed. This value provides an approximate solution that can be determined very quickly.

Rounding is the process of either bumping a number up or leaving it the same, based on a specified place value. First, the place value is specified. Then, the digit to its right is looked at. For example, if rounding to the nearest hundreds place, the digit in the tens place is used. If it is a 0, 1, 2, 3, or 4, the digit being rounded to is left alone. If it is a 5, 6, 7, 8 or 9, the digit being rounded to is increased by one. All other digits before the decimal point are then changed to zeros, and the digits in decimal places are dropped. If a decimal place is being rounded to, all subsequent digits are just dropped. For example, if 845,231.45 was to be rounded to the nearest thousands place, the answer would be 845,000. The 5 would remain the same due to the 2 in the hundreds place. Also, if 4.567 was to be rounded to the nearest tenths place, the answer would be 4.6. The 5 increased to 6 due to the 6 in the hundredths place, and the rest of the decimal is dropped.

Sometimes when performing operations such as multiplying numbers, the result can be estimated by *rounding*. For example, to estimate the value of 11.2×2.01, each number can be rounded to the nearest integer. This will yield a result of 22.

Rounding numbers helps with estimation because it changes the given number to a simpler, although less accurate, number than the exact given number. Rounding allows for easier calculations, which estimate the results of using the exact given number. The accuracy of the estimate and ease of use depends on the place value to which the number is rounded. Rounding numbers consists of:

- determining what place value the number is being rounded to
- examining the digit to the right of the desired place value to decide whether to round up or keep the digit
- replacing all digits to the right of the desired place value with zeros

To round 746,311 to the nearest ten thousand, the digit in the ten thousands place should be located first. In this case, this digit is 4 (7<u>4</u>6,311). Then, the digit to its right is examined. If this digit is 5 or greater, the number will be rounded up by increasing the digit in the desired place by one. If the digit to the right of the place value being rounded is 4 or less, the number will be kept the same. For the given example, the digit being examined is a 6, which means that the number will be rounded up by increasing the digit to the left by one. Therefore, the digit 4 is changed to a 5. Finally, to write the rounded number, any digits to the left of the place value being rounded remain the same and any to its right are replaced with zeros. For the given example, rounding 746,311 to the nearest ten thousand will produce 750,000. To round 746,311 to the nearest hundred, the digit to the right of the three in the hundreds place is examined to determine whether to round up or keep the same number. In this case, that digit is a 1, so the number will be kept the same and any digits to its right will be replaced with zeros. The resulting rounded number is 746,300.

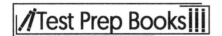

Rounding place values to the right of the decimal follows the same procedure, but digits being replaced by zeros can simply be dropped. To round 3.752891 to the nearest thousandth, the desired place value is located (3.75<u>2</u>891) and the digit to the right is examined. In this case, the digit 8 indicates that the number will be rounded up, and the 2 in the thousandths place will increase to a 3. Rounding up and replacing the digits to the right of the thousandths place produces 3.753000 which is equivalent to 3.753. Therefore, the zeros are not necessary, and the rounded number should be written as 3.753.

When rounding up, if the digit to be increased is a 9, the digit to its left is increased by 1 and the digit in the desired place value is changed to a zero. For example, the number 1,598 rounded to the nearest ten is 1,600. Another example shows the number 43.72961 rounded to the nearest thousandth is 43.730 or 43.73.

Mental math should always be considered as problems are worked through, and the ability to work through problems in one's head helps save time. If a problem is simple enough, such as $15 + 3 = 18$, it should be completed mentally. The ability to do this will increase once addition and subtraction in higher place values are grasped. Also, mental math is important in multiplication and division. The times tables multiplying all numbers from 1 to 12 should be memorized. This will allow for division within those numbers to be memorized as well. For example, we should know easily that $121 \div 11 = 11$ because it should be memorized that $11 \times 11 = 121$.

Here is the multiplication table to be memorized:

x	1	2	3	4	5	6	7	8	9	10	11	12	13	14	15
1	1	2	3	4	5	6	7	8	9	10	11	12	13	14	15
2	2	4	6	8	10	12	14	16	18	20	22	24	26	28	30
3	3	6	9	12	15	18	21	24	27	30	33	36	39	42	45
4	4	8	12	16	20	24	28	32	36	40	44	48	52	56	60
5	5	10	15	20	25	30	35	40	45	50	55	60	65	70	75
6	6	12	18	24	30	36	42	48	54	60	66	72	78	84	90
7	7	14	21	28	35	42	49	56	63	70	77	84	91	98	105
8	8	16	24	32	40	48	56	64	72	80	88	96	104	112	120
9	9	18	27	36	45	54	63	72	81	90	99	108	117	126	135
10	10	20	30	40	50	60	70	80	90	100	110	120	130	140	150
11	11	22	33	44	55	66	77	88	99	110	121	132	143	154	165
12	12	24	36	48	60	72	84	96	108	120	132	144	156	168	180
13	13	26	39	52	65	78	91	104	117	130	143	156	169	182	195
14	14	28	42	56	70	84	98	112	126	140	154	168	182	196	210
15	15	30	45	60	75	90	105	120	135	150	165	180	195	210	225

The values in yellow along the diagonal of the table consist of **perfect squares**. A perfect square is the product of two of the same numbers.

Estimating Absolute and Relative Error in the Numerical Answer to a Problem

Once a result is determined to be logical within the context of a given problem, the result should be evaluated by its nearness to the expected answer. This is performed by approximating given values to perform mental math. Numbers should be rounded to the nearest value possible to check the initial results.

Consider the following example:

A customer is buying a new sound system for their home. The customer purchases a stereo for $435, 2 speakers for $67 each, and the necessary cables for $12. The customer chooses an option that allows him to spread the costs over equal payments for 4 months. How much will the monthly payments be?

After making calculations for the problem, a student determines that the monthly payment will be $145.25. To check the accuracy of the results, the student rounds each cost to the nearest ten:

$$(440 + 70 + 70 + 10)$$

Then, the student determines that the total is approximately $590. Dividing by 4 months gives an approximate monthly payment of $147.50. Therefore, the student can conclude that the solution of $145.25 is very close to what should be expected.

When rounding, the place-value that is used in rounding can make a difference. Suppose the student had rounded to the nearest hundred for the estimation. The result:

$$400 + 100 + 100 + 0 = 600$$

$$600 \div 4 = 150$$

This will show that the answer is reasonable but not as close to the actual value as rounding to the nearest ten.

When considering the accuracy of estimates, the error in the estimated solution can be shown as absolute and relative. **Absolute error** tells the actual difference between the estimated value and the true, calculated value. The **relative error** tells how large the error is in relation to the true value. There may be two problems where the absolute error of the values (the estimated one and the calculated one) is 10. For one problem, this may mean the relative error in the estimate is very small because the estimated value is 15,000, and the true value is 14,990. Ten in relation to the true value of 15,000 is small: 0.06%. For the other problem, the estimated value is 50, and the true value is 40. In this case, the absolute error of 10 means a high relative error because the true value is smaller. The relative error is:

$$\frac{10}{40} = 0.25 \text{ or } 25\%$$

Comparing, Classifying, and Ordering Real/Rational Numbers

The mathematical number system is made up of two general types of numbers: real and complex. **Real numbers** are both irrational and rational numbers, while **complex numbers** are those composed of both a real number and an imaginary one. Imaginary numbers are the result of taking the square root of -1, and $\sqrt{-1} = i$.

The real number system is often explained using a Venn diagram similar to the one below. After a number has been labeled as a real number, further classification occurs when considering the other groups in this diagram. If a number is a never-ending, non-repeating decimal, it falls in the irrational category. Otherwise, it is rational. More information on these types of numbers is given in the section above. Furthermore, if a number does not have a

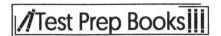
fractional part, it is classified as an integer, such as −2, 75, or 0. Whole numbers are an even smaller group that only includes positive integers and 0. The last group of natural numbers is made up of only positive integers, such as 2, 56, or 12.

Consider the diagram below:

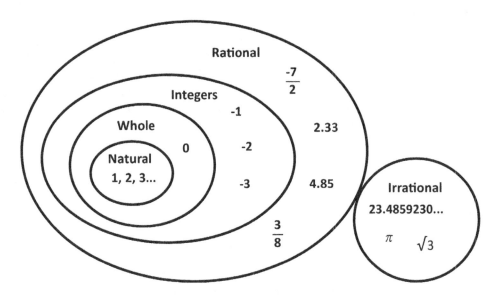

Real numbers can be compared and ordered using the number line. If a number falls to the left on the real number line, it is less than a number on the right. For example, −2 < 5 because −2 falls to the left of 0, and 5 falls to the right.

Complex numbers are made up of the sum of a real number and an imaginary number. Some examples of complex numbers include $6 + 2i$, $5 − 7i$, and $−3 + 12i$. Adding and subtracting complex numbers is similar to collecting like terms. The real numbers are added together, and the imaginary numbers are added together. For example, if the problem asks to simplify the given expression $6 + 2i − 3 + 7i$, the 6 and −3 would combine to make 3, and the $2i$ and $7i$ combine to make $9i$. Multiplying and dividing complex numbers is similar to working with exponents. One rule to remember when multiplying is that $i \times i = −1$. For example, if a problem asks to simplify the expression $4i(3 + 7i)$, the $4i$ should be distributed throughout the 3 and the $7i$. This leaves the final expression $12i − 28$. The 28 is negative because $i \times i$ results in a negative number. The last type of operation to consider with complex numbers is the conjugate. The **conjugate** of a complex number is a technique used to change the complex number into a real number. For example, the conjugate of $4 − 3i$ is $4 + 3i$. Multiplying $(4 − 3i)(4 + 3i)$ results in $16 + 12i − 12i + 9$, which has a final answer of $16 + 9 = 25$.

Integers are the whole numbers together with their negatives. They include numbers like 5, 24, 0, -6, and 15. They do not include fractions or numbers that have digits after the decimal point.

Rational numbers are all numbers that can be written as a fraction using integers. A **fraction** is written as $\frac{x}{y}$ and represents the quotient of x being divided by y. More practically, it means dividing the whole into y equal parts, then taking x of those parts.

Examples of rational numbers include $\frac{1}{2}$ and $\frac{5}{4}$. The **numerator** is the number on the top of the fraction, while the **denominator** is the number on the bottom. Because every integer can be written as a fraction with a denominator of 1, (e.g., $\frac{3}{1} = 3$), every integer is also a rational number.

42

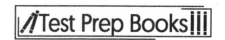
When adding integers and negative rational numbers, there are some basic rules to determine if the solution is negative or positive:

- Adding two positive numbers results in a positive value: $3.3 + 4.8 = 8.1$.
- Adding two negative numbers results in a negative number: $(-8) + (-6) = -14$.

Adding one positive and one negative number requires taking the absolute values and finding the difference between them. Then, the sign of the number that has the higher absolute value for the final solution is used.

For example, $(-9) + 11$, has a difference of absolute values of 2. The final solution is 2 because 11 has the higher absolute value. Another example is $9 + (-11)$, which has a difference of absolute values of 2. The final solution is -2 because 11 has the higher absolute value.

When subtracting integers and negative rational numbers, one has to change the problem to adding the opposite and then apply the rules of addition.

- Subtracting two positive numbers is the same as adding one positive and one negative number.

    For example, $4.9 - 7.1$ is the same as $4.9 + (-7.1)$. The solution is -2.2 since the absolute value of -7.1 is greater. Another example is $8.5 - 6.4$ which is the same as $8.5 + (-6.4)$. The solution is 2.1 since the absolute value of 8.5 is greater.

- Subtracting a positive number from a negative number results in negative value.

    For example, $(-12) - 7$ is the same as $(-12) + (-7)$ with a solution of -19.

- Subtracting a negative number from a positive number results in a positive value.

    For example, $12 - (-7)$ is the same as $12 + 7$ with a solution of 19.

- For multiplication and division of integers and rational numbers, if both numbers are positive or both numbers are negative, the result is a positive value.

    For example, $(-1.7)(-4)$ has a solution of 6.8 since both numbers are negative values.

- If one number is positive and another number is negative, the result is a negative value.

    For example, $(-15)/5$ has a solution of -3 since there is one negative number.

As mentioned, rational numbers are any number which can be written as a fraction or ratio. Within the set of rational numbers, several subsets exist which are referenced throughout the mathematics topics. Counting numbers are the first numbers learned as a child. Counting numbers consist of 1,2,3,4, and so on. Whole numbers include all counting numbers and zero (0,1,2,3,4,...). Integers include counting numbers, their opposites, and zero (...,-3,-2,-1,0,1,2,3,...). Rational numbers are inclusive of integers, fractions, and decimals that terminate, or end (1.7, 0.04213) or repeat (0.136).

A **number line** typically consists of integers (...3,2,1,0,-1,-2,-3...), and is used to visually represent the value of a rational number. Each rational number has a distinct position on the line determined by comparing its value with the displayed values on the line. For example, if plotting -1.5 on the number line below, it is necessary to recognize

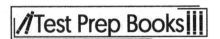

that the value of −1.5 is 0.5 less than −1 and 0.5 greater than −2. Therefore, −1.5 is plotted halfway between −1 and −2.

The number system that is used consists of only ten different digits or characters. However, this system is used to represent an infinite number of values. The **place value system** makes this infinite number of values possible. The position in which a digit is written corresponds to a given value. Starting from the decimal point (which is implied, if not physically present), each subsequent place value to the left represents a value greater than the one before it. Conversely, starting from the decimal point, each subsequent place value to the right represents a value less than the one before it.

The names for the place values to the left of the decimal point are as follows:

Billions	Hundred-Millions	Ten-Millions	Millions	Hundred-Thousands	Ten-Thousands	Thousands	Hundreds	Tens	Ones

*Note that this table can be extended infinitely further to the left.

The names for the place values to the right of the decimal point are as follows:

Decimal Point (.)	Tenths	Hundredths	Thousandths	Ten-Thousandths	...

*Note that this table can be extended indefinitely further to the right.

When given a multi-digit number, the value of each digit depends on its place value. Consider the number 682,174.953. Referring to the chart above, it can be determined that the digit 8 is in the ten-thousands place. It is in the fifth place to the left of the decimal point. Its value is 8 ten-thousands or 80,000. The digit 5 is two places to the right of the decimal point. Therefore, the digit 5 is in the hundredths place. Its value is 5 hundredths or $\frac{5}{100}$ (equivalent to 0.05).

In accordance with the **base-10 system**, the value of a digit increases by a factor of ten each place it moves to the left. For example, consider the number 7. Moving the digit one place to the left (70), increases its value by a factor of 10:

$$(7 \times 10 = 70)$$

Moving the digit two places to the left (700) increases its value by a factor of 10 twice:

$$(7 \times 10 \times 10 = 700)$$

Moving the digit three places to the left (7,000) increases its value by a factor of 10 three times (10^3), and so on.

Conversely, the value of a digit decreases by a factor of ten each place it moves to the right. (Note that multiplying by 10^{-1} is equivalent to dividing by 10). For example, consider the number 40. Moving the digit one place to the right (4) decreases its value by a factor of 10:

$$(40 \div 10 = 4)$$

Moving the digit two places to the right (0.4), decreases its value by a factor of 10 twice:

$$(40 \div 10 \div 10 = 0.4$$

or

$$(40 \times \frac{1}{10} \times \frac{1}{10} = 0.4)$$

Moving the digit three places to the right (0.04) decreases its value by a factor of 10 three times:

$$40 \div 10 \div 10 \div 10 = 0.04$$

or

$$40 \times \frac{1}{10} \times \frac{1}{10} \times \frac{1}{10} = 0.04$$

When comparing or ordering numbers, the numbers should be written in the same format (decimal or fraction), if possible. For example, $\sqrt{49}$, 7.3, and $\frac{15}{2}$ are easier to order if each one is converted to a decimal, such as 7, 7.3, and 7.5 (converting fractions and decimals is covered in the following section). A number line is used to order and compare the numbers. Any number that is to the right of another number is greater than that number. Conversely, a number positioned to the left of a given number is less than that number.

Ordering Numbers

A common question type asks to order rational numbers from least to greatest or greatest to least. The numbers will come in a variety of formats, including decimals, percentages, roots, fractions, and whole numbers. These questions test for knowledge of different types of numbers and the ability to determine their respective values.

Before discussing ordering all numbers, let's start with decimals.

To compare decimals and order them by their value, utilize a method similar to that of ordering large numbers.

The main difference is where the comparison will start. Assuming that any numbers to left of the decimal point are equal, the next numbers to be compared are those immediately to the right of the decimal point. If those are equal, then move on to compare the values in the next decimal place to the right.

For example:

Which number is greater, 12.35 or 12.38?

Check that the values to the left of the decimal point are equal:

$$12 = 12$$

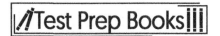

Next, compare the values of the decimal place to the right of the decimal:

$$12.3 = 12.3$$

Those are also equal in value.

Finally, compare the value of the numbers in the next decimal place to the right on both numbers:

$$12.3\mathbf{5} \text{ and } 12.3\mathbf{8}$$

Here the 5 is less than the 8, so the final way to express this inequality is:

$$12.35 < 12.38$$

Comparing decimals is regularly exemplified with money because the "cents" portion of money ends in the hundredths place. When paying for gasoline or meals in restaurants, and even in bank accounts, if enough errors are made when calculating numbers to the hundredths place, they can add up to dollars and larger amounts of money over time.

Now that decimal ordering has been explained, let's expand and consider all real numbers. Whether the question asks to order the numbers from greatest to least or least to greatest, the crux of the question is the same—convert the numbers into a common format. Generally, it's easiest to write the numbers as whole numbers and decimals so they can be placed on a number line. Follow these examples to understand this strategy.

1) Order the following rational numbers from greatest to least:

$$\sqrt{36}, 0.65, 78\%, \frac{3}{4}, 7, 90\%, \frac{5}{2}$$

Of the seven numbers, the whole number (7) and decimal (0.65) are already in an accessible form, so concentrate on the other five.

First, the square root of 36 equals 6. If the test asks for the root of a non-perfect root, determine which two whole numbers the root lies between. Next, convert the percentages to decimals. A percentage means "per hundred," so this conversion requires moving the decimal point two places to the left, leaving 0.78 and 0.9. Lastly, evaluate the fractions:

$$\frac{3}{4} = \frac{75}{100} = 0.75; \frac{5}{2} = 2\frac{1}{2} = 2.5$$

Now, the only step left is to list the numbers in the request order:

$$7, \sqrt{36}, \frac{5}{2}, 90\%, 78\%, \frac{3}{4}, 0.65$$

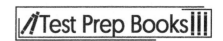
2) Order the following rational numbers from least to greatest:

$$2.5, \sqrt{9}, -10.5, 0.853, 175\%, \sqrt{4}, \frac{4}{5}$$

$$\sqrt{9} = 3$$

$$175\% = 1.75$$

$$\sqrt{4} = 2$$

$$\frac{4}{5} = 0.8$$

From least to greatest, the answer is:

$$-10.5, \frac{4}{5}, 0.853, 175\%, \sqrt{4}, 2.5, \sqrt{9}$$

Basic Concepts of Number Theory [ISEE]

Prime and Composite Numbers

Whole numbers are classified as either prime or composite. A **prime number** can only be divided evenly by itself and one. For example, the number 11 can only be divided evenly by 11 and one; therefore, 11 is a prime number. A helpful way to visualize a prime number is to use concrete objects and try to divide them into equal piles. If dividing 11 coins, the only way to divide them into equal piles is to create 1 pile of 11 coins or to create 11 piles of 1 coin each. Other examples of prime numbers include 2, 3, 5, 7, 13, 17, and 19.

A **composite number** is any whole number that is not a prime number. A composite number is a number that can be divided evenly by one or more numbers other than itself and one. For example, the number 6 can be divided evenly by 2 and 3. Therefore, 6 is a composite number. If dividing 6 coins into equal piles, the possibilities are 1 pile of 6 coins, 2 piles of 3 coins, 3 piles of 2 coins, or 6 piles of 1 coin. Other examples of composite numbers include 4, 8, 9, 10, 12, 14, 15, 16, 18, and 20.

To determine if a number is a prime or composite number, the number is divided by every whole number greater than one and less than its own value. If it divides evenly by any of these numbers, then the number is composite. If it does not divide evenly by any of these numbers, then the number is prime. For example, when attempting to divide the number 5 by 2, 3, and 4, none of these numbers divide evenly. Therefore, 5 must be a prime number.

Odd and Even Numbers

Even numbers are all divisible by the number 2. **Odd numbers** are not divisible by 2, and an odd quantity of items cannot be paired up into groups of 2 without having 1 item leftover. Examples of even numbers are 2, 4, 6, 20, 100, 242, etc. Examples of odd numbers are 1, 3, 5, 27, 99, 333, etc.

Factors, Multiples, and Divisibility

The **Fundamental Theorem of Arithmetic** states that any integer greater than 1 is either a prime number or can be written as a unique product of prime numbers. Factors can be used to find the combination of numbers to multiply to produce an integer that is not prime. The factors of a number are all integers that can be multiplied by another

47

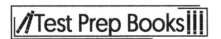
integer to produce the given number. For example, 2 is multiplied by 3 to produce 6. Therefore, 2 and 3 are both factors of 6. Similarly:

$$1 \times 6 = 6$$

and

$$2 \times 3 = 6$$

so 1, 2, 3, and 6 are all factors of 6. Another way to explain a factor is to say that a given number divides evenly by each of its factors to produce an integer. For example, 6 does not divide evenly by 5. Therefore, 5 is not a factor of 6.

Essentially, **factors** are the numbers multiplied to achieve a product. Thus, every product in a multiplication equation has, at minimum, two factors. Of course, some products will have more than two factors. For the sake of most discussions, assume that factors are positive integers.

To find a number's factors, start with 1 and the number itself. Then divide the number by 2, 3, 4, and so on, seeing if any divisors can divide the number without a remainder, keeping a list of those that do. Stop upon reaching either the number itself or another factor.

Let's find the factors of 45. Start with 1 and 45. Then try to divide 45 by 2, which fails. Now divide 45 by 3. The answer is 15, so 3 and 15 are now factors. Dividing by 4 doesn't work and dividing by 5 leaves 9. Lastly, dividing 45 by 6, 7, and 8 all don't work. The next integer to try is 9, but this is already known to be a factor, so the factorization is complete. The factors of 45 are 1, 3, 5, 9, 15 and 45.

A **common factor** is a factor shared by two numbers. Let's take 45 and 30 and find the common factors:

The factors of 45 are: 1, 3, 5, 9, 15, and 45.

The factors of 30 are: 1, 2, 3, 5, 6, 10, 15, and 30.

The common factors are 1, 3, 5, and 15.

The **greatest common factor** is the largest number among the shared, common factors. From the factors of 45 and 30, the common factors are 3, 5, and 15. Thus, 15 is the greatest common factor, as it's the largest number.

Multiples of a given number are found by taking that number and multiplying it by any other whole number. For example, 3 is a factor of 6, 9, and 12. Therefore, 6, 9, and 12 are multiples of 3. The multiples of any number are an infinite list. For example, the multiples of 5 are 5, 10, 15, 20, and so on. This list continues without end. A list of multiples is used in finding the **least common multiple**, or **LCM,** for fractions when a common denominator is needed. The denominators are written down and their multiples listed until a common number is found in both lists. This common number is the LCM.

If two numbers share no factors besides 1 in common, then their least common multiple will be simply their product. If two numbers have common factors, then their least common multiple will be their product divided by their greatest common factor. This can be visualized by the formula:

$$LCM = \frac{x \times y}{GCF}$$

here x and y are some integers, and LCM and GCF are their least common multiple and greatest common factor, respectively.

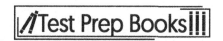

Prime factorization breaks down each factor of a whole number until only prime numbers remain. All composite numbers can be factored into prime numbers. For example, the prime factors of 12 are 2, 2, and 3 ($2 \times 2 \times 3 = 12$). To produce the prime factors of a number, the number is factored, and any composite numbers are continuously factored until the result is the product of prime factors only. A factor tree, such as the one below, is helpful when exploring this concept.

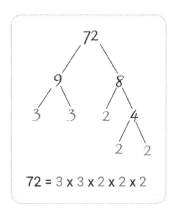

72 = 3 x 3 x 2 x 2 x 2

Let's break 129 down into its prime factors. First, the factors are 3 and 43. Both 3 and 43 are prime numbers, so we're done. But if 43 was not a prime number, then it would also need to be factorized until all of the factors are expressed as prime numbers.

Fractions

A **fraction** is an equation that represents a part of a whole but can also be used to present ratios or division problems. An example of a fraction is $\frac{x}{y}$. In this example, x is called the **numerator,** while y is the **denominator**. The numerator represents the number of parts, and the denominator is the total number of parts. They are separated by a line or slash, known as a fraction bar. In simple fractions, the numerator and denominator can be nearly any integer. However, the denominator of a fraction can never be zero because dividing by zero is a function that is undefined.

Imagine that an apple pie has been baked for a holiday party, and the full pie has eight slices. After the party, there are five slices left. How could the amount of the pie that remains be expressed as a fraction? The numerator is 5 since there are 5 pieces left, and the denominator is 8 since there were eight total slices in the whole pie. Thus, expressed as a fraction, the leftover pie totals $\frac{5}{8}$ of the original amount.

Fractions come in three different varieties: proper fractions, improper fractions, and mixed numbers. **Proper fractions** have a numerator less than the denominator, such as $\frac{3}{8}$, but **improper fractions** have a numerator greater than the denominator, such as $\frac{7}{2}$. **Mixed numbers** combine a whole number with a proper fraction, such as $3\frac{1}{2}$. Any mixed number can be written as an improper fraction by multiplying the integer by the denominator, adding the product to the value of the numerator, and dividing the sum by the original denominator. For example:

$$3\frac{1}{2} = \frac{3 \times 2 + 1}{2} = \frac{7}{2}$$

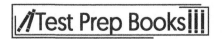

Whole numbers can also be converted into fractions by placing the whole number as the numerator and making the denominator 1. For example,

$$3 = \frac{3}{1}$$

One of the most fundamental concepts of fractions is their ability to be manipulated by multiplication or division. This is possible since $\frac{n}{n} = 1$ for any non-zero integer. As a result, multiplying or dividing by $\frac{n}{n}$ will not alter the original fraction since any number multiplied or divided by 1 doesn't change the value of that number. Fractions of the same value are known as equivalent fractions.

For example, $\frac{2}{4}, \frac{4}{8}, \frac{50}{100}$, and $\frac{75}{150}$ are equivalent, as they all equal $\frac{1}{2}$.

Although many equivalent fractions exist, they are easier to compare and interpret when reduced or simplified. The numerator and denominator of a simple fraction will have no factors in common other than 1. When reducing or simplifying fractions, divide the numerator and denominator by the greatest common factor. A simple strategy is to divide the numerator and denominator by low numbers, like 2, 3, or 5, until arriving at a simple fraction, but the same thing could be achieved by determining the greatest common factor for both the numerator and denominator and dividing each by it. Using the first method is preferable when both the numerator and denominator are even, end in 5, or are obviously a multiple of another number. However, if no numbers seem to work, it will be necessary to factor the numerator and denominator to find the GCF. For example:

1) Simplify the fraction $\frac{6}{8}$:

Dividing the numerator and denominator by 2 results in $\frac{3}{4}$, which is a simple fraction.

2) Simplify the fraction $\frac{12}{36}$:

Dividing the numerator and denominator by 2 leaves $\frac{6}{18}$. This isn't a simple fraction, as both the numerator and denominator have factors in common. Dividing each by 3 results in $\frac{2}{6}$, but this can be further simplified by dividing by 2 to get $\frac{1}{3}$. This is the simplest fraction, as the numerator is 1. In cases like this, multiple division operations can be avoided by determining the greatest common factor between the numerator and denominator.

3) Simplify the fraction $\frac{18}{54}$ by dividing by the greatest common factor:

First, determine the factors for the numerator and denominator. The factors of 18 are 1, 2, 3, 6, 9, and 18. The factors of 54 are 1, 2, 3, 6, 9, 18, 27, and 54. Thus, the greatest common factor is 18. Dividing $\frac{18}{54}$ by 18 leaves $\frac{1}{3}$, which is the simplest fraction. This method takes slightly more work, but it definitively arrives at the simplest fraction.

Of the four basic operations that can be performed on fractions, the one that involves the least amount of work is multiplication. To multiply two fractions, simply multiply the numerators together, multiply the denominators together, and place the products of each as a fraction. Whole numbers and mixed numbers can also be expressed as a fraction, as described above, to multiply with a fraction. Here are a few examples:

1) $\frac{2}{5} \times \frac{3}{4} = \frac{6}{20} = \frac{3}{10}$

2) $\frac{4}{9} \times \frac{7}{11} = \frac{28}{99}$

Dividing fractions is similar to multiplication with one key difference. To divide fractions, flip the numerator and denominator of the second fraction, and then proceed as if it were a multiplication problem:

1) $\frac{7}{8} \div \frac{4}{5} = \frac{7}{8} \times \frac{5}{4} = \frac{35}{32}$

2) $\frac{5}{9} \div \frac{1}{3} = \frac{5}{9} \times \frac{3}{1} = \frac{15}{9} = \frac{5}{3}$

Addition and subtraction require more steps than multiplication and division, as these operations require the fractions to have the same denominator, also called a common denominator. It is always possible to find a common denominator by multiplying the denominators. However, when the denominators are large numbers, this method is unwieldy, especially if the answer must be provided in its simplest form. Thus, it's beneficial to find the least common denominator of the fractions—the least common denominator is incidentally also the least common multiple.

Once equivalent fractions have been found with common denominators, simply add or subtract the numerators to arrive at the answer:

1) $\frac{1}{2} + \frac{3}{4} = \frac{2}{4} + \frac{3}{4} = \frac{5}{4}$

2) $\frac{3}{12} + \frac{11}{20} = \frac{15}{60} + \frac{33}{60} = \frac{48}{60} = \frac{4}{5}$

3) $\frac{7}{9} - \frac{4}{15} = \frac{35}{45} - \frac{12}{45} = \frac{23}{45}$

4) $\frac{5}{6} - \frac{7}{18} = \frac{15}{18} - \frac{7}{18} = \frac{8}{18} = \frac{4}{9}$

Decimals

The **decimal system** is a way of writing out numbers that uses ten different numerals: 0, 1, 2, 3, 4, 5, 6, 7, 8, and 9. This is also called a "base ten" or "base 10" system. Other bases are also used. For example, computers work with a base of 2. This means they only use the numerals 0 and 1.

The **decimal place** denotes how far to the right of the decimal point a numeral is. The first digit to the right of the decimal point is in the *tenths* place. The next is the **hundredths**. The third is the **thousandths**.

So, 3.142 has a 1 in the tenths place, a 4 in the hundredths place, and a 2 in the thousandths place.

The **decimal point** is a period used to separate the **ones** place from the **tenths** place when writing out a number as a decimal.

A **decimal number** is a number written out with a decimal point instead of as a fraction, for example, 1.25 instead of $\frac{5}{4}$. Depending on the situation, it can sometimes be easier to work with fractions and sometimes easier to work with decimal numbers.

A decimal number is **terminating** if it stops at some point. It is called **repeating** if it never stops but repeats over and over. It is important to note that every rational number can be written as a terminating decimal or as a repeating decimal.

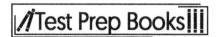

Addition with Decimals

To add decimal numbers, each number needs to be lined up by the decimal point in vertical columns. For each number being added, the zeros to the right of the last number need to be filled in so that each of the numbers has the same number of places to the right of the decimal. Then, the columns can be added together. Here is an example of $2.45 + 1.3 + 8.891$ written in column form:

$$
\begin{array}{r}
2.450 \\
1.300 \\
+8.891 \\
\hline
\end{array}
$$

Zeros have been added in the columns so that each number has the same number of places to the right of the decimal.

Added together, the correct answer is 12.641:

$$
\begin{array}{r}
2.450 \\
1.300 \\
+8.891 \\
\hline
12.641
\end{array}
$$

Subtraction with Decimals

Subtracting decimal numbers is the same process as adding decimals. Here is $7.89 - 4.235$ written in column form:

$$
\begin{array}{r}
7.890 \\
-4.235 \\
\hline
3.655
\end{array}
$$

A zero has been added in the column so that each number has the same number of places to the right of the decimal.

Multiplication with Decimals

The simplest way to multiply decimals is to calculate the product as if the decimals are not there, then count the number of decimal places in the original problem. Use that total to place the decimal the same number of places over in your answer, counting from right to left. For example, 0.5×1.25 can be rewritten and multiplied as:

$$5 \times 125 = 625$$

Then the decimal is added three places from the right for .625.

The final answer will have the same number of **decimal points** as the total number of decimal *places* in the problem. The first number has one decimal place, and the second number has two decimal places. Therefore, the final answer will contain three decimal places:

$$0.5 \times 1.25 = 0.625$$

Division with Decimals

Dividing a decimal by a whole number entails using long division first by ignoring the decimal point. Then, the decimal point is moved to the number of places given in the problem.

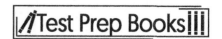

For example,

$$6.8 \div 4$$

This can be rewritten as:

$$68 \div 4$$

This is equal to 17. There is one non-zero integer to the right of the decimal point, so the final solution would have one decimal place to the right of the solution. In this case, the solution is 1.7.

Dividing a decimal by another decimal requires changing the divisor to a whole number by moving its decimal point. The decimal place of the dividend should be moved by the same number of places as the divisor. Then, the problem is the same as dividing a decimal by a whole number.

For example, $5.72 \div 1.1$ has a divisor with one decimal point in the denominator. The expression can be rewritten as $57.2 \div 11$ by moving each number one decimal place to the right to eliminate the decimal. The long division can be completed as $572 \div 11$ with a result of 52. Since there is one non-zero integer to the right of the decimal point in the problem, the final solution is 5.2.

In another example, $8 \div 0.16$ has a divisor with two decimal points in the denominator. The expression can be rewritten as $800 \div 16$ by moving each number two decimal places to the right to eliminate the decimal in the divisor. The long division can be completed with a result of 50.

Percentages [ISEE]

Think of **percentages** as fractions with a denominator of 100. In fact, percentage means "per hundred." Problems often require converting numbers from percentages, fractions, and decimals.

The basic percent equation is the following:

$$\frac{is}{of} = \frac{\%}{100}$$

The placement of numbers in the equation depends on what the question asks.

Example 1: Find 40% of 80.

Basically, the problem is asking, "What is 40% of 80?" The 40% is the percent, and 80 is the number to find the percent "of." The equation is:

$$\frac{x}{80} = \frac{40}{100}$$

Solving the equation by cross-multiplication, the problem becomes $100x = 80(40)$. Solving for x produces the answer: $x = 32$.

Example 2: What percent of 100 is 20?

20 fills in the "is" portion, while 100 fills in the "of." The question asks for the percent, so that will be x, the unknown. The following equation is set up:

$$\frac{20}{100} = \frac{x}{100}$$

Cross-multiplying yields the equation $100x = 20(100)$. Solving for x gives the answer: 20%.

Example 3: 30% of what number is 30?

The following equation uses the clues and numbers in the problem:

$$\frac{30}{x} = \frac{30}{100}$$

Cross-multiplying results in the equation $30(100) = 30x$. Solving for x gives the answer: $x = 100$.

Converting Fractions, Decimals, and Percentages [ISEE]

Decimals and Percentages

Since a percentage is based on "per hundred," decimals and percentages can be converted by multiplying or dividing by 100. Practically speaking, this always amounts to moving the decimal point two places to the right or left, depending on the conversion. To convert a percentage to a decimal, move the decimal point two places to the left and remove the % sign. To convert a decimal to a percentage, move the decimal point two places to the right and add a % sign. Here are some examples:

$$65\% = 0.65$$

$$0.33 = 33\%$$

$$0.215 = 21.5\%$$

$$99.99\% = 0.9999$$

$$500\% = 5.00$$

$$7.55 = 755\%$$

Fractions and Percentages

Remember that a percentage is a number per one hundred. So, a percentage can be converted to a fraction by making the number in the percentage the numerator and putting 100 as the denominator:

$$43\% = \frac{43}{100}$$

$$97\% = \frac{97}{100}$$

Note that the percent symbol (%) kind of looks like a 0, a 1, and another 0. So, think of a percentage like 54% as 54 over 100.

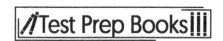

To convert a fraction to a percent, follow the same logic. If the fraction happens to have 100 in the denominator, you're in luck. Just take the numerator and add a percent symbol:

$$\frac{28}{100} = 28\%$$

Otherwise, divide the numerator by the denominator to get a decimal:

$$\frac{9}{12} = 0.75$$

Then convert the decimal to a percentage:

$$0.75 = 75\%$$

Another option is to make the denominator equal to 100. Be sure to multiply the numerator and the denominator by the same number. For example:

$$\frac{3}{20} \times \frac{5}{5} = \frac{15}{100}$$

$$\frac{15}{100} = 15\%$$

Changing Fractions to Decimals

To change a fraction into a decimal, divide the denominator into the numerator until there are no remainders. There may be repeating decimals, so rounding is often acceptable. A straight line above the repeating portion denotes that the decimal repeats.

Example: Express $\frac{4}{5}$ as a decimal.

Set up the division problem.

$$5\overline{)4}$$

5 does not go into 4, so place the decimal and add a zero.

$$5\overline{)4.0}$$

5 goes into 40 eight times. There is no remainder.

$$\begin{array}{r} 0.8 \\ 5\overline{)4.0} \\ -4.0 \\ \hline 0 \end{array}$$

The solution is 0.8.

Example: Express $33\frac{1}{3}$ as a decimal.

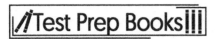

Since the whole portion of the number is known, set it aside to calculate the decimal from the fraction portion.

Set up the division problem.

$$3\overline{)1}$$

3 does not go into 1, so place the decimal and add zeros. 3 goes into 10 three times.

$$\begin{array}{r} 0.333 \\ 3\overline{)1.000} \end{array}$$

This will repeat with a remainder of 1, so placing a line over the 3 denotes the repetition.

$$\begin{array}{r} 0.333 \\ 3\overline{)1.000} \\ -9 \\ \hline 10 \\ -9 \\ \hline 10 \end{array}$$

The solution is $0.\overline{3}$

Changing Decimals to Fractions

To change decimals to fractions, place the decimal portion of the number, the numerator, over the respective place value, the denominator, then reduce, if possible.

Example: Express 0.25 as a fraction.

This is read as twenty-five hundredths, so put 25 over 100. Then reduce to find the solution.

$$\frac{25}{100} = \frac{1}{4}$$

Example: Express 0.455 as a fraction

This is read as four hundred fifty-five thousandths, so put 455 over 1,000. Then reduce to find the solution.

$$\frac{455}{1,000} = \frac{91}{200}$$

There are two types of problems that commonly involve percentages. The first is to calculate some percentage of a given quantity, where you convert the percentage to a decimal, and multiply the quantity by that decimal. Secondly, you are given a quantity and told it is a fixed percent of an unknown quantity. In this case, convert to a decimal, then divide the given quantity by that decimal.

Example: What is 30% of 760?

Convert the percent into a usable number. "Of" means to multiply.

$$30\% = 0.30$$

56

Set up the problem based on the givens and solve.

$$0.30 \times 760 = 228$$

Example: 8.4 is 20% of what number?

Convert the percent into a usable number.

$$20\% = 0.20$$

The given number is a percent of the answer needed, so divide the given number by this decimal rather than multiplying it.

$$\frac{8.4}{0.20} = 42$$

Representing Fractions, Decimals, and Percent Using Various Models [ISEE]

A **fraction** is a part of something that is whole. Items such as apples can be cut into parts to help visualize fractions. If an apple is cut into 2 equal parts, each part represents $\frac{1}{2}$ of the apple. If each half is cut into two parts, the apple now is cut into quarters. Each piece now represents $\frac{1}{4}$ of the apple. In this example, each part is equal because they all have the same size. Geometric shapes, such as circles and squares, can also be utilized in the classroom to help visualize the idea of fractions.

For example, a circle can be drawn on the board and divided into 6 equal parts:

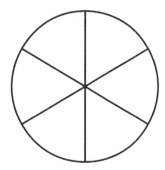

Shading can be used to represent parts of the circle that can be translated into fractions. The top of the fraction, the **numerator,** can represent how many segments are shaded. The bottom of the fraction, the **denominator,** can represent the number of segments that the circle is broken into. A pie is a good analogy to use in this example. If one piece of the circle is shaded, or one piece of pie is cut out, $\frac{1}{6}$ of the object is being referred to. An apple, a pie, or a circle can be utilized in order to compare simple fractions. For example, showing that $\frac{1}{2}$ is larger than $\frac{1}{4}$ and that $\frac{1}{4}$ is smaller than $\frac{1}{3}$ can be accomplished through shading. A **unit fraction** is a fraction in which the numerator is 1, and the denominator is a positive whole number. It represents one part of a whole—one piece of pie.

When representing fractions, it is important to remember the meaning of the word **fraction**. The number is a fraction, or portion, of a whole. The whole, or 1, is the number on the bottom part of the fraction, the denominator.

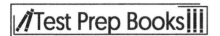
For example, the fraction $\frac{2}{5}$ represents a number of portions (the numerator, 2) of how many it would take to make a whole (the denominator, 5). So, $\frac{2}{5}$ represents 2 portions out of the 5 it would take to make a whole.

This could also be represented with blocks, as follows:

5 blocks = 1 whole

So, only 2 of the 5 are shaded.

This method could also be used to represent fractions with a higher number in the numerator than in the denominator.

What does the fraction $\frac{6}{5}$ look like with the block method?

Fractions can be broken apart into sums of fractions with the same denominator. For example, the fraction $\frac{5}{6}$ can be decomposed into sums of fractions with all denominators equal to 6 and the numerators adding to 5. The fraction $\frac{5}{6}$ is decomposed as the following:

$$\frac{3}{6} + \frac{2}{6}$$

$$\frac{2}{6} + \frac{2}{6} + \frac{1}{6}$$

$$\frac{3}{6} + \frac{1}{6} + \frac{1}{6}$$

$$\frac{1}{6} + \frac{1}{6} + \frac{1}{6} + \frac{2}{6}$$

$$\frac{1}{6} + \frac{1}{6} + \frac{1}{6} + \frac{1}{6} + \frac{1}{6}$$

As mentioned, unit fraction is a fraction in which the numerator is 1. If decomposing a fraction into unit fractions, the sum will consist of a unit fraction added the number of times equal to the numerator.

For example, unit fractions $\frac{1}{4}$ added 3 times:

$$\frac{3}{4} = \frac{1}{4} + \frac{1}{4} + \frac{1}{4}$$

Composing fractions is simply the opposite of decomposing. It is the process of adding fractions with the same denominators to produce a single fraction. For example,

$$\frac{3}{7} + \frac{2}{7} = \frac{5}{7}$$

and

$$\frac{1}{5} + \frac{1}{5} + \frac{1}{5} = \frac{3}{5}$$

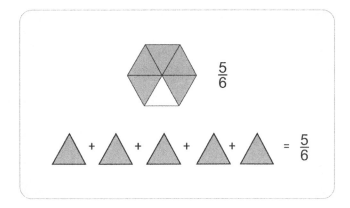

To represent fractions and decimals as distances beginning at zero on a number line, it's helpful to relate the fraction to a real-world application. For example, a charity walk covers $\frac{3}{10}$ of a mile. How could this distance be represented on a number line?

First, divide the number line into tenths, as follows:

If each division on the number line represents one-tenth of one, or $\frac{1}{10}$ then representing the distance of the charity walk, $\frac{3}{10}$, would cover 3 of those divisions and look as follows:

So, the fraction $\frac{3}{10}$ is represented by covering from 0 to 0.3 (or 3 sections) on the number line.

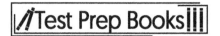

In general, to precisely understand a number being represented on a number line, the first step is to identify how the number line is divided up. When utilizing a number line to represent decimal portions of numbers, it is helpful to label the divisions, or insert additional divisions, as needed.

For example, what number, to the nearest hundredths place, is marked by the point on the following number line?

First, figure out how the number line is divided up. In this case, it has ten sections, so it is divided into tenths. To use this number line with the divisions, label the divisions as follows:

Because the dot is placed equally between 0.4 and 0.5, it is at 0.45.

What number, to the nearest tenths place, is marked by the point on the following number line?

First, determine what the number line is divided up into and mark it on the line.

This number line is divided up into half of the whole numbers it represents, or 0.5 increments. The division and labeling of the number line assists in easily reading the dot as marking 2.5.

Exponents [ISEE]

Exponents are used in mathematics to express a number or variable multiplied by itself a certain number of times. For example, x^3 means x is multiplied by itself three times. In this expression, x is called the **base**, and 3 is the **exponent.** Exponents can be used in more complex problems when they contain fractions and negative numbers.

Fractional exponents can be explained by looking first at the inverse of exponents, which are **roots.** Given the expression x^2, the square root can be taken, $\sqrt{x^2}$, canceling out the 2 and leaving x by itself, if x is positive.

Cancellation occurs because $\sqrt{x}$ can be written with exponents, instead of roots, as $x^{\frac{1}{2}}$. The numerator of 1 is the exponent, and the denominator of 2 is called the **root** (which is why it's referred to as a **square root**). Taking the square root of x^2 is the same as raising it to the $\frac{1}{2}$ power. Written out in mathematical form, it takes the following progression:

$$\sqrt{x^2} = (x^2)^{\frac{1}{2}} = x$$

From properties of exponents $2 \times \frac{1}{2} = 1$ is the actual exponent of x. Another example can be seen with $x^{\frac{4}{7}}$. The variable x, raised to four-sevenths, is equal to the seventh root of x to the fourth power: $\sqrt[7]{x^4}$. In general,

$$x^{\frac{1}{n}} = \sqrt[n]{x}$$

and

$$x^{\frac{m}{n}} = \sqrt[n]{x^m}$$

Negative exponents also involve fractions. Whereas y^3 can also be rewritten as $\frac{y^3}{1}$, y^{-3} can be rewritten as $\frac{1}{y^3}$. A negative exponent means the exponential expression must be moved to the opposite spot in a fraction to make the exponent positive. If the negative appears in the numerator, it moves to the denominator. If the negative appears in the denominator, it is moved to the numerator. In general, $a^{-n} = \frac{1}{a^n}$, and a^{-n} and a^n are reciprocals.

Take, for example, the following expression:

$$\frac{a^{-4}b^2}{c^{-5}}$$

Since a is raised to the negative fourth power, it can be moved to the denominator. Since c is raised to the negative fifth power, it can be moved to the numerator. The b variable is raised to the positive second power, so it does not move.

The simplified expression is as follows:

$$\frac{b^2 c^5}{a^4}$$

In mathematical expressions containing exponents and other operations, the order of operations must be followed. **PEMDAS** states that exponents are calculated after any parentheses and grouping symbols but before any multiplication, division, addition, and subtraction.

Scientific Notation [ISEE]

Scientific notation is used to represent numbers that are either very small or very large. For example, the distance to the Sun is approximately 150,000,000,000 meters. Instead of writing this number with so many zeros, it can be written in scientific notation as 1.5×10^{11} meters. The same is true for very small numbers, but the exponent becomes negative. If the mass of a human cell is 0.000000000001 kilograms, that measurement can be easily represented by 1.0×10^{-12} kilograms. In both situations, scientific notation makes the measurement easier to read and understand. Each number is translated to an expression with ones and tenths places multiplied by an expression corresponding to the zeros.

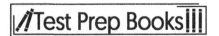

When two measurements are given and both involve scientific notation, it is important to know how these interact with each other:

- In addition and subtraction, the exponent on the ten must be the same before any operations are performed on the numbers. For example, $(1.3 \times 10^4) + (3.0 \times 10^3)$ cannot be added until one of the exponents on the ten is changed. The 3.0×10^3 can be changed to 0.3×10^4, then the 1.3 and 0.3 can be added. The answer comes out to be 1.6×10^4.

- For multiplication, the first numbers can be multiplied and then the exponents on the tens can be added. Once an answer is formed, it may have to be converted into scientific notation again depending on the change that occurred.

- The following is an example of multiplication with scientific notation:

$$(4.5 \times 10^3) \times (3.0 \times 10^{-5}) = 13.5 \times 10^{-2}$$

- Since this answer is not in scientific notation, the decimal is moved over to the left one unit, and 1 is added to the ten's exponent. This results in the final answer:

$$1.35 \times 10^{-1}$$

- For division, the first numbers are divided, and the exponents on the tens are subtracted. Again, the answer may need to be converted into scientific notation form, depending on the type of changes that occurred during the problem.

- **Order of magnitude** relates to scientific notation and is the total count of powers of 10 in a number. For example, there are 6 orders of magnitude in 1,000,000. If a number is raised by an order of magnitude, it is multiplied by 10. Order of magnitude can be helpful in estimating results using very large or small numbers. An answer should make sense in terms of its order of magnitude.

- For example, if area is calculated using two dimensions with 6 orders of magnitude, because area involves multiplication, the answer should have around 12 orders of magnitude. Also, answers can be estimated by rounding to the largest place value in each number. For example: 5,493,302 × 2,523,100 can be estimated by 5 × 3 = 15 with 12 orders of magnitude.

Simplifying and Approximating Radicals [ISEE]

The **square root symbol** is expressed as $\sqrt{}$ and is commonly known as the **radical.** Taking the root of a number is the inverse operation of multiplying that number by itself some amount of times. For example, squaring the number 7 is equal to 7×7, or 49. Finding the square root is the opposite of finding an exponent, as the operation seeks a number that when multiplied by itself equals the number in the square root symbol.

For example,

$$\sqrt{36} = 6$$

6 multiplied by 6 equals 36. Note, the square root of 36 is also -6 since:

$$-6 \times -6 = 36$$

This can be indicated using a plus/minus symbol like this: ± 6. However, square roots are often just expressed as a positive number for simplicity with it being understood that the true value can be either positive or negative.

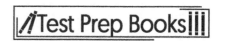

Perfect squares are numbers with whole number square roots. The list of perfect squares begins with 0, 1, 4, 9, 16, 25, 36, 49, 64, 81, and 100.

Determining the square root of imperfect squares requires a calculator to reach an exact figure. It's possible, however, to approximate the answer by finding the two perfect squares that the number fits between. For example, the square root of 40 is between 6 and 7 since the squares of those numbers are 36 and 49, respectively.

Square roots are the most common root operation. If the radical doesn't have a number to the upper left of the symbol, $\sqrt{\ }$, then it's a square root. Sometimes a radical includes a number in the upper left, like $\sqrt[3]{27}$, as in the other common root type—the cube root. Complicated roots like the cube root often require a calculator.

Sequences and Series [SSAT]

Patterns within a sequence can come in 2 distinct forms: the items (shapes, numbers, etc.) either repeat in a constant order, or the items change from one step to another in some consistent way. The core is the smallest unit, or number of items, that repeats in a repeating pattern. For example, the pattern ○○▲○○▲○... has a core that is ○○▲. Knowing only the core, the pattern can be extended. Knowing the number of steps in the core allows the identification of an item in each step without drawing/writing the entire pattern out. For example, suppose the tenth item in the previous pattern must be determined. Because the core consists of three items (○○▲), the core repeats in multiples of 3. In other words, steps 3, 6, 9, 12, etc. will be ▲ completing the core with the core starting over on the next step. For the above example, the 9th step will be ▲ and the 10th will be ○.

The most common patterns in which each item changes from one step to the next are arithmetic and geometric sequences. An arithmetic sequence is one in which the items increase or decrease by a constant difference. In other words, the same thing is added or subtracted to each item or step to produce the next. To determine if a sequence is arithmetic, determine what must be added or subtracted to step one to produce step two. Then, check if the same thing is added/subtracted to step two to produce step three. The same thing must be added/subtracted to step three to produce step four, and so on. Consider the pattern 13, 10, 7, 4 ... To get from step one (13) to step two (10) by adding or subtracting requires subtracting by 3. The next step is checking if subtracting 3 from step two (10) will produce step three (7), and subtracting 3 from step three (7) will produce step four (4). In this case, the pattern holds true. Therefore, this is an arithmetic sequence in which each step is produced by subtracting 3 from the previous step. To extend the sequence, 3 is subtracted from the last step to produce the next. The next three numbers in the sequence are 1, -2, -5.

A geometric sequence is one in which each step is produced by multiplying or dividing the previous step by the same number. To determine if a sequence is geometric, decide what step one must be multiplied or divided by to produce step two. Then check if multiplying or dividing step two by the same number produces step three, and so on. Consider the pattern 2, 8, 32, 128 ... To get from step one (2) to step two (8) requires multiplication by 4. The next step determines if multiplying step two (8) by 4 produces step three (32), and multiplying step three (32) by 4 produces step four (128). In this case, the pattern holds true. Therefore, this is a geometric sequence in which each step is produced by multiplying the previous step by 4. To extend the sequence, the last step is multiplied by 4 and repeated. The next three numbers in the sequence are 512; 2,048; 8,192.

Although arithmetic and geometric sequences typically use numbers, these sequences can also be represented by shapes. For example, an arithmetic sequence could consist of shapes with three sides, four sides, and five sides (add one side to the previous step to produce the next). A geometric sequence could consist of eight blocks, four blocks, and two blocks (each step is produced by dividing the number of blocks in the previous step by 2).

63

Frequencies [SSAT]

In mathematics, frequencies refer to how often an event occurs or the number of times a particular quantity appears in a given series. To find the number of times a specific value appears, frequency tables are used to record the occurrences, which can then be summed. To construct a frequency table, one simply inputs the values into a tabular format with a column denoting each value, typically in ascending order, with a second column to tally up the number of occurrences for each value, and a third column to give a numerical frequency based on the number of tallies.

A **frequency distribution communicates** the number of outcomes of a given value or number in a data set. When displayed as a bar graph or histogram, a frequency distribution can visually indicate the spread and distribution of the data. A histogram resembling a bell curve approximates a normal distribution. A frequency distribution can also be displayed as a **stem-and-leaf plot**, which arranges data in numerical order and displays values similar to a tally chart with the stem being a range within the set and the leaf indicating the exact value (i.e., stems are whole numbers and leaves are tenths).

	Movie Ratings
4	7
5	2 6 9
6	1 4 6 8 8
7	0 3 5 9
8	1 3 5 6 8 8 9
9	0 0 1 3 4 6 6 9

Key	6 │ 1 represents 61

Stem	Leaf
2	0 2 3 6 8 8 9
3	2 6 7 7
4	7 9
5	4 6 9

This plot provides more detail about individual data points and allows for easy identification of the median, as well as any repeated values in the set.

Data that isn't described using numbers is known as **categorical data.** For example, age is numerical data but hair color is categorical data. Categorical data can also be summarized using two-way frequency tables. A **two-way frequency table** counts the relationship between two sets of categorical data. There are rows and columns for each category, and each cell represents frequency information that shows the actual data count between each combination.

For example, below is a two-way frequency table showing the gender and breed of cats in an animal shelter:

	Domestic Shorthair	Persian	Domestic Longhair	Total
Male	12	2	7	21
Female	8	4	5	17
Total	20	6	12	38

Entries in the middle of the table are known as the **joint frequencies**. For example, the number of females that are Persians is 4, which is a joint frequency. The totals are the **marginal frequencies**. For example, the total number of males is 21, which is a marginal frequency. If the frequencies are changed into percentages based on totals, the table is known as a **two-way relative frequency table**. Percentages can be calculated using the table total, the row totals, or the column totals. Two-way frequency tables can help in making conclusions about the data.

Algebra

Algebraic Expressions and Equations

An algebraic expression is a statement about an unknown quantity expressed in mathematical symbols. A variable is used to represent the unknown quantity, usually denoted by a letter. An equation is a statement in which two expressions (at least one containing a variable) are equal to each other. An algebraic expression can be thought of as a mathematical phrase and an equation can be thought of as a mathematical sentence.

Algebraic expressions and equations both contain numbers, variables, and mathematical operations. The following are examples of algebraic expressions: $5x + 3$, $7xy - 8(x^2 + y)$, and $\sqrt{a^2 + b^2}$. An expression can be simplified or evaluated for given values of variables. The following are examples of equations: $2x + 3 = 7$, $a^2 + b^2 = c^2$, and $2x + 5 = 3x - 2$. An equation contains two sides separated by an equal sign. Equations can be solved to determine the value(s) of the variable for which the statement is true.

Adding and Subtracting Linear Algebraic Expressions

An algebraic expression is simplified by combining like terms. A term is a number, variable, or product of a number and variables separated by addition and subtraction. For the algebraic expression $3x^2 - 4x + 5 - 5x^2 + x - 3$, the terms are $3x^2$, $-4x$, 5, $-5x^2$, x, and -3. Like terms have the same variables raised to the same powers (exponents). The like terms for the previous example are $3x^2$ and $-5x^2$, $-4x$ and x, 5 and -3. To combine like

65

terms, the coefficients (numerical factor of the term including sign) are added, and the variables and their powers are kept the same. Note that if a coefficient is not written, it is an implied coefficient of 1 ($x = 1x$). The previous example will simplify to $-2x^2 - 3x + 2$.

When adding or subtracting algebraic expressions, each expression is written in parentheses. The negative sign is distributed when necessary, and like terms are combined. Consider the following: add $2a + 5b - 2$ to $a - 2b + 8c - 4$. The sum is set as follows: $(a - 2b + 8c - 4) + (2a + 5b - 2)$. In front of each set of parentheses is an implied positive one, which, when distributed, does not change any of the terms. Therefore, the parentheses are dropped and like terms are combined:

$$a - 2b + 8c = 4 + 2a + 5b - 2 = 3a + 3b + 8c - 6$$

Consider the following problem: Subtract $2a + 5b - 2$ from $a - 2b + 8c - 4$. The difference is set as follows:

$$(a - 2b + 8c - 4) - (2a + 5b - 2)$$

The implied one in front of the first set of parentheses will not change those four terms. However, distributing the implied -1 in front of the second set of parentheses will change the sign of each of those three terms:

$$a - 2b + 8c - 4 - 2a - 5b + 2$$

Combining like terms yields the simplified expression $-a - 7b + 8c - 2$.

Distributive Property

The distributive property states that multiplying a sum (or difference) by a number produces the same result as multiplying each value in the sum (or difference) by the number and adding (or subtracting) the products. Using mathematical symbols, the distributive property states $a(b + c) = ab + ac$. The expression $4(3 + 2)$ is simplified using the order of operations. Simplifying inside the parentheses first produces 4×5, which equals 20. The expression $4(3 + 2)$ can also be simplified using the distributive property:

$$4(3 + 2) = 4 \times 3 + 4 \times 2 = 12 + 8 = 20$$

Consider the following example: $4(3x - 2)$. The expression cannot be simplified inside the parentheses because $3x$ and -2 are not like terms and therefore cannot be combined. However, the expression can be simplified by using the distributive property and multiplying each term inside of the parentheses by the term outside of the parentheses: $12x - 8$. The resulting equivalent expression contains no like terms, so it cannot be further simplified.

Consider the expression $(3x + 2y + 1) - (5x - 3) + 2(3y + 4)$. Again, there are no like terms, but the distributive property is used to simplify the expression. Note there is an implied one in front of the first set of parentheses and an implied -1 in front of the second set of parentheses. Distributing the 1, -1, and 2 produces:

$$1(3x) + 1(2y) + 1(1) - 1(5x) - 1(-3) + 2(3y) + 2(4) = 3x + 2y + 1 - 5x + 3 + 6y + 8$$

This expression contains like terms that are combined to produce the simplified expression $-2x + 8y + 12$.

Algebraic expressions are tested to be equivalent by choosing values for the variables and evaluating both expressions. For example, $4(3x - 2)$ and $12x - 8$ are tested by substituting 3 for the variable x and calculating to determine if equivalent values result.

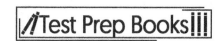

Simple Expressions for Given Values

An algebraic expression is a statement written in mathematical symbols, typically including one or more unknown values represented by variables. For example, the expression $2x + 3$ states that an unknown number (x) is multiplied by 2 and added to 3. If given a value for the unknown number, or variable, the value of the expression is determined. For example, if the value of the variable x is 4, the value of the expression 4 is multiplied by 2, and 3 is added. This results in a value of 11 for the expression.

When given an algebraic expression and values for the variable(s), the expression is evaluated to determine its numerical value. To evaluate the expression, the given values for the variables are substituted (or replaced), and the expression is simplified using the order of operations. Parentheses should be used when substituting. Consider the following: Evaluate $a - 2b + ab$ for $a = 3$ and $b = -1$. To evaluate, any variable a is replaced with 3 and any variable b with -1, producing $(3) - 2(-1) + 3(-1)$. Next, the order of operations is used to calculate the value of the expression, which is 2.

Parts of Expressions

Algebraic expressions consist of variables, numbers, and operations. A term of an expression is any combination of numbers and/or variables, and terms are separated by addition and subtraction. For example, the expression $5x^2 - 3xy + 4 - 2$ consists of 4 terms: $5x^2, -3xy, 4y$, and -2. Note that each term includes its given sign ($+$ or $-$). The variable part of a term is a letter that represents an unknown quantity. The coefficient of a term is the number by which the variable is multiplied. For the term $4y$, the variable is y, and the coefficient is 4. Terms are identified by the power (or exponent) of its variable.

A number without a variable is referred to as a constant. If the variable is to the first power (x^1 or simply x), it is referred to as a linear term. A term with a variable to the second power (x^2) is quadratic, and a term to the third power (x^3) is cubic. Consider the expression $x^3 + 3x - 1$. The constant is -1. The linear term is $3x$. There is no quadratic term. The cubic term is x^3.

An algebraic expression can also be classified by how many terms exist in the expression. Any like terms should be combined before classifying. A monomial is an expression consisting of only one term. Examples of monomials are: $17, 2x$, and $-5ab^2$. A binomial is an expression consisting of two terms separated by addition or subtraction. Examples include $2x - 4$ and $-3y^2 + 2y$. A trinomial consists of 3 terms. For example, $5x^2 - 2x + 1$ is a trinomial.

Verbal Statements and Algebraic Expressions

An algebraic expression is a statement about unknown quantities expressed in mathematical symbols. The statement *five times a number added to forty* is expressed as $5x + 40$. An equation is a statement in which two expressions (with at least one containing a variable) are equal to one another. The statement *five times a number added to forty is equal to ten* is expressed as $5x + 40 = 10$.

Real world scenarios can also be expressed mathematically. Suppose a job pays its employees $300 per week and $40 for each sale made. The weekly pay is represented by the expression $40x + 300$ where x is the number of sales made during the week.

Consider the following scenario: Bob had $20 and Tom had $4. After selling 4 ice cream cones to Bob, Tom has as much money as Bob. The cost of an ice cream cone is an unknown quantity and can be represented by a variable (x). The amount of money Bob has after his purchase is four times the cost of an ice cream cone subtracted from his original $20 → $20 - 4x$. The amount of money Tom has after his sale is four times the cost of an ice cream cone

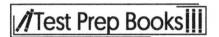

added to his original \$4 → $4x + 4$. After the sale, the amount of money that Bob and Tom have is equal → $20 - 4x = 4x + 4$.

When expressing a verbal or written statement mathematically, it is vital to understand words or phrases that can be represented with symbols. The following are examples:

Symbol	Phrase
+	Added to; increased by; sum of; more than
−	Decreased by; difference between; less than; take away
×	Multiplied by; 3(4,5...) times as large; product of
÷	Divided by; quotient of; half (third, etc.) of
=	Is; the same as; results in; as much as; equal to
x,t,n, etc.	A number; unknown quantity; value of; variable

Use of Formulas

Formulas are mathematical expressions that define the value of one quantity, given the value of one or more different quantities. Formulas look like equations because they contain variables, numbers, operators, and an equal sign. All formulas are equations, but not all equations are formulas. A formula must have more than one variable. For example, $2x + 7 = y$ is an equation and a formula (it relates the unknown quantities x and y). However, $2x + 7 = 3$ is an equation but not a formula (it only expresses the value of the unknown quantity x).

Formulas are typically written with one variable alone (or isolated) on one side of the equal sign. This variable can be thought of as the *subject* in that the formula is stating the value of the *subject* in terms of the relationship between the other variables. Consider the distance formula: $distance = rate \times time$ or $d = rt$. The value of the subject variable d (distance) is the product of the variable r and t (rate and time). Given the rate and time, the distance traveled can easily be determined by substituting the values into the formula and evaluating.

The formula $P = 2l + 2w$ expresses how to calculate the perimeter of a rectangle (P) given its length (l) and width (w). To find the perimeter of a rectangle with a length of 3 ft and a width of 2 ft, these values are substituted into the formula for l and w:

$$P = 2(3 \text{ ft}) + 2(2 \text{ ft})$$

Following the order of operations, the perimeter is determined to be 10 ft. When working with formulas such as these, including units is an important step.

Given a formula expressed in terms of one variable, the formula can be manipulated to express the relationship in terms of any other variable. In other words, the formula can be rearranged to change which variable is the *subject*.

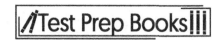

To solve for a variable of interest by manipulating a formula, the equation may be solved as if all other variables were numbers. The same steps for solving are followed, leaving operations in terms of the variables instead of calculating numerical values. For the formula $P = 2l + 2w$, the perimeter is the subject expressed in terms of the length and width. To write a formula to calculate the width of a rectangle, given its length and perimeter, the previous formula relating the three variables is solved for the variable w. If P and l were numerical values, this is a two-step linear equation solved by subtraction and division. To solve the equation $P = 2l + 2w$ for w, $2l$ is first subtracted from both sides: $P - 2l = 2w$. Then both sides are divided by 2:

$$\frac{P - 2l}{2} = w$$

Dependent and Independent Variables

A variable represents an unknown quantity and, in the case of a formula, a specific relationship exists between the variables. Within a given scenario, variables are the quantities that are changing. If two variables exist, one is dependent and one is independent. The value of one variable depends on the other variable. If a scenario describes distance traveled and time traveled at a given speed, distance is dependent and time is independent. The distance traveled depends on the time spent traveling. If a scenario describes the cost of a cab ride and the distance traveled, the cost is dependent and the distance is independent. The cost of a cab ride depends on the distance travelled. Formulas often contain more than two variables and are typically written with the dependent variable alone on one side of the equation. This lone variable is the *subject* of the statement. If a formula contains three or more variables, one variable is dependent and the rest are independent. The values of all independent variables are needed to determine the value of the dependent variable.

The formula $P = 2l + 2w$ expresses the dependent variable P in terms of the independent variables, l and w. The perimeter of a rectangle depends on its length and width. The formula $d = rt$ ($distance = rate \times time$) expresses the dependent variable d in terms of the independent variables, r and t. The distance traveled depends on the rate (or speed) and the time traveled.

Multi-step One-Variable Linear Equations and Inequalities

Linear equations and linear inequalities are both comparisons of two algebraic expressions. However, unlike equations in which the expressions are equal, linear inequalities compare expressions that may be unequal. Linear equations typically have one value for the variable that makes the statement true. Linear inequalities generally have an infinite number of values that make the statement true.

When solving a linear equation, the desired result requires determining a numerical value for the unknown variable. If given a linear equation involving addition, subtraction, multiplication, or division, working backwards isolates the variable. Addition and subtraction are inverse operations, as are multiplication and division. Therefore, they can be used to cancel each other out.

The first steps to solving linear equations are distributing, if necessary, and combining any like terms on the same side of the equation. Sides of an equation are separated by an *equal* sign. Next, the equation is manipulated to show the variable on one side. Whatever is done to one side of the equation must be done to the other side of the equation to remain equal. Inverse operations are then used to isolate the variable and undo the order of operations backwards. Addition and subtraction are undone, then multiplication and division are undone.

For example, solve $4(t - 2) + 2t - 4 = 2(9 - 2t)$

Distributing: $4t - 8 + 2t - 4 = 18 - 4t$

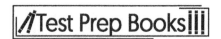

Combining like terms: $6t - 12 = 18 - 4t$

Adding $4t$ to each side to move the variable: $10t - 12 = 18$

Adding 12 to each side to isolate the variable: $10t = 30$

Dividing each side by 10 to isolate the variable: $t = 3$

The answer can be checked by substituting the value for the variable into the original equation, ensuring that both sides calculate to be equal.

Linear inequalities express the relationship between unequal values. More specifically, they describe in what way the values are unequal. A value can be greater than ($>$), less than ($<$), greater than or equal to ($\geq$), or less than or equal to ($\leq$) another value. $5x + 40 > 65$ is read as *five times a number added to forty is greater than sixty-five.*

When solving a linear inequality, the solution is the set of all numbers that make the statement true. The inequality $x + 2 \geq 6$ has a solution set of 4 and every number greater than 4 (4.01; 5; 12; 107; etc.). Adding 2 to 4 or any number greater than 4 results in a value that is greater than or equal to 6. Therefore, $x \geq 4$ is the solution set.

To algebraically solve a linear inequality, follow the same steps as those for solving a linear equation. The inequality symbol stays the same for all operations *except* when multiplying or dividing by a negative number. If multiplying or dividing by a negative number while solving an inequality, the relationship reverses (the sign flips). In other words, $>$ switches to $<$ and vice versa. Multiplying or dividing by a positive number does not change the relationship, so the sign stays the same. An example is shown below.

Solve $-2x - 8 \leq 22$ for the value of x.

Add 8 to both sides to isolate the variable: $-2x \leq 30$

Divide both sides by -2 to solve for x: $x \geq -15$

Solutions of a linear equation or a linear inequality are the values of the variable that make a statement true. In the case of a linear equation, the solution set (list of all possible solutions) typically consists of a single numerical value. To find the solution, the equation is solved by isolating the variable. For example, solving the equation $3x - 7 = -13$ produces the solution $x = -2$. The only value for x which produces a true statement is -2. This can be checked by substituting -2 into the original equation to check that both sides are equal. In this case, $3(-2) - 7 = -13 \rightarrow -13 = -13$; therefore, -2 is a solution.

Although linear equations generally have one solution, this is not always the case. If there is no value for the variable that makes the statement true, there is no solution to the equation. Consider the equation $x + 3 = x - 1$. There is no value for x in which adding 3 to the value produces the same result as subtracting one from the value. Conversely, if any value for the variable makes a true statement, the equation has an infinite number of solutions. Consider the equation $3x + 6 = 3(x + 2)$. Any number substituted for x will result in a true statement (both sides of the equation are equal).

By manipulating equations like the two above, the variable of the equation will cancel out completely. If the remaining constants express a true statement (ex. $6 = 6$), then all real numbers are solutions to the equation. If the constants left express a false statement (ex. $3 = -1$), then no solution exists for the equation.

Solving a linear inequality requires all values that make the statement true to be determined. For example, solving $3x - 7 \geq -13$ produces the solution $x \geq -2$. This means that -2 and any number greater than -2 produces a true statement. Solution sets for linear inequalities will often be displayed using a number line. If a value is included in the set ($\geq$ or $\leq$), a shaded dot is placed on that value and an arrow extending in the direction of the solutions. For a variable $>$ or $\geq$ a number, the arrow will point right on a number line, the direction where the numbers increase. If a variable is $<$ or $\leq$ a number, the arrow will point left on a number line, which is the direction where the numbers decrease. If the value is not included in the set ($>$ or $<$), an open (unshaded) circle on that value is used with an arrow in the appropriate direction.

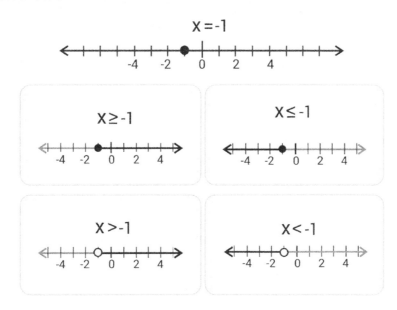

Similar to linear equations, a linear inequality may have a solution set consisting of all real numbers, or can contain no solution. When solved algebraically, a linear inequality in which the variable cancels out and results in a true statement (ex. $7 \geq 2$) has a solution set of all real numbers. A linear inequality in which the variable cancels out and results in a false statement (ex. $7 \leq 2$) has no solution.

Linear Relationships

Linear relationships describe the way two quantities change with respect to each other. The relationship is defined as linear because a line is produced if all the sets of corresponding values are graphed on a coordinate grid. When expressing the linear relationship as an equation, the equation is often written in the form $y = mx + b$ (slope-intercept form) where m and b are numerical values and x and y are variables (for example, $y = 5x + 10$). Given a linear equation and the value of either variable (x or y), the value of the other variable can be determined.

Suppose a teacher is grading a test containing 20 questions with 5 points given for each correct answer, adding a curve of 10 points to each test. This linear relationship can be expressed as the equation $y = 5x + 10$ where x represents the number of correct answers, and y represents the test score. To determine the score of a test with a given number of correct answers, the number of correct answers is substituted into the equation for x and evaluated. For example, for 10 correct answers, 10 is substituted for x:

$$y = 5(10) + 10 \rightarrow y = 60$$

Therefore, 10 correct answers will result in a score of 60. The number of correct answers needed to obtain a certain score can also be determined. To determine the number of correct answers needed to score a 90, 90 is substituted for y in the equation (y represents the test score) and solved:

$$90 = 5x + 10 \rightarrow 80 = 5x \rightarrow 16 = x$$

71

Therefore, 16 correct answers are needed to score a 90.

Linear relationships may be represented by a table of 2 corresponding values. Certain tables may determine the relationship between the values and predict other corresponding sets.

Consider the table below, which displays the money in a checking account that charges a monthly fee:

Month	0	1	2	3	4
Balance	$210	$195	$180	$165	$150

An examination of the values reveals that the account loses $15 every month (the month increases by one and the balance decreases by 15). This information can be used to predict future values. To determine what the value will be in month 6, the pattern can be continued, and it can be concluded that the balance will be $120. To determine which month the balance will be $0, $210 is divided by $15 (since the balance decreases $15 every month), resulting in month 14.

Similar to a table, a graph can display corresponding values of a linear relationship.

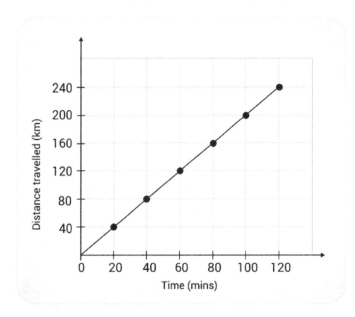

The graph above represents the relationship between distance traveled and time. To find the distance traveled in 80 minutes, the mark for 80 minutes is located at the bottom of the graph. By following this mark directly up on the graph, the corresponding point for 80 minutes is directly across from the 160-kilometer mark. This information indicates that the distance traveled in 80 minutes is 160 kilometers. To predict information not displayed on the graph, the way in which the variables change with respect to one another is determined. In this case, distance increases by 40 kilometers as time increases by 20 minutes. This information can be used to continue the data in the graph or convert the values to a table.

Conjectures, Predictions, or Generalizations Based on Patterns

An arithmetic or geometric sequence can be written as a formula and used to determine unknown steps without writing out the entire sequence. (Note that a similar process for repeating patterns is covered in the previous section.) An arithmetic sequence progresses by a **common difference**. To determine the common difference, any step is subtracted by the step that precedes it. In the sequence $4, 9, 14, 19$ ... the common difference, or d, is 5. By expressing each step as a_1, a_2, a_3, etc., a formula can be written to represent the sequence. a_1 is the first step. To produce step two, step 1 (a_1) is added to the common difference (d): $a_2 = a_1 + d$. To produce step three, the common difference (d) is added twice to a_1: $a_3 = a_1 + 2d$. To produce step four, the common difference (d) is added three times to a_1: $a_4 = a_1 + 3d$. Following this pattern allows a general rule for arithmetic sequences to be written. For any term of the sequence (a_n), the first step (a_1) is added to the product of the common difference (d) and one less than the step of the term $(n - 1)$: $a_1 + (n - 1)d$. Suppose the 8th term (a_8) is to be found in the previous sequence. By knowing the first step (a_1) is 4 and the common difference (d) is 5, the formula can be used:

$$a_n = a_1 + (n - 1)d \rightarrow a_8 = 4 + (7)5 \rightarrow a_8 = 39$$

In a geometric sequence, each step is produced by multiplying or dividing the previous step by the same number. The **common ratio**, or (r), can be determined by dividing any step by the previous step. In the sequence $1, 3, 9, 27$ ... the common ratio (r) is 3 $\left(\frac{3}{1} = 3 \ or \ \frac{9}{3} = 3 \ or \ \frac{27}{9} = 3\right)$. Each successive step can be expressed as a product of the first step a_1 and the common ratio (r) to some power. For example,

$$a_2 = a_1 \times r$$

$$a_3 = a_1 \times r \times r \ or \ a_3 = a_1 \times r^2$$

$$a_4 = a_1 \times r \times r \times r \ or \ a_4 = a - 1 \times r^3$$

Following this pattern, a general rule for geometric sequences can be written. For any term of the sequence (a_n), the first step (a_1) is multiplied by the common ratio (r) raised to the power one less than the step of the term $(n - 1)$: $a_n = a_1 \times r^{(n-1)}$. Suppose for the previous sequence, the 7th term (a_7) is to be found. Knowing the first step (a_1) is one, and the common ratio (r) is 3, the formula can be used:

$$a_n = a_1 \times r^{(n-1)} \rightarrow a_7 = (1) \times 3^6 \rightarrow a_7 = 729$$

Corresponding Terms of Two Numerical Patterns

When given two numerical patterns, the corresponding terms should be examined to determine if a relationship exists between them. Corresponding terms between patterns are the pairs of numbers that appear in the same step of the two sequences. Consider the following patterns $1, 2, 3, 4$ ... and $3, 6, 9, 12$ ... The corresponding terms are: 1 and 3; 2 and 6; 3 and 9; and 4 and 12. To identify the relationship, each pair of corresponding terms is examined and the possibilities of performing an operation $(+, -, \times, \div)$ to the term from the first sequence to produce the corresponding term in the second sequence are determined. In this case:

$$1 + 2 = 3 \quad or \quad 1 \times 3 = 3$$

$$2 + 4 = 6 \quad or \quad 2 \times 3 = 6$$

$$3 + 6 = 9 \quad or \quad 3 \times 3 = 9$$

$$4 + 8 = 12 \quad or \quad 4 \times 3 = 12$$

73

The consistent pattern is that the number from the first sequence multiplied by 3 equals its corresponding term in the second sequence. By assigning each sequence a label (input and output) or variable (x and y), the relationship can be written as an equation. If the first sequence represents the inputs, or x, and the second sequence represents the outputs, or y, the relationship can be expressed as: $y = 3x$.

Consider the following sets of numbers:

a	2	4	6	8
b	6	8	10	12

To write a rule for the relationship between the values for a and the values for b, the corresponding terms (2 and 6; 4 and 8; 6 and 10; 8 and 12) are examined. The possibilities for producing b from a are:

$$2 + 4 = 6 \quad \text{or} \quad 2 \times 3 = 6$$

$$4 + 4 = 8 \quad \text{or} \quad 4 \times 2 = 8$$

$$6 + 4 = 10$$

$$8 + 4 = 12 \quad \text{or} \quad 8 \times 1.5 = 12$$

The consistent pattern is that adding 4 to the value of a produces the value of b. The relationship can be written as the equation $a + 4 = b$.

Geometry/Measurement

Geometry is part of mathematics. It deals with shapes and their properties. Geometry means knowing the names and properties of shapes. It is also similar to measurement and number operations. The basis of geometry involves being able to label and describe shapes and their properties. That knowledge will lead to working with formulas such as area, perimeter, and volume. This knowledge will help to solve word problems involving shapes.

Flat or two-dimensional shapes include circles, triangles, hexagons, and rectangles, among others. Three-dimensional solid shapes, such as spheres and cubes, are also used in geometry. A shape can be classified based on whether it is open like the letter U or closed like the letter O. Further classifications involve counting the number of sides and vertices (corners) on the shapes. This will help you tell the difference between shapes.

Polygons can be drawn by sketching a fixed number of line segments that meet to create a closed shape. In addition, **triangles** can be drawn by sketching a closed space using only three-line segments. **Quadrilaterals** are closed shapes with four-line segments. Note that a triangle has three vertices, and a quadrilateral has four vertices.

To draw circles, one curved line segment must be drawn that has only one endpoint. This creates a closed shape. Given such direction, every point on the line would be the same distance away from its center. The radius of a circle goes from an endpoint on the center of the circle to an endpoint on the circle. The diameter is the line segment created by placing an endpoint on the circle, drawing through the radius, and placing the other endpoint on the circle. A compass can be used to draw circles of a more precise size and shape.

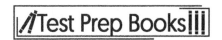
Classifying Two-Dimensional Figures [ISEE]

A **polygon** is a closed geometric figure in a plane (flat surface) consisting of at least 3 sides formed by line segments. These are often defined as two-dimensional shapes. Common two-dimensional shapes include circles, triangles, squares, rectangles, pentagons, and hexagons. Note that a circle is a two-dimensional shape without sides.

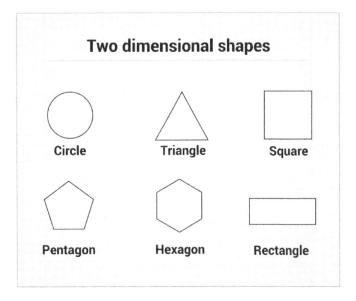

Polygons can be either convex or concave. A polygon that has interior angles all measuring less than 180° is convex. A concave polygon has one or more interior angles measuring greater than 180°. Examples are shown below.

Polygons can be classified by the number of sides (also equal to the number of angles) they have. The following are the names of polygons with a given number of sides or angles:

# of Sides	Name of Polygon
3	Triangle
4	Quadrilateral
5	Pentagon
6	Hexagon
7	Septagon (or heptagon)
8	Octagon
9	Nonagon
10	Decagon

Equiangular polygons are polygons in which the measure of every interior angle is the same. The sides of equilateral polygons are always the same length. If a polygon is both equiangular and equilateral, the polygon is defined as a regular polygon.

Triangles can be further classified by their sides and angles. A triangle with its largest angle measuring 90° is a right triangle. A triangle with the largest angle less than 90° is an acute triangle. A triangle with the largest angle greater than 90° is an obtuse triangle. Below is an example of a right triangle.

A triangle consisting of two equal sides and two equal angles is an **isosceles triangle**. A triangle with three equal sides and three equal angles is an **equilateral triangle**. A triangle with no equal sides or angles is a **scalene triangle**.

Isosceles triangle:

Equilateral triangle:

Scalene triangle:

Quadrilaterals can be further classified according to their sides and angles. A quadrilateral with exactly one pair of parallel sides is called a **trapezoid**. A quadrilateral that shows both pairs of opposite sides parallel is a **parallelogram**. Parallelograms include rhombuses, rectangles, and squares. A r**hombus** has four equal sides. A

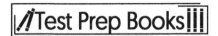

rectangle has four equal angles (90° each). A **square** has four 90° angles and four equal sides. Therefore, a square is both a rhombus and a rectangle.

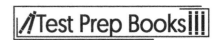

Properties of Three-Dimensional Shapes [ISEE]

A **solid** is a three-dimensional figure that encloses a part of space. Common three-dimensional shapes include spheres, prisms, cubes, pyramids, cylinders, and cones.

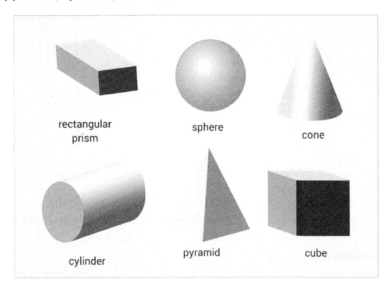

Solids consisting of all flat surfaces that are polygons are called **polyhedrons**. The two-dimensional surfaces that make up a polyhedron are called faces. Types of polyhedrons include prisms and pyramids. A **prism** consists of two parallel faces that are congruent (or the same shape and same size), and **lateral faces** going around (which are parallelograms).

A prism is further classified by the shape of its base, as shown below:

79

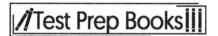
A pyramid consists of lateral faces (triangles) that meet at a common point called the vertex and one other face that is a polygon, called the base. A pyramid can be further classified by the shape of its base, as shown below.

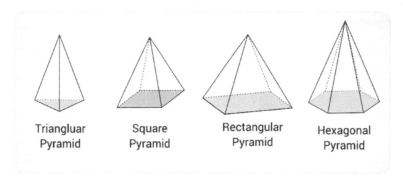

| Triangluar Pyramid | Square Pyramid | Rectangular Pyramid | Hexagonal Pyramid |

A tetrahedron is another name for a triangular pyramid. All the faces of a tetrahedron are triangles.

Solids that are not polyhedrons include spheres, cylinders, and cones. A sphere is the set of all points a given distance from a given center point. A sphere is commonly thought of as a three-dimensional circle. A cylinder consists of two parallel, congruent (same size) circles and a lateral curved surface. A cone consists of a circle as its base and a lateral curved surface that narrows to a point called the vertex.

Similar polygons are the same shape but different sizes. More specifically, their corresponding angle measures are congruent (or equal) and the length of their sides is proportional. For example, all sides of one polygon may be double the length of the sides of another. Likewise, similar solids are the same shape but different sizes. Any corresponding faces or bases of similar solids are the same polygons that are proportional by a consistent value.

Three-Dimensional Figures with Nets

A **net** is a construction of two-dimensional figures that can be folded to form a given three-dimensional figure. More than one net may exist to fold and produce the same solid, or three-dimensional figure. The bases and faces of the solid figure are analyzed to determine the polygons (two-dimensional figures) needed to form the net.

Consider the following triangular prism:

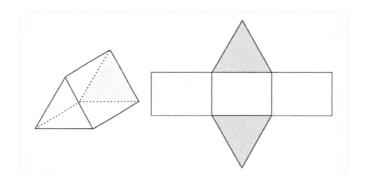

The surface of the prism consists of two triangular bases and three rectangular faces. The net beside it can be used to construct the triangular prism by first folding the triangles up to be parallel to each other, and then folding the two outside rectangles up and to the center with the outer edges touching.

Consider the following cylinder:

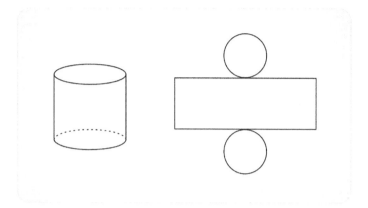

The surface consists of two circular bases and a curved lateral surface that can be opened and flattened into a rectangle. The net beside the cylinder can be used to construct the cylinder by first folding the circles up to be parallel to each other, and then curving the sides of the rectangle up to touch each other. The top and bottom of the folded rectangle should be touching the outside of both circles.

Consider the following square pyramid below on the left. The surface consists of one square base and four triangular faces. The net below on the right can be used to construct the square pyramid by folding each triangle towards the center of the square. The top points of the triangle meet at the vertex.

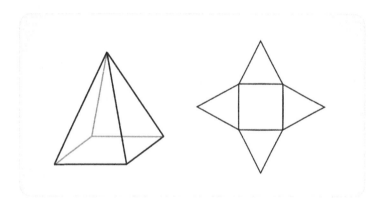

Perimeter and Area of Geometric Shapes

Perimeter is the measurement of a distance around something or the sum of all sides of a polygon. Think of perimeter as the length of the boundary, like a fence. In contrast, **area** is the space occupied by a defined enclosure, like a field enclosed by a fence.

When thinking about perimeter, think about walking around the outside of something. When thinking about area, think about the amount of space or **surface area** something takes up.

Square
The perimeter of a square is measured by adding together all of the sides. Since a square has four equal sides, its perimeter can be calculated by multiplying the length of one side by 4. Thus, the formula is $4 \times s$, where s equals one side.

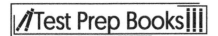
For example, the following square has side lengths of 5 meters:

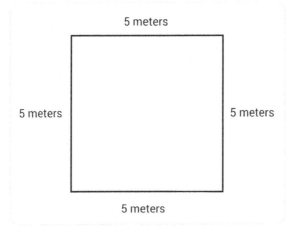

The perimeter is 20 meters because 4 times 5 is 20.

The area of a square is the length of a side squared. For example, if a side of a square is 7 centimeters, then the area is 49 square centimeters. The formula for this example is:

$$A = s^2 = 7^2 = 49 \text{ square centimeters}$$

An example is if the rectangle has a length of 6 inches and a width of 7 inches, then the area is 42 square inches:

$$A = lw = 6(7) = 42 \text{ square inches}$$

Rectangle

Like a square, a rectangle's perimeter is measured by adding together all of the sides. But as the sides are unequal, the formula is different. A rectangle has equal values for its lengths (long sides) and equal values for its widths (short sides), so the perimeter formula for a rectangle is:

$$P = l + l + w + w = 2l + 2w$$

l equals length

w equals width

The area is found by multiplying the length by the width, so the formula is $A = l \times w$.

For example, if the length of a rectangle is 10 inches and the width 8 inches, then the perimeter is 36 inches because:

$$P = 2l + 2w = 2(10) + 2(8)$$

$$20 + 16 = 36 \text{ inches}$$

Triangle

A triangle's perimeter is measured by adding together the three sides, so the formula is:

$$P = a + b + c$$

82

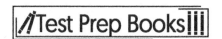

a, b, and c are the values of the three sides. The area is the product of one-half the base and height, so the formula is:

$$A = \frac{1}{2} \times b \times h$$

It can be simplified to:

$$A = \frac{bh}{2}$$

The base is the bottom of the triangle, and the height is the distance from the base to the peak. If a problem asks to calculate the area of a triangle, it will provide the base and height.

For example, if the base of the triangle is 2 feet and the height 4 feet, then the area is 4 square feet. The following equation shows the formula used to calculate the area of the triangle:

$$A = \frac{1}{2}bh = \frac{1}{2}(2)(4) = 4 \text{ square feet}$$

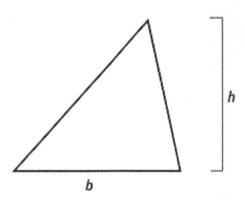

Circle

A circle's perimeter—also known as its **circumference**—is measured by multiplying the diameter by π.

Diameter is the straight line measured from a point on one side of the circle to a point directly across on the opposite side of the circle. π is referred to as pi and is equal to 3.14 (with rounding). So, the formula is $\pi \times d$. This is sometimes expressed by the formula:

$$C = 2 \times \pi \times r$$

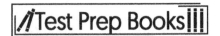
r is the radius of the circle. These formulas are equivalent, as the radius equals half of the diameter.

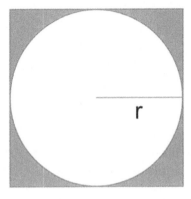

The area of a circle is calculated through the formula:

$$A = \pi \times r^2$$

The test will indicate either to leave the answer with π attached or to calculate to the nearest decimal place, which means multiplying by 3.14 for π.

Parallelogram

The perimeter of a parallelogram is measured by adding the lengths and widths together. Thus, the formula is the same as for a rectangle:

$$P = l + l + w + w = 2l + 2w$$

However, the area formula differs from the rectangle. For a parallelogram, the area is calculated by multiplying the length by the height:

$$A = h \times l$$

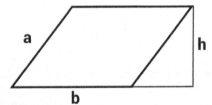

Area = bh

Perimeter = 2(a + b)

Trapezoid

The perimeter of a trapezoid is calculated by adding the two unequal bases and two equal sides, so the formula is:

$$P = a + b_1 + c + b_2$$

Although unlikely to be a test question, the formula for the area of a trapezoid is:

$$A = \frac{b_1 + b_2}{2} \times h$$

h equals height, and b_1 and b_2 equal the bases.

Irregular Shapes

The perimeter of an irregular polygon is found by adding the lengths of all of the sides. In cases where all of the sides are given, this will be very straightforward, as it will simply involve finding the sum of the provided lengths. Other times, a side length may be missing and must be determined before the perimeter can be calculated. Consider the example below:

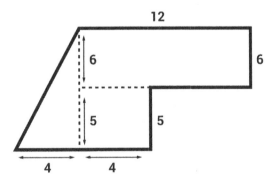

All of the side lengths are provided except for the angled side on the left. Test takers should notice that this is the hypotenuse of a right triangle. The other two sides of the triangle are provided (the base is 4 and the height is $6 + 5 = 11$). The Pythagorean Theorem can be used to find the length of the hypotenuse, remembering that $a^2 + b^2 = c^2$. Substituting the side values provided yields:

$$(4)^2 + (11)^2 = c^2$$

Therefore,

$$c = \sqrt{16 + 121} = 11.7$$

85

Finally, the perimeter can be found by adding this new side length with the other provided lengths to get the total length around the figure:

$$4 + 4 + 5 + 8 + 6 + 12 + 11.7 = 50.7$$

Although units are not provided in this figure, remember that reporting units with a measurement is important.

The area of an irregular polygon is found by decomposing, or breaking apart, the figure into smaller shapes. When the area of the smaller shapes is determined, these areas are added together to produce the total area of the original figure. Consider the same example provided before:

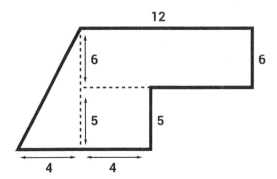

The irregular polygon is decomposed into two rectangles and a triangle. The area of the large rectangle is 72 square units.

$$A = l \times w \rightarrow A = 12 \times 6$$

The area of the small rectangle is 20 square units ($A = 4 \times 5$). The area of the triangle is 22 square units.

$$A = \frac{1}{2} \times b \times h \rightarrow A = \frac{1}{2} \times 4 \times 11$$

The sum of the areas of these figures produces the total area of the original polygon:

$$A = 72 + 20 + 22 \rightarrow A = 114 \text{ square units}$$

Surface Area and Volume of Geometric Shapes

The area of a two-dimensional figure refers to the number of square units needed to cover the interior region of the figure. This concept is similar to wallpaper covering the flat surface of a wall. For example, if a rectangle has an area of 8 square inches (written 8 in^2), it will take 8 squares, each with sides one inch in length, to cover the interior region of the rectangle.

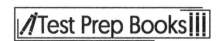

Note that area is measured in square units such as: square feet or ft²; square yards or yd²; square miles or mi².

2 in

4 in

The **surface area** of a three-dimensional figure refers to the number of square units needed to cover the entire surface of the figure. This concept is similar to using wrapping paper to completely cover the outside of a box. For example, if a triangular pyramid has a surface area of 17 square inches (written 17 in²), it will take 17 squares, each with sides one inch in length, to cover the entire surface of the pyramid. Surface area is also measured in square units.

Many three-dimensional figures (solid figures) can be represented by nets consisting of rectangles and triangles. The surface area of such solids can be determined by adding the areas of each of its faces and bases. Finding the surface area using this method requires calculating the areas of rectangles and triangles. To find the area (A) of a rectangle, the length (l) is multiplied by the width (w):

$$A = l \times w$$

The area of a rectangle with a length of 8 cm and a width of 4 cm is calculated:

$$A = (8 \text{ cm}) \times (4 \text{ cm}) \rightarrow A = 32 \text{ cm}^2$$

To calculate the area (A) of a triangle, the product of $\frac{1}{2}$, the base (b), and the height (h) is found:

$$A = \frac{1}{2} \times b \times h$$

Note that the height of a triangle is measured from the base to the vertex opposite of it forming a right angle with the base. The area of a triangle with a base of 11 cm and a height of 6 cm is calculated:

$$A = \frac{1}{2} \times (11 \text{ cm}) \times (6 \text{ cm}) \rightarrow A = 33 \text{ cm}^2$$

Consider the following triangular prism, which is represented by a net consisting of two triangles and three rectangles.

The surface area of the prism can be determined by adding the areas of each of its faces and bases. The surface area $(SA) = area\ of\ triangle + area\ of\ triangle + area\ of\ rectangle + area\ of\ rectangle + area\ of\ rectangle$.

$$SA = (\frac{1}{2} \times b \times h) + (\frac{1}{2} \times b \times h) + (l \times w) + (l \times w) + (l \times w)$$

$$SA = (\frac{1}{2} \times 6 \times 4) + (\frac{1}{2} \times 6 \times 4) + (6 \times 10) + (6 \times 10) + (6 \times 10)$$

$$SA = (12) + (12) + (60) + (60) + (60)$$

$$SA = 204 \text{ square units}$$

Volume is the measurement of how much space an object occupies, like how much space is in the cube. Volume is useful in determining the space within a certain three-dimensional object. Volume can be calculated for a cube, rectangular prism, cylinder, pyramid, cone, and sphere. By knowing specific dimensions of the objects, the volume of the object is computed with these figures. The units for the volumes of solids can include cubic centimeters, cubic meters, cubic inches, and cubic feet.

Cube

The **cube** is the simplest figure for which volume can be determined because all dimensions in a cube are equal. In the following example, the length, width, and height of the cube are all represented by the variable a because these measurements are equal lengths.

The volume of any rectangular, three-dimensional object is found by multiplying its length by its width by its height. In the case of a cube, the length, width, and height are all equal lengths, represented by the variable a. Therefore, the equation used to calculate the volume is $(a \times a \times a)$ or a^3. In a real-world example of this situation, if the length of a side of the cube is 3 centimeters, the volume is calculated by utilizing the formula:

$$(3 \times 3 \times 3) = 27 \text{ cm}^3$$

Rectangular Prism

The dimensions of a **rectangular prism** are not necessarily equal as those of a cube. Therefore, the formula for a rectangular prism recognizes that the dimensions vary and use different variables to represent these lengths. The length, width, and height of a rectangular prism can be represented with the variables a, b, and c.

The equation used to calculate volume is length times width times height. Using these variables, this means $a \times b \times c$.

88

In a real-world application of this situation, if $a = 2$ cm, $b = 3$ cm, and $c = 4$ cm, the volume is calculated by utilizing the formula:

$$3 \times 4 \times 5 = 60 \text{ cm}^3$$

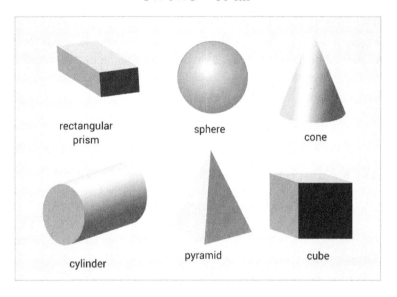

rectangular prism

sphere

cone

cylinder

pyramid

cube

Cylinder

Discovering a cylinder's volume requires the measurement of the cylinder's base, length of the radius, and height. The height of the cylinder can be represented with variable h, and the radius can be represented with variable r.

The formula to find the volume of a cylinder is $\pi r^2 h$. Notice that πr^2 is the formula for the area of a circle. This is because the base of the cylinder is a circle. To calculate the volume of a cylinder, the slices of circles needed to build the entire height of the cylinder are added together. For example, if the radius is 5 feet and the height of the cylinder is 10 feet, the cylinder's volume is calculated by using the following equation:

$$\pi 5^2 \times 10$$

Substituting 3.14 for the volume is 785.4 ft³.

Pyramid

To calculate the volume of a pyramid, the area of the base of the pyramid is multiplied by the pyramid's height by $\frac{1}{3}$. The area of the base of the pyramid is found by multiplying the base length by the base width.

Therefore, the formula to calculate a pyramid's volume is:

$$(L \times W \times H) \div 3$$

Cone

The formula to calculate the volume of a circular cone is similar to the formula for the volume of a pyramid. The primary difference in determining the area of a cone is that a circle serves as the base of a cone. Therefore, the area of a circle is used for the cone's base.

The variable r represents the radius, and the variable h represents the height of the cone. The formula used to calculate the volume of a cone is:

$$\frac{1}{3}\pi r^2 h$$

Essentially, the area of the base of the cone is multiplied by the cone's height. In a real-life example where the radius of a cone is 2 meters and the height of a cone is 5 meters, the volume of the cone is calculated by utilizing the formula:

$$\frac{1}{3}\pi 2^2 \times 5 = 21 \text{ m}^3$$

Sphere
The volume of a sphere uses π due to its circular shape.

The length of the radius, r, is the only variable needed to determine the sphere's volume. The formula to calculate the volume of a sphere is:

$$\frac{4}{3}\pi r^3$$

Therefore, if the radius of a sphere is 8 centimeters, the volume of the sphere is calculated by utilizing the formula:

$$\frac{4}{3}\pi(8)^3 = 2,144 \text{ cm}^3$$

Lines and Angles
In geometry, a line connects two points, has no thickness, and extends indefinitely in both directions beyond the points. If it does end at two points, it is known as a **line segment**. It is important to distinguish between a line and a line segment.

An angle can be visualized as a corner. It is defined as the formation of two rays connecting at a vertex that extend indefinitely. Angles are measured in degrees. Their measurement is a measure of rotation. A full rotation equals 360 degrees and represents a circle. Half of a rotation equals 180 degrees and represents a half-circle. Subsequently, 90 degrees represents a quarter-circle. Similar to the hands on a clock, an angle begins at the center point, and two lines extend indefinitely from that point in two different directions.

A clock can be useful when learning how to measure angles. At 3:00, the big hand is on the 12 and the small hand is on the 3. The angle formed is 90 degrees and is known as a **right angle**. Any angle less than 90 degrees, such as the one formed at 2:00, is known as an **acute angle**. Any angle greater than 90 degrees is known as an *obtuse angle*. The entire clock represents 360 degrees, and each clockwise increment on the clock represents an addition of 30 degrees. Therefore, 6:00 represents 180 degrees, 7:00 represents 210 degrees, etc. Angle measurement is additive. An angle can be broken into two non-overlapping angles. The total measure of the larger angle is equal to the sum of the measurements of the two smaller angles.

A **ray** is a straight path that has an endpoint on one end and extends indefinitely in the other direction. Lines are known as being **coplanar** if they are located in the same plane. Coplanar lines exist within the same two-dimensional surface. Two lines are **parallel** if they are coplanar, extend in the same direction, and never cross. They are known as being **equidistant** because they are always the same distance from each other. If lines do cross, they are known as **intersecting lines**. As discussed previously, angles are utilized throughout geometry, and their

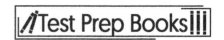
measurement can be seen through the use of an analog clock. An angle is formed when two rays begin at the same endpoint. **Adjacent angles** can be formed by forming two angles out of one shared ray. They are two side-by-side angles that also share an endpoint.

Perpendicular lines are coplanar lines that form a right angle at their point of intersection. A triangle that contains a right angle is known as a **right triangle**. The sum of the angles within any triangle is always 180 degrees. Therefore, in a right triangle, the sum of the two angles that are not right angles is 90 degrees. Any two angles that sum up to 90 degrees are known as **complementary angles**. A triangle that contains an obtuse angle is known as an **obtuse triangle**. A triangle that contains three acute angles is known as an **acute triangle**. Here is an example of a 180-degree angle, split up into an acute and obtuse angle:

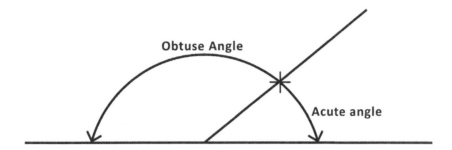

The vocabulary regarding many two-dimensional shapes is important to understand and use appropriately. Many four-sided figures can be identified using properties of angles and lines. A **quadrilateral** is a closed shape with four sides. A **parallelogram** is a specific type of quadrilateral that has two sets of parallel lines having the same length. A **trapezoid** is a quadrilateral having only one set of parallel sides. A **rectangle** is a parallelogram that has four right angles. A **rhombus** is a parallelogram with four equal sides and sometimes two acute angles and two obtuse angles. The acute angles are of equal measure, and the obtuse angles are of equal measure. Finally, a **square** is a rhombus consisting of four right angles. It is important to note that some of these shapes share common attributes. For instance, all four-sided shapes are quadrilaterals. All squares are rectangles, but not all rectangles are squares.

Symmetry is another concept in geometry. If a two-dimensional shape can be folded along a straight line and the halves line up exactly, the figure is **symmetric**. The line is known as a **line of symmetry**. Circles, squares, and rectangles are examples of symmetric shapes.

Applying Angle Relationships to Solve Problems

An **angle** consists of two rays that have a common endpoint. This common endpoint is called the **vertex** of the angle. The two rays can be called **sides** of the angle. The angle below has a vertex at point B and the sides consist of ray BA and ray BC. An angle can be named in three ways:

1. Using the vertex and a point from each side, with the vertex letter in the middle.

2. Using only the vertex. This can only be used if it is the only angle with that vertex.

3. Using a number that is written inside the angle.

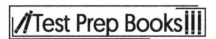

The angle below can be written (read angle ABC), $\angle CBA$, $\angle B$, or $\angle 1$.

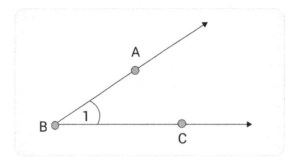

An angle divides a plane, or flat surface, into three parts: the angle itself, the interior (inside) of the angle, and the exterior (outside) of the angle. The figure below shows point M on the interior of the angle and point N on the exterior of the angle.

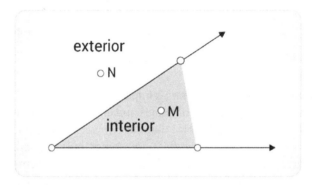

Angles can be measured in units called degrees, with the symbol °. The degree measure of an angle is between 0° and 180°, is a measure of rotation, and can be obtained by using a protractor.

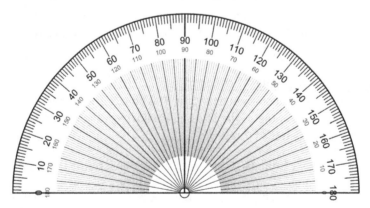

A straight angle (or simply a line) measures exactly 180°. A right angle's sides meet at the vertex to create a square corner. A right angle measures exactly 90° and is typically indicated by a box drawn in the interior of the angle. An acute angle has an interior that is narrower than a right angle. The measure of an acute angle is any value less than 90° and greater than 0°. For example, 89.9°, 47°, 12°, and 1°. An obtuse angle has an interior that is wider than a

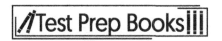

right angle. The measure of an obtuse angle is any value greater than 90° but less than 180°. For example, 90.1°, 110°, 150°, and 179.9°. Any two angles that sum up to 90 degrees are known as **complementary angles**.

- Acute angles: Less than 90°
- Obtuse angles: Greater than 90°
- Right angles: 90°
- Straight angles: 180°

To determine angle measures for adjacent angles, angles that share a common side and vertex, at least one of the angles must be known. Other information that is necessary to determine such measures include that there are 90° in a right angle, and there are 180° in a straight line. Therefore, if two adjacent angles form a right angle, they will add up to 90°, and if two adjacent angles form a straight line, they add up to 180°.

If the measurement of one of the adjacent angles is known, the other can be found by subtracting the known angle from the total number of degrees.

For example, given the following situation, if angle a measures 55°, find the measure of unknown angle b:

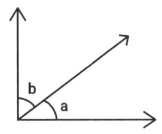

To solve this, subtract the known angle measure from 90°.

$$90° - 55° = 35°$$

The measure of $b = 35°$.

Given the following situation, if angle 1 measures 45°, find the measure of the unknown angle 2:

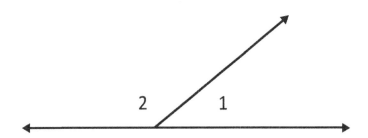

To solve this, subtract the known angle measure from 180°.

$$180° - 45° = 135°$$

The measure of angle $2 = 135°$

In the case that more than two angles are given, use the same method of subtracting the known angles from the total measure.

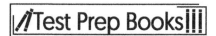

For example, given the following situation, if angle $y = 40°$, and angle $z = 25°$, find unknown angle x.

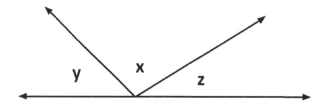

Subtract the known angles from 180°.

$$180° − 45° = 135°$$

The measure of angle $x = 115°$.

Measuring Lengths of Objects

The length of an object can be measured using standard tools such as rulers, yard sticks, meter sticks, and measuring tapes. The following image depicts a yardstick:

Choosing the right tool to perform the measurement requires determining whether United States customary units or metric units are desired, and having a grasp of the approximate length of each unit and the approximate length of each tool. The measurement can still be performed by trial and error without the knowledge of the approximate size of the tool.

For example, to determine the length of a room in feet, a United States customary unit, various tools can be used for this task. These include a ruler (typically 12 inches/1 foot long), a yardstick (3 feet/1 yard long), or a tape measure displaying feet (typically either 25 feet or 50 feet). Because the length of a room is much larger than the length of a ruler or a yardstick, a tape measure should be used to perform the measurement.

When the correct measuring tool is selected, the measurement is performed by first placing the tool directly above or below the object (if making a horizontal measurement) or directly next to the object (if making a vertical measurement). The next step is aligning the tool so that one end of the object is at the mark for zero units, then recording the unit of the mark at the other end of the object. To give the length of a paperclip in metric units, a ruler displaying centimeters is aligned with one end of the paper clip to the mark for zero centimeters.

Directly down from the other end of the paperclip is the mark that measures its length. In this case, that mark is two small dashes past the 3-centimeter mark. Each small dash is 1 millimeter (or .1 centimeters). Therefore, the length of the paper clip is 3.2 centimeters.

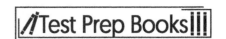

To compare the lengths of objects, each length must be expressed in the same unit. If possible, the objects should be measured with the same tool or with tools utilizing the same units. For example, a ruler and a yardstick can both measure length in inches. If the lengths of the objects are expressed in different units, these different units must be converted to the same unit before comparing them. If two lengths are expressed in the same unit, the lengths may be compared by subtracting the smaller value from the larger value. For example, suppose the lengths of two gardens are to be compared. Garden A has a length of 4 feet, and garden B has a length of 2 yards. 2 yards is converted to 6 feet so that the measurements have similar units. Then, the smaller length (4 ft) is subtracted from the larger length (6 ft): 6 ft − 4 ft = 2 ft. Therefore, garden B is 2 feet larger than garden A.

Relative Sizes of United States Customary Units and Metric Units

The United States customary system and the metric system each consist of distinct units to measure lengths and volume of liquids. The U.S. customary units for length, from smallest to largest, are: inch (in), foot (ft), yard (yd), and mile (mi). The metric units for length, from smallest to largest, are: millimeter (mm), centimeter (cm), decimeter (dm), meter (m), and kilometer (km). The relative size of each unit of length is shown below.

U.S. Customary	Metric	Conversion
12 in = 1 ft	10 mm = 1 cm	1 in = 2.54 cm
36 in = 3 ft = 1 yd	10 cm = 1 dm (decimeter)	1 m ≈ 3.28 ft ≈ 1.09 yd
5,280 ft = 1,760 yd = 1 mi	100 cm = 10 dm = 1 m	1 mi ≈ 1.6 km
	1,000 m = 1 km	

The U.S. customary units for volume of liquids, from smallest to largest, are: fluid ounces (fl oz), cup (c), pint (pt), quart (qt), and gallon (gal). The metric units for volume of liquids, from smallest to largest, are: milliliter (mL), centiliter (cL), deciliter (dL), liter (L), and kiloliter (kL). The relative size of each unit of liquid volume is shown below.

U.S. Customary	Metric	Conversion
8 fl oz = 1 c	10 mL = 1 cL	1 pt ≈ 0.473 L
2 c = 1 pt	10 cL = 1 dL	1 L ≈ 1.057 qt
4 c = 2 pt = 1 qt	1,000 mL = 100 cL = 10 dL = 1 L	1 gal ≈ 3.785 L
4 qt = 1 gal	1,000 L = 1 kL	

The U.S. customary system measures weight (how strongly Earth is pulling on an object) in the following units, from least to greatest: ounce (oz), pound (lb), and ton. The metric system measures mass (the quantity of matter within an object) in the following units, from least to greatest: milligram (mg), centigram (cg), gram (g), kilogram (kg), and metric ton (MT). The relative sizes of each unit of weight and mass are shown below.

U.S. Measures of Weight	Metric Measures of Mass
16 oz = 1 lb	10 mg = 1 cg
2,000 lb = 1 ton	100 cg = 1 g
	1,000 g = 1 kg
	1,000 kg = 1 MT

Note that weight and mass DO NOT measure the same thing.

Time is measured in the following units, from shortest to longest: second (sec), minute (min), hour (h), day (d), week (wk), month (mo), year (yr), decade, century, millennium. The relative sizes of each unit of time is shown below.

- 60 sec = 1 min
- 60 min = 1 h
- 24 hr = 1 d
- 7 d = 1 wk
- 52 wk = 1 yr
- 12 mo = 1 yr
- 10 yr = 1 decade
- 100 yrs = 1 century
- 1,000 yrs = 1 millennium

Conversion of Units

Converting measurements in different units between the two systems can be difficult because they follow different rules. The best method is to look up an English to Metric system conversion factor and then use a series of equivalent fractions to set up an equation to convert the units of one of the measurements into those of the other. The table below lists some common conversion values that are useful for problems involving measurements with units in both systems:

English System	Metric System
1 inch	2.54 cm
1 foot	0.3048 m
1 yard	0.914 m
1 mile	1.609 km
1 ounce	28.35 g
1 pound	0.454 kg
1 fluid ounce	29.574 mL
1 quart	0.946 L
1 gallon	3.785 L

Consider the example where a scientist wants to convert 6.8 inches to centimeters. One method for converting units is to write and solve a proportion. The arrangement of values in a proportion is extremely important. The table above is used to find that there are 2.54 centimeters in every inch, so the following equation should be set up and solved:

$$\frac{6.8 \text{ in}}{1} \times \frac{2.54 \text{ cm}}{1 \text{ in}} = 17.272 \text{ cm}$$

Notice how the inches in the numerator of the initial figure and the denominator of the conversion factor cancel out. (This equation could have been written simply as:

$$6.8 \text{ in} \times 2.54 \text{ cm} = 17.272 \text{ cm}$$

but it was shown in detail to illustrate the steps). The goal in any conversion equation is to set up the fractions so that the units you are trying to convert from cancel out and the units you desire remain.

97

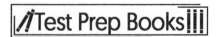

For a more complicated example, consider converting 2.15 kilograms into ounces. The first step is to convert kilograms into grams and then grams into ounces. Note that the measurement you begin with does not have to be put in a fraction.

So, in this case, 2.15 kg is by itself although it's technically the numerator of a fraction:

$$2.15 \text{ kg} \times \frac{1{,}000 \text{ g}}{\text{kg}} = 2150 \text{ g}$$

Then, use the conversion factor from the table to convert grams to ounces:

$$2150 \text{ g} \times \frac{1 \text{ oz}}{28.35 \text{ g}} = 75.8 \text{ oz}$$

When working with different systems of measurement, conversion from one unit to another may be necessary. The conversion rate must be known to convert units. One method for converting units is to write and solve a proportion. The arrangement of values in a proportion is extremely important. Suppose that a problem requires converting 20 fluid ounces to cups. To do so, a proportion can be written using the conversion rate of 8 fl oz = 1 c with x representing the missing value.

The proportion can be written in any of the following ways:

$$\frac{1}{8} = \frac{x}{20} \left(\frac{c \; for \; conversion}{fl \; oz \; for \; conversion} = \frac{unknown \; c}{fl \; oz \; given} \right); \; \frac{8}{1} = \frac{20}{x} \left(\frac{fl \; oz \; for \; conversion}{c \; for \; conversion} = \frac{fl \; oz \; given}{unknown \; c} \right);$$

$$\frac{1}{x} = \frac{8}{20} \left(\frac{c \; for \; conversion}{unknown \; c} = \frac{fl \; oz \; for \; conversion}{fl \; oz \; given} \right)$$

$$\frac{x}{1} = \frac{20}{8} \left(\frac{unknown \; c}{c \; for \; conversion} = \frac{fl \; oz \; given}{fl \; oz \; for \; conversion} \right)$$

To solve a proportion, the ratios are cross-multiplied and the resulting equation is solved. When cross-multiplying, all four proportions above will produce the same equation:

$$(8)(x) = (20)(1) \rightarrow 8x = 20$$

Divide by 8 to isolate the variable x, the result is $x = 2.5$. The variable x represents the unknown number of cups. Therefore, the conclusion is that 20 fluid ounces converts (is equal) to 2.5 cups.

Sometimes converting units requires writing and solving more than one proportion. Suppose an exam question asks to determine how many hours are in 2 weeks. Without knowing the conversion rate between hours and weeks, this can be determined knowing the conversion rates between weeks and days, and between days and hours. First, weeks are converted to days, then days are converted to hours. To convert from weeks to days, the following proportion can be written:

$$\frac{7}{1} = \frac{x}{2} \left(\frac{days \; conversion}{weeks \; conversion} = \frac{days \; unknown}{weeks \; given} \right)$$

Cross-multiplying produces:

$$(7)(2) = (x)(1) \rightarrow 14 = x$$

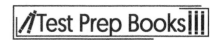
Therefore, 2 weeks is equal to 14 days. Next, a proportion is written to convert 14 days to hours:

$$\frac{24}{1} = \frac{x}{14} \left(\frac{conversion\ hours}{conversion\ days} = \frac{unknown\ hours}{given\ days} \right)$$

Cross-multiplying produces:

$$(24)(14) = (x)(1) \rightarrow 336 = x$$

Therefore, the answer is that there are 336 hours in 2 weeks.

Locating Ordered Pairs in All Four Quadrants of a Rectangular Coordinate System [ISEE]

The **coordinate plane**, sometimes referred to as the Cartesian plane, is a two-dimensional surface consisting of a horizontal and a vertical number line. The horizontal number line is referred to as the x-axis, and the vertical number line is referred to as the y-axis. The x-axis and y-axis intersect (or cross) at a point called the origin. At the origin, the value of the x-axis is zero, and the value of the y-axis is zero. The coordinate plane identifies the exact location of a point that is plotted on the two-dimensional surface. Like a map, the location of all points on the plane are in relation to the origin. Along the x-axis (horizontal line), numbers to the right of the origin are positive and increasing in value (1,2,3, ...) and to the left of the origin numbers are negative and decreasing in value (-1,-2,-3, ...). Along the y-axis (vertical line), numbers above the origin are positive and increasing in value and numbers below the origin are negative and decreasing in value.

The x- and y-axis divide the coordinate plane into four sections. These sections are referred to as quadrant one, quadrant two, quadrant three, and quadrant four, and are often written with Roman numerals I, II, III, and IV.

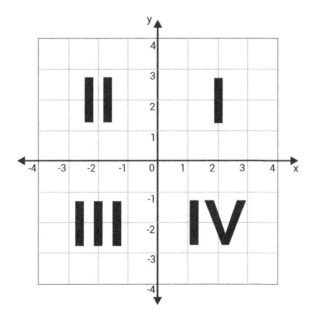

The upper right section is Quadrant I and consists of points with positive x-values and positive y-values. The upper left section is Quadrant II and consists of points with negative x-values and positive y-values. The bottom left section is Quadrant III and consists of points with negative x-values and negative y-values. The bottom right section is Quadrant IV and consists of points with positive x-values and negative y-values.

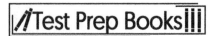

Any point within the plane can be defined by a set of **coordinates** (x, y). The coordinates consist of two numbers, x and y, which represent a position on each number line. The coordinates can also be referred to as an **ordered pair,** and $(0, 0)$ is the ordered pair known as the **vertex**, or the origin, the point in which the axes intersect. Positive x-coordinates go to the right of the vertex, and positive y-coordinates go up. Negative x-coordinates go left, and negative y-coordinates go down.

Here is an example of the coordinate plane with a point plotted:

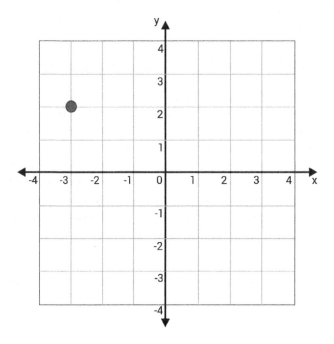

In order to plot a point on the coordinate plane, each coordinate must be considered individually. The value of x represents how many units away from the vertex the point lies on the x-axis. The value of y represents the number of units away from the vertex that the point lies on the y-axis.

The points on the coordinate plane are labeled based on their position in relation to the origin. If a point is found 4 units to the right and 2 units up from the origin, the location is described as $(4, 2)$. These numbers are the x- and y-coordinates, always written in the order (x, y). This point is also described as lying in the first quadrant. Every point in the first quadrant has a location that is positive in the x and y directions.

100

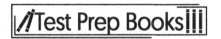

The following figure shows the coordinate plane with examples of points that lie in each quadrant:

The Coordinate Plane

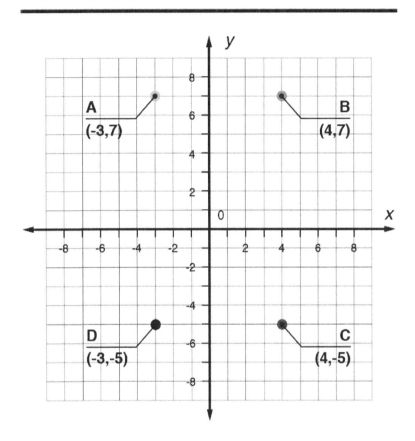

Point B lies in the first quadrant, described with positive x- and y-values, above the x-axis and to the right of the y-axis. Point A lies in the second quadrant, where the x-value is negative and the y-value is positive. This quadrant is above the x-axis and to the left of the y-axis. Point D lies in the third quadrant, where both the x- and y-values are negative. Points in this quadrant are described as being below the x-axis and to the left of the y-axis. Point C is in the fourth quadrant, where the x-value is positive and the y-value is negative.

Graphing on the Coordinate Plane Using Mathematical Problems, Tables, and Patterns

Data can be recorded using a coordinate plane. Graphs are utilized frequently in real-world applications and can be seen in many facets of everyday life. A relationship can exist between the x- and y-coordinates that are plotted on a graph, and those values can represent a set of data that can be listed in a table. Going back and forth between the table and the graph is an important concept and defining the relationship between the variables is the key that links the data to a real-life application.

For example, temperature increases during a summer day. The x-coordinate can be used to represent hours in the day, and the y-coordinate can be used to represent the temperature in degrees. The graph would show the temperature at each hour of the day. Time is almost always plotted on the x-axis, and utilizing different units on each axis, if necessary, is important. Labeling the axes with units is also important.

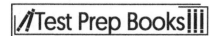
Within the first quadrant of the coordinate plane, both the x and y values are positive. Most real-world problems can be plotted in this quadrant because most real-world quantities, such as time and distance, are positive.

Consider the following table of values:

X	Y
1	2
2	4
3	6
4	8

Each row gives a coordinate pair. For example, the first row gives the coordinates $(1, 2)$. Each x-value tells you how far to move from the origin, the point $(0, 0)$, to the right, and each y-value tells you how far to move up from the origin. Here is the graph of the points listed above in the table in addition to the origin:

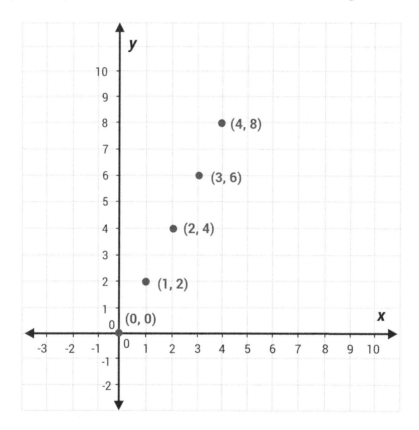

Notice that each y-value is found by doubling the x-value that forms the other portion of its coordinate pair.

Data Analysis/Probability

Measures of Center and Range

The center of a set of data (statistical values) can be represented by its mean, median, or mode. These are sometimes referred to as measures of central tendency. The mean is the average of the data set. The mean can be

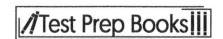

calculated by adding the data values and dividing by the sample size (the number of data points). Suppose a student has test scores of 93, 84, 88, 72, 91, and 77.

To find the mean, or average, the scores are added and the sum is divided by 6 because there are 6 test scores:

$$\frac{93 + 84 + 88 + 72 + 91 + 77}{6} = \frac{505}{6} = 84.17$$

Given the mean of a data set and the sum of the data points, the sample size can be determined by dividing the sum by the mean. Suppose you are told that Kate averaged 12 points per game and scored a total of 156 points for the season. The number of games that she played (the sample size or the number of data points) can be determined by dividing the total points (sum of data points) by her average (mean of data points): $\frac{156}{12} = 13$. Therefore, Kate played in 13 games this season.

If given the mean of a data set and the sample size, the sum of the data points can be determined by multiplying the mean and sample size. Suppose you are told that Tom worked 6 days last week for an average of 5.5 hours per day. The total number of hours worked for the week (sum of data points) can be determined by multiplying his daily average (mean of data points) by the number of days worked (sample size): $5.5 \times 6 = 33$. Therefore, Tom worked a total of 33 hours last week.

The median of a data set is the value of the data point in the middle when the sample is arranged in numerical order. To find the median of a data set, the values are written in order from least to greatest. The lowest and highest values are simultaneously eliminated, repeating until the value in the middle remains. Suppose the salaries of math teachers are: $35,000; $38,500; $41,000; $42,000; $42,000; $44,500; $49,000. The values are listed from least to greatest to find the median. The lowest and highest values are eliminated until only the middle value remains. Repeating this step three times reveals a median salary of $42,000. If the sample set has an even number of data points, two values will remain after all others are eliminated. In this case, the mean of the two middle values is the median. Consider the following data set: 7, 9, 10, 13, 14, 14. Eliminating the lowest and highest values twice leaves two values, 10 and 13, in the middle. The mean of these values ($\frac{10+13}{2}$) is the median. Therefore, the set has a median of 11.5.

The mode of a data set is the value that appears most often. A data set may have a single mode, multiple modes, or no mode. If different values repeat equally as often, multiple modes exist. If no value repeats, no mode exists. Consider the following data sets:

- A: 7, 9, 10, 13, 14, 14
- B: 37, 44, 33, 37, 49, 44, 51, 34, 37, 33, 44
- C: 173, 154, 151, 168, 155

Set A has a mode of 14. Set B has modes of 37 and 44. Set C has no mode.

The range of a data set is the difference between the highest and the lowest values in the set. The range can be considered the span of the data set. To determine the range, the smallest value in the set is subtracted from the largest value. The ranges for the data sets A, B, and C above are calculated as follows: $A: 14 - 7 = 7$; $B: 51 - 33 = 18$; $C: 173 - 151 = 22$.

Best Description of a Set of Data

Measures of central tendency, namely mean, median, and mode, describe characteristics of a set of data. Specifically, they are intended to represent a *typical* value in the set by identifying a central position of the set.

103

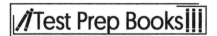
Depending on the characteristics of a specific set of data, different measures of central tendency are more indicative of a typical value in the set.

When a data set is grouped closely together with a relatively small range and the data is spread out somewhat evenly, the mean is an effective indicator of a typical value in the set. Consider the following data set representing the height of sixth grade boys in inches: 61 inches, 54 inches, 58 inches, 63 inches, 58 inches. The mean of the set is 58.8 inches. The data set is grouped closely (the range is only 9 inches) and the values are spread relatively evenly (three values below the mean and two values above the mean). Therefore, the mean value of 58.8 inches is an effective measure of central tendency in this case.

When a data set contains a small number of values either extremely large or extremely small when compared to the other values, the mean is not an effective measure of central tendency. Consider the following data set representing annual incomes of homeowners on a given street: $71,000; $74,000; $75,000; $77,000; $340,000. The mean of this set is $127,400. This figure does not indicate a typical value in the set, which contains four out of five values between $71,000 and $77,000. The median is a much more effective measure of central tendency for data sets such as these. Finding the middle value diminishes the influence of outliers, or numbers that may appear out of place, like the $340,000 annual income. The median for this set is $75,000 which is much more typical of a value in the set.

The mode of a data set is a useful measure of central tendency for categorical data when each piece of data is an option from a category. Consider a survey of 31 commuters asking how they get to work with results summarized below.

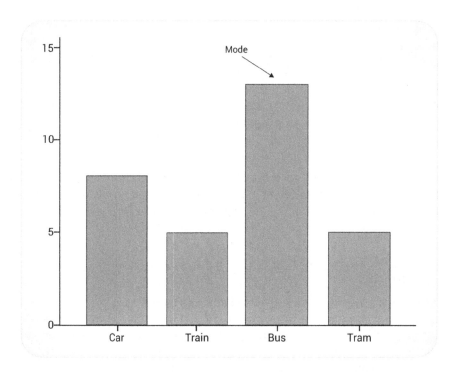

The mode for this set represents the value, or option, of the data that repeats most often. This indicates that the bus is the most popular method of transportation for the commuters.

Effects of Changes in Data

Changing all values of a data set in a consistent way produces predictable changes in the measures of the center and range of the set. A linear transformation changes the original value into the new value by either adding a given

104

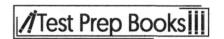

number to each value, multiplying each value by a given number, or both. Adding (or subtracting) a given value to each data point will increase (or decrease) the mean, median, and any modes by the same value. However, the range will remain the same due to the way that range is calculated. Multiplying (or dividing) a given value by each data point will increase (or decrease) the mean, median, and any modes, and the range by the same factor.

Consider the following data set, call it set P, representing the price of different cases of soda at a grocery store: $4.25, $4.40, $4.75, $4.95, $4.95, $5.15. The mean of set P is $4.74. The median is $4.85. The mode of the set is $4.95. The range is $0.90. Suppose the state passes a new tax of $0.25 on every case of soda sold. The new data set, set T, is calculated by adding $0.25 to each data point from set P. Therefore, set T consists of the following values: $4.50, $4.65, $5.00, $5.20, $5.20, $5.40. The mean of set T is $4.99. The median is $5.10. The mode of the set is $5.20. The range is $.90. The mean, median and mode of set T is equal to $0.25 added to the mean, median, and mode of set P. The range stays the same.

Now suppose, due to inflation, the store raises the cost of every item by 10 percent. Raising costs by 10 percent is calculated by multiplying each value by 1.1. The new data set, set I, is calculated by multiplying each data point from set T by 1.1. Therefore, set I consists of the following values: $4.95, $5.12, $5.50, $5.72, $5.72, $5.94. The mean of set I is $5.49. The median is $5.61. The mode of the set is $5.72. The range is $0.99. The mean, median, mode, and range of set I is equal to 1.1 multiplied by the mean, median, mode, and range of set T because each increased by a factor of 10 percent.

Describing a Set of Data

A set of data can be described in terms of its center, spread, shape and any unusual features. The center of a data set can be measured by its mean, median, or mode. Measures of central tendency are covered in the *Measures of Center and Range* section. The spread of a data set refers to how far the data points are from the center (mean or median). The spread can be measured by the range or by the quartiles and interquartile range. A data set with all its data points clustered around the center will have a small spread. A data set covering a wide range of values will have a large spread.

When a data set is displayed as a histogram or frequency distribution plot, the shape indicates if a sample is normally distributed, symmetrical, or has measures of skewness or kurtosis. When graphed, a data set with a normal distribution will resemble a bell curve.

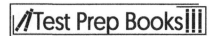
If the data set is symmetrical, each half of the graph when divided at the center is a mirror image of the other. If the graph has fewer data points to the right, the data is skewed right. If it has fewer data points to the left, the data is skewed left.

Right-Skewed   Symmetric   Left-Skewed

Kurtosis is a measure of whether the data is heavy-tailed with a high number of outliers, or light-tailed with a low number of outliers.

A description of a data set should include any unusual features such as gaps or outliers. A gap is a span within the range of the data set containing no data points. An outlier is a data point with a value either extremely large or extremely small when compared to the other values in the set.

Interpreting Displays of Data

A set of data can be visually displayed in various forms allowing for quick identification of characteristics of the set. Histograms, such as the one shown below, display the number of data points (vertical axis) that fall into given intervals (horizontal axis) across the range of the set. Suppose the histogram below displays IQ scores of students. Histograms can describe the center, spread, shape, and any unusual characteristics of a data set.

Histogram

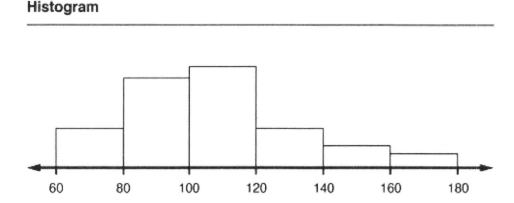

A box plot, also called a box-and-whisker plot, divides the data points into four groups and displays the five-number summary for the set as well as any outliers. The five-number summary consists of:

- The lower extreme: the lowest value that is not an outlier
- The higher extreme: the highest value that is not an outlier
- The median of the set: also referred to as the second quartile or Q_2
- The first quartile or Q_1: the median of values below Q_2
- The third quartile or Q_3: the median of values above Q_2

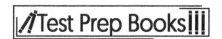

Calculating each of these values is covered in the next section, *Graphical Representation of Data*.

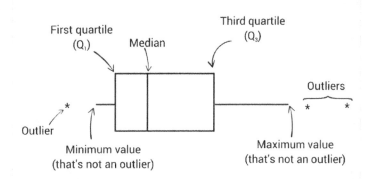

Suppose the box plot displays IQ scores for 12th grade students at a given school. The five number summary of the data consists of: lower extreme (67); upper extreme (127); Q_2 or median (100); Q_1 (91); Q_3 (108); and outliers (135 and 140). Although all data points are not known from the plot, the points are divided into four quartiles each, including 25% of the data points. Therefore, 25% of students scored between 67 and 91, 25% scored between 91 and 100, 25% scored between 100 and 108, and 25% scored between 108 and 127. These percentages include the normal values for the set and exclude the outliers. This information is useful when comparing a given score with the rest of the scores in the set.

A scatter plot is a mathematical diagram that visually displays the relationship or connection between two variables. The independent variable is placed on the x-axis, or horizontal axis, and the dependent variable is placed on the y-axis, or vertical axis. When visually examining the points on the graph, if the points model a linear relationship, or if a line of best-fit can be drawn through the points with the points relatively close on either side, then a correlation exists. If the line of best-fit has a positive slope (rises from left to right), then the variables have a positive correlation. If the line of best-fit has a negative slope (falls from left to right), then the variables have a negative correlation. If a line of best-fit cannot be drawn, then no correlation exists. A positive or negative correlation can be categorized as strong or weak, depending on how closely the points are graphed around the line of best-fit.

107

Graphical Representation of Data

Various graphs can be used to visually represent a given set of data. Each type of graph requires a different method of arranging data points and different calculations of the data. Examples of histograms, box plots, and scatter plots are discussed in the previous section **Interpreting Displays of Data**. To construct a histogram, the range of the data points is divided into equal intervals. The frequency for each interval is then determined, which reveals how many points fall into each interval. A graph is constructed with the vertical axis representing the frequency and the horizontal axis representing the intervals. The lower value of each interval should be labeled along the horizontal axis. Finally, for each interval, a bar is drawn from the lower value of each interval to the lower value of the next interval with a height equal to the frequency of the interval. Because of the intervals, histograms do not have any gaps between bars along the horizontal axis.

To construct a box (or box-and-whisker) plot, the five-number summary for the data set is calculated as follows: the second quartile (Q_2) is the median of the set. The first quartile (Q_1) is the median of the values below Q_2. The third quartile (Q_3) is the median of the values above Q_2. The upper extreme is the highest value in the data set if it is not an outlier (greater than 1.5 times the interquartile range $Q_3 - Q_1$). The lower extreme is the least value in the data set if it is not an outlier (more than 1.5 times lower than the interquartile range).

To construct the box-and-whisker plot, each value is plotted on a number line, along with any outliers. The box consists of Q_1 and Q_3 as its top and bottom and Q_2 as the dividing line inside the box. The whiskers extend from the lower extreme to Q_1 and from Q_3 to the upper extreme.

Box Plot

A scatter plot displays the relationship between two variables. Values for the independent variable, typically denoted by x, are paired with values for the dependent variable, typically denoted by y. Each set of corresponding values are written as an ordered pair (x, y). To construct the graph, a coordinate grid is labeled with the x-axis representing the independent variable and the y-axis representing the dependent variable. Each ordered pair is graphed.

Like a scatter plot, a line graph compares variables that change continuously, typically over time. Paired data values (ordered pairs) are plotted on a coordinate grid with the x- and y-axis representing the variables. A line is drawn from each point to the next, going from left to right.

The line graph below displays cell phone use for given years (two variables) for men, women, and both sexes (three data sets).

A line plot, also called dot plot, displays the frequency of data (numerical values) on a number line. To construct a line plot, a number line is used that includes all unique data values. It is marked with x's or dots above the value the number of times that the value occurs in the data set.

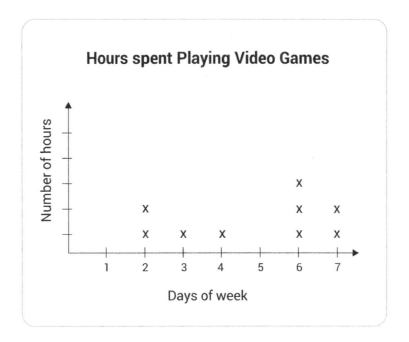

A bar graph looks similar to a histogram but displays categorical data. The horizontal axis represents each category and the vertical axis represents the frequency for the category. A bar is drawn for each category (often different colors) with a height extending to the frequency for that category within the data set. A double bar graph displays two sets of data that contain data points consisting of the same categories.

The double bar graph below indicates that two girls and four boys like Pad Thai the most out of all the foods, two boys and five girls like pizza, and so on.

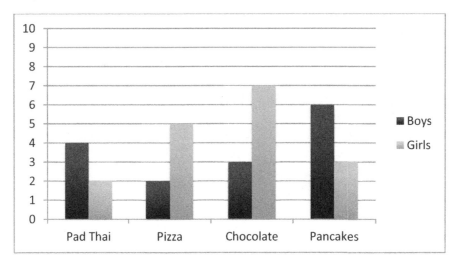

A circle graph, also called a pie chart, displays categorical data with each category representing a percentage of the whole data set. To construct a circle graph, the percent of the data set for each category must be determined. To do so, the frequency of the category is divided by the total number of data points and converted to a percent. For

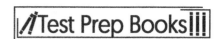

example, if 80 people were asked their favorite pizza topping and 20 responded cheese, then cheese constitutes 25% of the data ($\frac{20}{80} = .25 = 25\%$).

Each category in a data set is represented by a **slice** of the circle proportionate to its percentage of the whole.

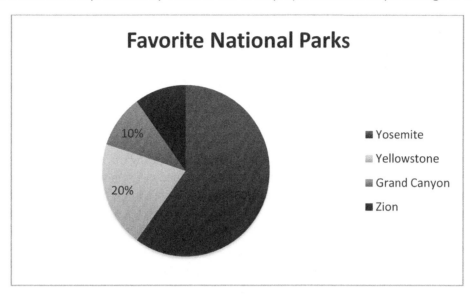

Choice of Graphs to Display Data

Choosing the appropriate graph to display a data set depends on what type of data is included in the set and what information must be displayed. Histograms and box plots can be used for data sets consisting of individual values across a wide range. Examples include test scores and incomes. Histograms and box plots will indicate the center, spread, range, and outliers of a data set. A histogram will show the shape of the data set, while a box plot will divide the set into quartiles (25% increments), allowing for comparison between a given value and the entire set.

Scatter plots and line graphs can be used to display data consisting of two variables. Examples include height and weight, or distance and time. A correlation between the variables is determined by examining the points on the graph. Line graphs are used if each value for one variable pairs with a distinct value for the other variable. Line graphs show relationships between variables.

Line plots, bar graphs, and circle graphs are all used to display categorical data, such as surveys. Line plots and bar graphs both indicate the frequency of each category within the data set. A line plot is used when the categories consist of numerical values. For example, the number of hours of TV watched by individuals is displayed on a line plot. A bar graph is used when the categories consist of words. For example, the favorite ice cream of individuals is displayed with a bar graph. A circle graph can be used to display either type of categorical data. However, unlike line plots and bar graphs, a circle graph does not indicate the frequency of each category. Instead, the circle graph represents each category as its percentage of the whole data set.

Probabilities Relative to Likelihood of Occurrence [ISEE]

Probability is a measure of how likely an event is to occur. Probability is written as a fraction between zero and one. If an event has a probability of zero, the event will never occur. If an event has a probability of one, the event will definitely occur. If the probability of an event is closer to zero, the event is unlikely to occur. If the probability of an event is closer to one, the event is more likely to occur. For example, a probability of $\frac{1}{2}$ means that the event is equally as likely to occur as it is not to occur. An example of this is tossing a coin. The probability of an event can be calculated by dividing the number of favorable outcomes by the number of total outcomes. For example, suppose you have 2 raffle tickets out of 20 total tickets sold. The probability that you win the raffle is calculated:

$$\frac{number\ of\ favorable\ outcomes}{total\ number\ of\ outcomes} = \frac{2}{20} = \frac{1}{10}\ \text{(always reduce fractions)}$$

Therefore, the probability of winning the raffle is $\frac{1}{10}$ or 0.1.

Chance is the measure of how likely an event is to occur, written as a percent. If an event will never occur, the event has a 0% chance. If an event will certainly occur, the event has a 100% chance. If an event will sometimes occur, the event has a chance somewhere between 0% and 100%. To calculate chance, probability is calculated, and the fraction is converted to a percent.

The probability of multiple events occurring can be determined by multiplying the probability of each event. For example, suppose you flip a coin with heads and tails, and roll a six-sided die numbered one through six. To find the probability that you will flip heads AND roll a two, the probability of each event is determined, and those fractions are multiplied. The probability of flipping heads is $\frac{1}{2}$ ($\frac{1\ side\ with\ heads}{2\ sides\ total}$), and the probability of rolling a two is $\frac{1}{6}$ ($\frac{1\ side\ with\ a\ 2}{6\ total\ sides}$). The probability of flipping heads AND rolling a 2 is:

$$\frac{1}{2} \times \frac{1}{6} = \frac{1}{12}$$

The above scenario with flipping a coin and rolling a die is an example of independent events. Independent events are circumstances in which the outcome of one event does not affect the outcome of the other event. Conversely, dependent events are ones in which the outcome of one event affects the outcome of the second event. Consider the following scenario: a bag contains 5 black marbles and 5 white marbles. What is the probability of picking 2 black marbles without replacing the marble after the first pick?

The probability of picking a black marble on the first pick is $\frac{5}{10}$ $\left(\frac{5\ black\ marbles}{10\ total\ marbles}\right)$. Assuming that a black marble was picked, there are now 4 black marbles and 5 white marbles for the second pick. Therefore, the probability of picking a black marble on the second pick is $\frac{4}{9}$ $\left(\frac{4\ black\ marbles}{9\ total\ marbles}\right)$. To find the probability of picking two black marbles, the probability of each is multiplied:

$$\frac{5}{10} \times \frac{4}{9} = \frac{20}{90} = \frac{2}{9}$$

Practice Quiz

1. At the beginning of the day, Xavier has 20 apples. At lunch, he meets his sister Emma and gives her half of his apples. After lunch, he stops by his neighbor Jim's house and gives him six of his apples. He then uses $\frac{3}{4}$ of his remaining apples to make an apple pie for dessert at dinner. At the end of the day, how many apples does Xavier have left?
   - a.   4
   - b.   6
   - c.   2
   - d.   1
   - e.   3

2. If $\frac{5}{2} \div \frac{1}{3} = n$, then n is between which of the following?
   - a.   5 and 7
   - b.   7 and 9
   - c.   9 and 11
   - d.   3 and 5
   - e.   11 and 13

3. Apples cost $2 each, while bananas cost $3 each. Maria purchased a total of 10 pieces of fruit and spent $22. How many apples did she buy?
   - a.   4
   - b.   5
   - c.   6
   - d.   7
   - e.   8

4. A rectangle has a length that is 5 feet longer than 3 times its width. If the perimeter is 90 feet, what is the length in feet?
   - a.   10
   - b.   20
   - c.   25
   - d.   30
   - e.   35

5. Five of six numbers have a sum of 25. The average of all six numbers is 6. What is the sixth number?
   - a.   8
   - b.   10
   - c.   13
   - d.   12
   - e.   11

See answers on the next page.

113

Answer Explanations

1. D: This problem can be solved using basic arithmetic. Xavier starts with 20 apples, then gives his sister half, so 20 is divided by 2.

$$\frac{20}{2} = 10$$

He then gives his neighbor six apples, so 6 is subtracted from 10.

$$10 - 6 = 4$$

Finally, he uses $\frac{3}{4}$ of his remaining apples to make a pie. Since $\frac{3}{4}$ of 4 is 3, he uses 3 apples, so 3 is subtracted from 4.

$$4 - 3 = 1$$

2. B: $\frac{5}{2} \div \frac{1}{3} = \frac{5}{2} \times \frac{3}{1} = \frac{15}{2} = 7.5$

3. E: Let a be the number of apples and b be the number of bananas. The total cost is:

$$2a + 3b = 22$$

While it also known that:

$$a + b = 10$$

Using the knowledge of systems of equations, cancel the b variables by multiplying the second equation by -3. This makes the equation:

$$-3a - 3b = -30$$

Adding this to the first equation, the b values cancel to get $-a = -8$, which simplifies to $a = 8$.

4. E: Denote the width as w and the length as l. Then, $l = 3w + 5$. The perimeter is $2w + 2l = 90$. Substituting the first expression for l into the second equation yields:

$$2(3w + 5) + 2w = 90$$

$$6w + 10 + 2w = 90$$

$$8w = 80$$

$$w = 10$$

Putting this into the first equation, it yields:

$$l = 3(10) + 5 = 35$$

5. E: The average is calculated by adding all six numbers, then dividing by 6. The first five numbers have a sum of 25. This scenario can be expressed by the equation $\frac{25+n}{6} = 6$, where n is the unknown number. After multiplying both sides by 6, we get $25 + n = 36$, which means $n = 11$.

Reading Comprehension

Main Idea

Recognizing the Main Idea

Typically, in a piece of narrative writing there are only a couple of ideas that the author is trying to convey to the reader. Be careful to understand the difference between a topic and a main idea. A topic might be "horses," but the main idea should be a complete sentence such as, "Racehorses run faster when they have a good relationship with the jockey." Here are some guidelines, tips, and tricks to follow that will help identify the main idea:

Identifying the Main Idea
The most important part of the text
Text title and pictures may reveal clues
Opening sentences and final sentences may reveal clues
Key vocabulary words that are repeatedly used may reveal clues

Topic versus the Main Idea

It is very important to know the difference between the **topic** and the **main idea** of the text. Even though these two are similar because they both present the central point of a text, they have distinctive differences. A **topic** is the subject of the text; This can usually be described in a concise one- to two-word phrase. On the other hand, the **main idea** is more detailed and provides the author's central point of the text. It can be expressed through a complete sentence and is often found in the beginning, the middle, or at the end of a paragraph. In most nonfiction books, the first sentence of the passage usually (but not always) states the main idea. Take a look at the passage below to review the **topic** versus the **main idea**:

Cheetahs

> Cheetahs are one of the fastest mammals on the land, reaching up to 70 miles an hour over short distances. Even though cheetahs can run as fast as 70 miles an hour, they usually only have to run half that speed to catch up with their choice of prey. Cheetahs cannot maintain a fast pace over long periods of time because they will overheat their bodies. After a chase, cheetahs need to rest for approximately 30 minutes prior to eating or returning to any other activity.

In the example above, the *topic* of the passage is "Cheetahs" simply because that is the subject of the text. The *main idea* of the text is "Cheetahs are one of the fastest mammals on the land but can only maintain a fast pace for shorter distances." While it covers the topic, it is more detailed and refers to the text in its entirety. The text continues to provide additional details called **supporting details**.

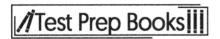

Theme

The **theme** of a text is the central message of the story. The theme can be about a moral or lesson that the author wants to share with the audience. Although authors do not directly state the theme of a story, it is the "big picture" that they intend readers to walk away with. For example, the fairy tale *The Boy Who Cried Wolf* features the tale of a little boy who continued to lie about seeing a wolf. When the little boy actually saw a wolf, no one believed him because of all of the previous lies. The author of this fairy tale does not directly tell readers, "Don't lie because people will question the credibility of the story." The author simply portrays the story of the little boy and presents the moral through the tale.

The theme of a text centers around varying subjects such as courage, friendship, love, bravery, facing challenges, or adversity. It often leaves readers with more questions than answers. Authors tend to insinuate certain themes in texts; however, readers are left to interpret the true meaning of the story.

Supporting Ideas

Locating Details

Supporting details of texts are defined as those elements of a text that help readers make sense of the main idea. They either qualitatively and/or quantitatively describe the main idea, strengthening the reader's understanding.

Supporting details answer questions like *who, what, where, when, why,* and *how.* Different types of supporting details include examples, facts and statistics, anecdotes, and sensory details.

Persuasive and informative texts often use supporting details. In persuasive texts, authors attempt to make readers agree with their points of view, and supporting details are often used as "selling points." If authors make a statement, they need to support the statement with evidence in order to adequately persuade readers. Informative texts use supporting details such as examples, facts, and details to inform readers. Take a look at the "Cheetahs" example again below to find examples of supporting details.

Cheetahs

Cheetahs are one of the fastest mammals on the land, reaching up to 70 miles an hour over short distances. Even though cheetahs can run as fast as 70 miles an hour, they usually only have to run half that speed to catch up with their choice of prey. Cheetahs cannot maintain a fast pace over long periods of time because they will overheat their bodies. After a chase, cheetahs need to rest for approximately 30 minutes prior to eating or returning to any other activity.

In the previous example, supporting details include:

- Cheetahs reach up to 70 miles per hour over short distances.
- They usually only have to run half that speed to catch up with their prey.
- Cheetahs will overheat their bodies if they exert a high speed over longer distances.
- They need to rest for 30 minutes after a chase.

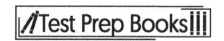
Look at the diagram below (applying the cheetah example) to help determine the hierarchy of *topic, main idea,* and *supporting details.*

Making Inferences

Simply put, an **inference** is an educated guess drawn from evidence, logic, and reasoning. The key to making inferences is identifying clues within a passage, and then using common sense to arrive at a reasonable conclusion. Consider it "reading between the lines."

One way to make an inference is to look for main topics. When doing so, pay particular attention to any titles, headlines, or opening statements made by the author. Topic sentences or repetitive ideas can be clues in gleaning inferred ideas. For example, if a passage contains the phrase *While some consider DNA testing to be infallible, it is an inherently flawed technique,* the test taker can infer the rest of the passage will contain information that points to problems with DNA testing.

The test taker may be asked to make an inference based on prior knowledge but may also be asked to make predictions based on new ideas. For example, the test taker may have no prior knowledge of DNA other than its genetic property to replicate. However, if the reader is given passages on the flaws of DNA testing with enough factual evidence, the test taker may arrive at the inferred conclusion that the author does not support the infallibility of DNA testing in all identification cases.

When making inferences, it is important to remember that the critical thinking process involved must be fluid and open to change. While a reader may infer an idea from a main topic, general statement, or other clues, he or she must be open to receiving new information within a particular passage. New ideas presented by an author may require the test taker to alter an inference. Similarly, when asked questions that require making an inference, it's

117

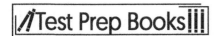

important to read the entire test passage and all of the answer options. Often, a test taker will need to refine a general inference based on new ideas that may be presented within the test itself.

Inferences also refer to the ability to make logical assumptions based on clues from the text. People make inferences about the world around them on a daily basis but may not be aware of what they are doing. For example, a young boy may infer that it is likely cold outside if he wakes up and his bedroom is chilly or the floor is cold. While being driven somewhere on the highway and a girl notices a person at the side of the road with a parked car, that girl will likely infer that the individual is having car problems and is awaiting some assistance. Both of these are example of how inferences are used every day and the same skill can be applied to different stories and texts.

In a way, making inferences is similar to detective work by collecting evidence. Sometimes clues can be found in the pictures or visual aids (like diagrams) that accompany a story or text. For example, a story may show a picture of a school in which all children are gathered in the parking lot. Upon closer examination, careful readers might spot a fire truck parked at the side of the road and may infer that the school had a fire drill or an actual fire.

Conclusions

Determining **conclusions** requires being an active reader, as a reader must make a prediction and analyze facts to identify a conclusion. There are a few ways to determine a logical conclusion, but careful reading is the most important. It's helpful to read a passage a few times, noting details that seem important to the text. A reader should also identify key words in a passage to determine the logical conclusion or determination that flows from the information presented.

Textual evidence helps readers draw a conclusion about a passage. **Textual evidence** refers to information—facts and examples that support the main point; it will likely come from outside sources and can be in the form of quoted or paraphrased material. In order to draw a conclusion from evidence, it's important to examine the credibility and validity of that evidence as well as how (and if) it relates to the main idea.

If an author presents a differing opinion or a **counterargument** in order to refute it, the reader should consider how and why the information is being presented. It is meant to strengthen the original argument and shouldn't be confused with the author's intended conclusion, but it should also be considered in the reader's final evaluation.

Sometimes, authors explicitly state the conclusion they want readers to understand. Alternatively, a conclusion may not be directly stated. In that case, readers must rely on the implications to form a logical conclusion:

> On the way to the bus stop, Michael realized his homework wasn't in his backpack. He ran back to the house to get it and made it back to the bus just in time.

In this example, though it's never explicitly stated, it can be inferred that Michael is a student on his way to school in the morning. When forming a conclusion from implied information, it's important to read the text carefully to find several pieces of evidence to support the conclusion.

Synthesis

Synthesis also requires a reader to make inferences while reading. Inference has been addressed earlier in this guide. Review the section and take note of the required skills in making inferences.

In order to achieve synthesis and full reading comprehension, a reader must take their prior knowledge, the knowledge or main ideas an author presents, and fill in the gaps to reach a logical conclusion. In a testing situation, a test taker may be asked to infer ideas from a given passage, asked to choose from a set of inferences that best

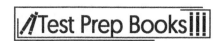

express a summary of what the author hints at, or arrive at a logical conclusion based on their inferences. This is not an easy task, but it is approachable.

While inference requires a reader to make educated guesses based on stated information, it's important that the reader does not assume too much. It's important the reader does not insert information into a passage that's not there. It's important to make an inference based solely on the presented information and to make predictions using a logical thought process.

After reviewing the earlier section on making inferences, keep the following in mind:

- Do not jump to conclusions early in the passage. Read the full text before trying to infer meaning.

- Rely on asking questions (see the above section). What is the author stating? More important, what is the author not saying? What information is missing? What conclusions can be made about that missing information, if any.

- Make an inference then apply it back to the text passage. Does the inference make sense? Is it likely an idea with which the author would agree?

- What inferences can be made from any data presented? Are these inferences sound, logical, and do they hold water?

While this is not an exhaustive list of questions related to making inferences, it should help the reader with the skill of synthesis in achieving full reading comprehension.

Deriving the Meaning of a Word or Phrase from its Context

It's common to find words that aren't familiar in writing. When you don't know a word, there are some "tricks" that can be used to find out its meaning. *Context clues* are words or phrases in a sentence or paragraph that provide hints about a word and what it means. For example, if an unknown word is attached to a noun with other surrounding words as clues, these can help you figure out the word's meaning. Consider the following example:

> After the treatment, Grandma's natural rosy cheeks looked *wan* and ghostlike.

The word we don't know is *wan*. The first clue to its meaning is in the phrase *After the treatment,* which tells us that something happened after a procedure (possibly medical). A second clue is the word *rosy*, which describes Grandma's natural cheek color that changed after the treatment. Finally, the word *ghostlike* infers that Grandma's cheeks now look white. By using the context clues in the sentence, we can figure out that the meaning of the word *wan* means *pale*.

Contrasts

Look for context clues that **contrast** the unknown word. When reading a sentence with a word we don't know, look for an opposite word or idea. Here's an example:

> Since Mary didn't cite her research sources, she lost significant points for *plagiarizing* the content of her report.

In this sentence, *plagiarizing* is the word we don't know. Notice that when Mary *didn't cite her research sources,* it resulted in her losing points for *plagiarizing the content of her report*. These contrasting ideas tell us that Mary did something wrong with the content. This makes sense because the definition of *plagiarizing* is "taking the work of someone else and passing it off as your own."

Contrasts often use words like *but, however, although,* or phrases like *on the other hand.* For example:

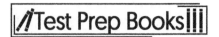
The *gargantuan* television won't fit in my car, but it will cover the entire wall in the den.

The word we don't know is *gargantuan*. Notice that the television is too big to fit in a car, <u>but</u> *it will cover the entire wall in the den*. This tells us that the television is extremely large. The word *gargantuan* means *enormous*.

Synonyms

Another way to find out a word you don't know is to think of synonyms for that word. **Synonyms** are words with the same meaning. To do this, replace synonyms one at a time. Then read the sentence after each synonym to see if the meaning is clear. By replacing a word we don't know with a word we do know, it's easier to uncover its meaning. For example:

Gary's clothes were *saturated* after he fell into the swimming pool.

In this sentence, we don't know the word *saturated*. To brainstorm synonyms for *saturated*, think about what happens to Gary's clothes after falling into the swimming pool. They'd be *soaked* or *wet*. These both turn out to be good synonyms to try. The actual meaning of *saturated* is "thoroughly soaked."

Antonyms

Sometimes sentences contain words or phrases that oppose each other. Opposite words are known as **antonyms**. An example of an antonym is *hot* and *cold*. For example:

Although Mark seemed *tranquil*, you could tell he was actually nervous as he paced up and down the hall.

The word we don't know is *tranquil*. The sentence says that Mark was in fact not *tranquil*. He was *actually nervous*. The opposite of the word *nervous* is *calm*. *Calm* is the meaning of the word *tranquil*.

Explanations or Descriptions

Explanations or descriptions of other things in the sentence can also provide clues to an unfamiliar word. Take the following example:

Golden Retrievers, Great Danes, and Pugs are the top three *breeds* competing in the dog show.

We don't know the word *breeds*. Look at the sentence for a clue. The subjects (*Golden Retrievers*, *Great Danes*, and *Pugs*) describe different types of dogs. This description helps uncover the meaning of the word *breeds*. The word *breeds* means "a particular type of animal."

Inferences

Inferences are clues to an unknown word that tell us its meaning. These inferences can be found within the sentence where the word appears. Or, they can be found in a sentence before the word or after the word. Look at the following example:

The *wretched* old lady was kicked out of the restaurant. She was so mean and nasty to the waiter!

Here, we don't know the word *wretched*. The first sentence says that the *old lady was kicked out of the restaurant*, but it doesn't say why. The sentence after tells us why: *She was so mean and nasty to the waiter!* This infers that the old lady was *kicked out* because she was *so mean and nasty* or, in other words, *wretched*.

When you prepare for a vocabulary test, try reading harder materials to learn new words. If you don't know a word on the test, look for prefixes and suffixes to find out what the word means and get rid of wrong answers. If two answers both seem right, see if there are any differences between them. Then select the word that best fits.

120

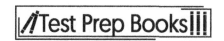

Context clues in the sentence or paragraph can also help you find the meaning of a word you don't know. By learning new words, a person can expand their knowledge. They can also improve the quality of their writing.

Determining the Author's Purpose

Authors want to capture the interest of the reader. An effective reader is attentive to an author's *position*. Authors write with intent, whether implicit or explicit. An author may hold a bias or use emotional language, which in turn creates a very clear *position*. Finding an author's *purpose* is usually easier than figuring out their position. An author's **purpose** of a text may be to persuade, inform, entertain, or be descriptive. Most narratives are written with the intent to entertain the reader, although some may also be informative or persuasive. When an author tries to persuade a reader, the reader must be cautious of the intent or argument. Therefore, the author keeps the persuasion lighthearted and friendly to maintain the entertainment value in narrative texts even though he or she is still trying to convince the reader of something.

An author's **purpose** will influence their writing style. As mentioned previously, the purpose can inform, entertain, or persuade a reader. If an author writes an informative text, their purpose is to educate the reader about a certain topic. Informative texts are usually nonfiction, and the author rarely states their opinion. The **purpose** of an informative text is also indicated by the outline of the text itself. In some cases, an informative text may have headings, subtitles, and bold key words. The purpose for this type of text is to educate the reader.

Entertaining texts, whether fiction or nonfiction, are meant to captivate readers' attention. Entertaining texts are usually stories that describe real or fictional people, places, or things. These narratives often use expressive language, emotions, imagery, and figurative language to captivate the readers. If readers do not want to put the entertaining text down, the author has fulfilled their purpose for this type of text.

Descriptive texts use adjectives and adverbs to describe people, places, or things to provide a clear image to the reader throughout the story. If an author fails to provide detailed descriptions, readers may find texts boring or confusing. Descriptive texts are almost always informative but can also be persuasive or entertaining pending the author's purpose.

Determining the Author's Attitude and Tone

Tone refers to the writer's attitude toward the subject matter. Tone conveys how the writer feels about characters, situations, events, ideas, etc. Nonfiction writing is sometimes thought to have no tone at all, but this is incorrect.

A lot of nonfiction writing has a neutral tone, which is an extremely important tone for the writer to take. A neutral tone demonstrates that the writer is presenting a topic impartially and letting the information speak for itself. On the other hand, nonfiction writing can be just as effective and appropriate if the tone isn't neutral. For instance, take the previous examples involving seat belt use. In them, the writer mostly chooses to retain a neutral tone when presenting information. If the writer would instead include their own personal experience of losing a friend or family member in a car accident, the tone would change dramatically. The tone would no longer be neutral. Now it would show that the writer has a personal stake in the content, allowing them to interpret the information in a different way. When analyzing tone, consider what the writer is trying to achieve in the passage, and how they *create* the tone using style.

Understanding and Evaluating Opinions/Arguments

A **fact** is information that is true. If information can be disproven, it is not a fact. For example, water freezes at or below thirty-two degrees Fahrenheit. An argument stating that water freezes at seventy degrees Fahrenheit cannot be supported by data and is therefore not a fact. Facts tend to be associated with science, mathematics, and statistics.

Opinions are information open for debate. Opinions are often tied to subjective concepts like feelings, desires, or manners. They can also be controversial.

Stereotypes and **biases** are viewpoints based in opinion and held despite evidence that they are incorrect. A stereotype is a widely held belief projected onto a group, while a bias is an individual's belief. Biased people ignore evidence that contradicts their position while offering as proof any evidence that supports it. Those who stereotype tend to make assumptions based on what others have told them and usually have little firsthand experience with the group or item in question.

Readers should always identify the author's position or stance in a text. No matter how objective a text may seem, assume the author has preconceived beliefs. Reduce the likelihood of accepting an invalid argument, by looking for multiple articles on the topic, including those with varying opinions. If several opinions point in the same direction, and are backed by reputable peer-reviewed sources, it's more likely the author has a valid argument. Positions that run contrary to widely held beliefs and existing data should invite scrutiny. There are exceptions to the rule, so be a careful consumer of information.

Making Predictions Based on Information in the Passage

An active reader uses prior knowledge while reading to make accurate predictions. Prior knowledge is best utilized when readers make links between the current text, previously read texts, and life experiences. Some texts use suspense and foreshadowing to captivate readers. For example, an intriguing aspect of murder mysteries is that the reader is never sure of the culprit until the author reveals the individual's identity. Authors often build suspense, and add depth and meaning to a work by leaving clues to provide hints or predict future events in the story; this is called foreshadowing. While some instances of foreshadowing are subtle, others are quite obvious.

Another way to read actively is to identify examples of inference within text. Authors employ literary devices such as tone, characterization, and theme to engage the audience by showing details of the story instead of merely telling them. For example, if an author said *Bob is selfish*, there's little left to infer. If the author said, *Bob cheated on his test, ignored his mom's calls, and parked illegally*, the reader can infer Bob is selfish. Authors also make implications through character dialogue, thoughts, effects on others, actions, and looks. Like in life, readers must assemble all the clues to form a complete picture.

Active readers should also draw conclusions. A conclusion should be based only on the text details, not personal experiences. This means the reader should first determine the author's intent. Identify the author's viewpoint and connect relevant evidence to support it. Readers may then move to the most important step: deciding whether to agree and whether they are correct. Always read cautiously and critically. Interact with text and record reactions in the margins. These active reading skills help determine not only what the author thinks, but what the reader thinks.

Understanding the Effect of Word Choice [ISEE]

An author's choice of words—also referred to as **diction**—helps to convey meaning in a particular way. Through diction, an author can convey a particular tone—e.g., a humorous tone, a serious tone—in order to support the thesis in a meaningful way to the reader.

Connotation and Denotation

Connotation is when an author chooses words or phrases that invoke ideas or feelings other than their literal meaning. An example of the use of connotation is the word *cheap*, which suggests something is poor in value or

122

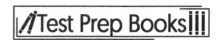

negatively describes a person as reluctant to spend money. When something or someone is described this way, the reader is more inclined to have a particular image or feeling. Thus, connotation can be a very effective language tool in creating emotion and swaying opinion. However, connotations are sometimes hard to pin down because varying emotions can be associated with a word. Generally, though, connotative meanings tend to be fairly consistent within a specific cultural group.

Denotation refers to words or phrases that mean exactly what they say. It is helpful when a writer wants to present hard facts or vocabulary terms with which readers may be unfamiliar. Some examples of denotation are the words *inexpensive* and *frugal*. *Inexpensive* refers to the cost of something, not its value, and *frugal* indicates that a person is conscientiously watching their spending. These terms do not elicit the same emotions that *cheap* does.

Authors sometimes choose to use both, but what they choose and when they use it is what critical readers need to differentiate. One method isn't inherently better than the other; however, one may create a better effect, depending upon an author's intent. If, for example, an author's purpose is to inform, to instruct, and to familiarize readers with a difficult subject, their use of connotation may be helpful. However, it may also undermine credibility and confuse readers. An author who wants to create a credible, scholarly effect in their text would most likely use denotation, which emphasizes literal, factual meaning and examples.

Technical Language

Test takers and critical readers alike should be very aware of technical language used within informational text. **Technical language** refers to terminology that is specific to a particular industry and is best understood by those specializing in that industry. This language is fairly easy to differentiate since it will most likely be unfamiliar to readers. It's critical to be able to define technical language either by the author's written definition, through the use of an included glossary—if offered—or through context clues that help readers clarify word meaning.

Organization/Logic [ISEE]

Types of Passages

Authors write with different purposes in mind. They use a variety of writing passages to appeal to their chosen audience. There are four types of writing passages:

- Narrative
- Expository
- Technical
- Persuasive

Narrative

Narrative writing tells a story or a series of events. A narrative can either be fiction or nonfiction, although in order to still be categorized as a narrative, certain elements need to be present.
A narrative must have:

- **Plot:** what happens in the story, or what is going to happen

- **Series of events:** beginning, middle, and end, but not necessarily in that order

- **Characters:** people, animals, or inanimate objects

- **Figurative language:** metaphors, similes, personification, etc.

- **Setting:** when and where the story takes place

Expository

Expository passages are informative texts usually written as memoirs or autobiographies. These nonfiction passages often use transitional words and phrases like *first, next,* and *therefore* to provide readers with a clear sense of direction of where they are within the text. Because expository passages are meant to educate readers, they often do not use flamboyant language, unless the subject area requires it.

Technical

Technical passages are written to describe how to do or make something. Technical passages are often manuals or guides written in a very organized and logical manner. The texts usually have outlines with subtitles and very little jargon. The vocabulary used in technical passages is very straightforward so as not to confuse readers. Technical texts often explore cause and effect relationships and can also include authors' purposes.

Persuasive

Persuasive passages are written with the intent to convince readers to agree with the author's viewpoint on the subject. Authors generally stick to one main point and present smaller arguments that concur with the initial central claim. The author's intent or purpose is to persuade readers by presenting them with evidence or clues (such as facts, statistics, and observations) to make them stray away from their own thoughts on the matter and agree with the author's ideas. By using evidence and clues to support their ideas, authors may or may not be strategically placing strong thoughts and emotions in their readers' minds, causing them to lean in one direction more than the other.

Readers' opinions are formed from these strong thoughts and emotions. Authors need to be wary of misleading their readers because it is not ethical, nor is it appropriate. In the same sense, readers also need to be skeptical of an author's intent if the persuasion comes from an emotional standpoint.

For example, during an election year, candidates often post slanderous advertisements about one another. These malicious ads do not state what the candidate will do for their country or district. They are meant to show why readers or viewers should not elect the other candidate. These ads are trying to persuade viewers' opinions of opposing candidates. On the other hand, there are other ads that show the positive impacts that candidates have made. These types of advertisements also persuade voters into liking those candidates because of the positive claims portrayed. Are these advertisements right or wrong? Are they ethical? It is up to the viewer or reader to decide.

Identifying Characteristics of Major Forms Within Each Genre [ISEE]

Fictional Prose

Fiction written in prose can be further broken down into **fiction genres**—types of fiction. Some of the more common genres of fiction are as follows:

- **Classical fiction**: A work of fiction considered timeless in its message or theme, remaining noteworthy and meaningful over decades or centuries—e.g., Charlotte Brontë's *Jane Eyre*, Mark Twain's *Adventures of Huckleberry Finn*

- **Fables**: Short fiction that generally features animals, fantastic creatures, or other forces within nature that assume human-like characters and has a moral lesson for the reader—e.g., *Aesop's Fables*

- **Fairy tales**: Children's stories with magical characters in imaginary, enchanted lands, usually depicting a struggle between good and evil, a sub-genre of folklore—e.g., Hans Christian Anderson's *The Little Mermaid*, *Cinderella* by the Brothers Grimm

124

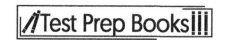

- **Fantasy**: Fiction with magic or supernatural elements that cannot occur in the real world, sometimes involving medieval elements in language, usually includes some form of sorcery or witchcraft and sometimes set on a different world—e.g., J.R.R. Tolkien's *The Hobbit*, J.K. Rowling's *Harry Potter and the Sorcerer's Stone*, George R.R. Martin's *A Game of Thrones*

- **Folklore**: Types of fiction passed down from oral tradition, stories indigenous to a particular region or culture, with a local flavor in tone, designed to help humans cope with their condition in life and validate cultural traditions, beliefs, and customs—e.g., William Laughead's *Paul Bunyan and The Blue Ox*, the Buddhist story of "The Banyan Deer"

- **Mythology**: Closely related to folklore but more widespread, features mystical, otherworldly characters and addresses the basic question of why and how humans exist, relies heavily on allegory, and features gods or heroes captured in some sort of struggle—e.g., Greek myths, Genesis I and II in the Bible, Arthurian legends

- **Science fiction**: Fiction that uses the principle of extrapolation—loosely defined as a form of prediction—to imagine future realities and problems of the human experience—e.g., Robert Heinlein's *Stranger in a Strange Land*, Ayn Rand's *Anthem*, Isaac Asimov's *I, Robot*, Philip K. Dick's *Do Androids Dream of Electric Sheep?*

- **Short stories**: Short works of prose fiction with fully-developed themes and characters, focused on mood, generally developed with a single plot, with a short period of time for settings—e.g., Edgar Allan Poe's "Fall of the House of Usher," Shirley Jackson's "The Lottery," Isaac Bashevis Singer's "Gimpel the Fool"

Drama

Drama refers to a form of literature written for the purpose of performance for an audience. Like prose fiction, drama has several genres. The following are the most common ones:

- **Comedy**: A humorous play designed to amuse and entertain, often with an emphasis on the common person's experience, generally resolved in a positive way—e.g., Richard Sheridan's *School for Scandal*, Shakespeare's *Taming of the Shrew*, Neil Simon's *The Odd Couple*

- **History**: A play based on recorded history where the fate of a nation or kingdom is at the core of the conflict—e.g., Christopher Marlowe's *Edward II*, Shakespeare's *King Richard III*, Arthur Miller's *The Crucible*

- **Tragedy**: A serious play that often involves the downfall of the protagonist. In modern tragedies, the protagonist is not necessarily in a position of power or authority—e.g., Jean Racine's *Phèdre*, Arthur Miller's *Death of a Salesman*, John Steinbeck's *Of Mice and Men*

- **Melodrama**: A play that emphasizes heightened emotion and sensationalism, generally with stereotypical characters in exaggerated or realistic situations and with moral polarization—e.g., Jean-Jacques Rousseau's *Pygmalion*

- **Tragi-comedy**: A play that has elements of both tragedy—a character experiencing a tragic loss—and comedy—the resolution is often positive with no clear distinctive mood for either—e.g., Shakespeare's *The Merchant of Venice*, Anton Chekhov's *The Cherry Orchard*

Poetry

The genre of **poetry** refers to literary works that focus on the expression of feelings and ideas through the use of structure and linguistic rhythm to create a desired effect.

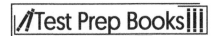

Different poetic structures and devices are used to create the various major forms of poetry. Some of the most common forms are discussed in the following chart.

Type	Poetic Structure	Example
Ballad	A poem or song passed down orally which tells a story and in English tradition usually uses an ABAB or ABCB rhyme scheme	William Butler Yeats' "The Ballad of Father O'Hart"
Epic	A long poem from ancient oral tradition which narrates the story of a legendary or heroic protagonist	Homer's *The Odyssey* Virgil's *The Aeneid*
Haiku	A Japanese poem of three unrhymed lines with five, seven, and five syllables (in English) with nature as a common subject matter	Matsuo Bashō "An old silent pond ... A frog jumps into the pond, splash! Silence again."
Limerick	A five-line poem written in an AABBA rhyme scheme, with a witty focus	From Edward Lear's *Book of Nonsense*: "There was a Young Person of Smyrna Whose grandmother threatened to burn her ..."
Ode	A formal lyric poem that addresses and praises a person, place, thing, or idea	Edna St. Vincent Millay's "Ode to Silence"
Sonnet	A fourteen-line poem written in iambic pentameter	Shakespeare's Sonnets 18 and 130

Literary Nonfiction

Nonfiction works are best characterized by their subject matter, which must be factual and real, describing true life experiences. There are several common types of literary non-fiction.

Biography

A **biography** is a work written about a real person (historical or currently living). It involves factual accounts of the person's life, often in a re-telling of those events based on available, researched factual information. The re-telling and dialogue, especially if related within quotes, must be accurate and reflect reliable sources. A biography reflects the time and place in which the person lived, with the goal of creating an understanding of the person and their human experience. Examples of well-known biographies include *The Life of Samuel Johnson* by James Boswell and *Steve Jobs* by Walter Isaacson.

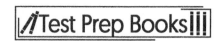

Autobiography

An **autobiography** is a factual account of a person's life written by that person. It may contain some or all of the same elements as a biography, but the author is the subject matter. An autobiography will be told in first person narrative. Examples of well-known autobiographies in literature include *Night* by Elie Wiesel and *Margaret Thatcher: The Autobiography* by Margaret Thatcher.

Memoir

A **memoir** is a historical account of a person's life and experiences written by one who has personal, intimate knowledge of the information. The line between memoir, autobiography, and biography is often muddled, but generally speaking, a memoir covers a specific timeline of events as opposed to the other forms of nonfiction. A memoir is less all-encompassing. It is also less formal in tone and tends to focus on the emotional aspect of the presented timeline of events. Some examples of memoirs in literature include *Angela's Ashes* by Frank McCourt and *All Creatures Great and Small* by James Herriot.

Journalism

Some forms of **journalism** can fall into the category of literary non-fiction—e.g., travel writing, nature writing, sports writing, the interview, and sometimes, the essay. Some examples include Elizabeth Kolbert's "The Lost World, in the Annals of Extinction series for *The New Yorker* and Gary Smith's "Ali and His Entourage" for *Sports Illustrated*.

Organization of the Text

The **structure of the text** is how authors organize information in their writing. The organization of text depends on the authors' intentions and writing purposes for the text itself. Text structures can vary from paragraph to paragraph or from piece to piece, depending on the author. There are various types of patterns in which authors can organize texts, some of which include problem and solution, cause and effect, chronological order, and compare and contrast. These four text structures are described below.

Problem and Solution

One way authors can organize their text is by following a **problem and solution** pattern. This type of structure may present the problem first without offering an immediately clear solution. The problem and solution pattern may also offer the solution first and then hint at the problem throughout the text. Some texts offer multiple solutions to the same problem, which then leaves the decision as to the "best" solution to the minds of readers.

Even though the problem and solution text may seem easy to recognize, it is often confused with another organizational text pattern, cause and effect. One way of determining the difference between the two patterns is by searching for key words that indicate a problem and solution organizational text pattern is being followed, such as *propose, answer, prevention, issue, fix,* and *problematic*. Also, in problem and solution patterned texts, solutions are offered to all problems, even negative problems, unlike the cause-and-effect pattern.

Cause and Effect

Cause and effect is one of the more common ways that authors organize texts. In a cause and effect patterned text, the author explains what caused something to happen. For example, "It rained, so we got all wet." In this sentence, the cause is "the rain," and the effect is "we got all wet." Authors tend to use key words such as *because, as a result, due to, effected, caused, since, in order,* and *so* when writing cause and effect patterned texts.

Persuasive and expository writing models frequently use a cause and effect organizational pattern as well. In **persuasive texts**, authors try to convince readers to sway their opinions to align with the authors' thoughts. Authors may use cause and effect patterns or relationships to present supporting evidence to try to persuade the readers' judgment on a particular subject.

In **expository texts**, authors write to inform and educate readers about certain subjects. By using cause and effect patterns in expository writing, authors show relationships between events—basically, how one event may affect the other in chronological order.

Chronological Order

When using a **chronological order** organizational pattern, authors simply state information in the order in which it occurs. Nonfiction texts often include specific dates listing events in chronological order (such as timelines), whereas fiction texts may list events in order but not provide detailed dates (such as describing a daily routine: wake up, eat breakfast, get dressed, and so on). Narratives usually follow the chronological order pattern of beginning, middle, and end, with the occasional flashback in between.

Compare and Contrast

The **compare and contrast** organizational text pattern explores the differences and similarities of two or more objects. If authors describe how two or more objects are similar, they are comparing the items. If they describe how two or more objects are different, they are contrasting them. In order for texts to follow a compare and contrast organizational pattern, authors must include both similarities and differences within the text and hold each to the same guidelines. The following Venn diagram compares and contrasts oranges and apples.

Compare and Contrast Example

Oranges		Apples
Tropical	**Fruit**	Moderate to subtropical
Thick peel	**Grow on trees**	Thin peel
Came to Europe from India	**Give juice**	Center of diversity: Turkey
Fruit is in sections	**Contain seeds**	Solid fruit around a core

In this diagram, readers should notice how the author uses the same guidelines when comparing and contrasting oranges and apples. The origin, peel type, climate, outcomes, and classifications are all used for both fruits. The author does not use different categories for each fruit to compare or contrast the two fruits.

Even though authors may agree or disagree with each side of an argument, they should remain impartial when presenting the facts in a compare and contrast text(s). Authors should present all information using neutral language and allow readers to form their individual conclusions about the subject matter. Authors tend to use key words such as *like, unlike, different, similar, both,* and *neither* when following a compare and contrast pattern.

Overall, organization of texts helps readers better understand an author's intent and purpose.

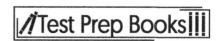

Opinions, Facts, and Fallacies

As mentioned previously, authors write with a purpose. They adjust their writing for an intended audience. It is the readers' responsibility to comprehend the writing style or purpose of the author. When readers understand a writer's purpose, they can then form their own thoughts about the text(s) regardless of whether their thoughts are the same as or different from the author's. The following section will examine different writing tactics that authors use, such as facts versus opinions, bias and stereotypes, appealing to the readers' emotions, and fallacies.

Facts Versus Opinions

Readers need to be aware of the writer's purpose to help discern facts and opinions within texts. A **fact** is a piece of information that is true. It can either prove or disprove claims or arguments presented in texts. Facts cannot be changed or altered. For example, the statement: *Abraham Lincoln was assassinated on April 15, 1865*, is a fact. The date and related events cannot be altered.

Authors not only present facts in their writing to support or disprove their claim(s), but they may also express their opinions. Authors may use facts to support their own opinions, especially in a persuasive text; however, that does not make their opinion fact. An **opinion** is a belief or view formed about something that is not necessarily based on the truth. Opinions often express authors' personal feelings about a subject and use words like *believe, think,* or *feel.* For example, the statement: *Abraham Lincoln was the best president who has ever lived*, expresses the writer's opinion. Not all writers or readers agree or disagree with the statement. Therefore, the statement can be altered or adjusted to express opposing or supporting beliefs, such as "Abraham Lincoln was the worst president who has ever lived" or "I also think Abraham Lincoln was a great president."

When authors include facts and opinions in their writing, readers may be less influenced by the text(s). Readers need to be conscious of the distinction between facts and opinions while going through texts. Not only should the intended audience be vigilant in following authors' thoughts versus valid information, readers need to check the source of the facts presented. Facts should have reliable sources derived from credible outlets like almanacs, encyclopedias, medical journals, and so on.

Bias and Stereotypes

Not only can authors state facts or opinions in their writing, they sometimes intentionally or unintentionally show bias or portray a stereotype. A **bias** is when someone demonstrates a prejudice in favor of or against something or someone in an unfair manner. When an author is biased in their writing, readers should be skeptical despite the fact that the author's bias may be correct. For example, two athletes competed for the same position. One athlete is related to the coach and is a mediocre athlete, while the other player excels and deserves the position. The coach chose the less talented player who is related to him for the position. This is a biased decision because it favors someone in an unfair way.

Similar to a bias, a **stereotype** shows favoritism or opposition but toward a specific group or place. Stereotypes create an oversimplified or overgeneralized idea about a certain group, person, or place.

For example,

Women are horrible drivers.

This statement basically labels *all* women as horrible drivers. While there may be some terrible female drivers, the stereotype implies that *all* women are bad drivers when, in fact, not *all* women are. While many readers are aware of several vile ethnic, religious, and cultural stereotypes, audiences should be cautious of authors' flawed assumptions because they can be less obvious than the despicable examples that are unfortunately pervasive in society.

129

Fallacies [ISEE]

A **fallacy** is a mistaken belief or faulty reasoning, otherwise known as a **logical fallacy**. It is important for readers to recognize logical fallacies because they discredit the author's message. Readers should continuously self-question as they go through a text to identify logical fallacies. Readers cannot simply complacently take information at face value. There are six common types of logical fallacies, explained in detail below.

False Analogy

A **false analogy** is when the author assumes two objects or events are alike in all aspects despite the fact that they may be vastly different. Authors intend on making unfamiliar objects relatable to convince readers of something. For example, the letters *A* and *E* are both vowels; therefore, *A* = *E*. Readers cannot assume that because *A* and *E* are both vowels that they perform the same function in words or independently. If authors tell readers, *A* = *E*, then that is a false analogy. While this is a simple example, other false analogies may be less obvious.

Circular Reasoning

Circular reasoning is when the reasoning is decided based upon the outcome or conclusion and then vice versa. Basically, those who use circular reasoning start out with the argument and then use false logic to try to prove it, and then, in turn, the reasoning supports the conclusion in one big circular pattern. For example, consider the two thoughts, "I don't have time to get organized" and "My disorganization is costing me time." Which is the argument? What is the conclusion? If there is not time to get organized, will more time be spent later trying to find whatever is needed? In turn, if so much time is spent looking for things, there is not time to get organized. The cycle keeps going in an endless series. One problem affects the other; therefore, there is a circular pattern of reasoning.

False Dichotomy

A **false dichotomy**, also known as a false dilemma, is when the author tries to make readers believe that there are only two options to choose from when, in fact, there are more. The author creates a false sense of the situation because he or she wants the readers to believe that their claim is the most logical choice. If the author does not present the readers with options, then the author is purposefully limiting what readers may believe. In turn, the author hopes that readers will believe that their point of view is the most sensible choice. For example, in the statement: *you either love running, or you are lazy*, the fallacy lies in the options of loving to run or being lazy. Even though both statements do not necessarily have to be true, the author tries to make one option seem more appealing than the other.

Overgeneralization

An **overgeneralization** is a logical fallacy that occurs when authors write something so extreme that it cannot be proved or disproved. Words like *all, never, most,* and *few* are commonly used when an overgeneralization is being made. For example,

> All kids are crazy when they eat sugar; therefore, my son will not have a cupcake at the birthday party.

Not *all* kids are crazy when they eat sugar, but the extreme statement can influence the readers' points of view on the subject. Readers need to be wary of overgeneralizations in texts because authors may try to sneak them in to sway the readers' opinions.

Slippery Slope

A **slippery slope** is when an author implies that something will inevitably happen as a result of another action. A slippery slope may or may not be true, even though the order of events or gradations may seem logical. For example, in the children's book *If You Give a Mouse a Cookie*, the author goes off on tangents such as "If you give a mouse a cookie, he will ask for some milk. When you give him the milk, he'll probably ask you for a straw." The

130

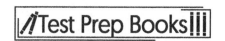
mouse in the story follows a series of logical events as a result of a previous action. The slippery slope continues on and on throughout the story. Even though the mouse made logical decisions, it very well could have made a different choice, changing the direction of the story.

Hasty Generalization

A **hasty generalization** is when the reader comes to a conclusion without reviewing or analyzing all the evidence. It is never a good idea to make a decision without all the information, which is why hasty generalizations are considered fallacies. For example, if two friends go to a hairdresser and give the hairdresser a positive recommendation, that does not necessarily mean that a new client will have the same experience. Two referrals are not quite enough information to form an educated and well-formed conclusion.

Overall, readers should carefully review and analyze authors' arguments to identify logical fallacies and come to sensible conclusions.

Summarizing [ISEE]

At the end of a text or passage, it is important to summarize what the readers read. **Summarizing** is a strategy in which readers determine what is important throughout the text or passage, shorten those ideas, and rewrite or retell it in their own words. A summary should identify the main idea of the text or passage. Important details or supportive evidence should also be accurately reported in the summary. If writers provide irrelevant details in the summary, it may cloud the greater meaning of the text or passage. When summarizing, writers should not include their opinions, quotes, or what they thought the author should have said. A clear summary provides clarity of the text or passage to the readers.

The following checklist lists items that writers should include in a summary:

Summary Checklist

- Title of the story
- Someone: Who is or are the main character(s)?
- Wanted: What did the character(s) want?
- But: What was the problem?
- So: How did the character(s) solve the problem?
- Then: How did the story end? What was the resolution?

Paraphrasing

Another strategy readers can use to help them fully comprehend a text or passage is paraphrasing. **Paraphrasing** is when readers take the author's words and put them into their own words. When readers and writers paraphrase, they need to avoid copying the text—that is plagiarism. It is also important to include as many details as possible when restating the facts. Not only will this help readers and writers recall information, but by putting the information into their own words, they demonstrate if they fully comprehend the text or passage. The example below shows an original text and how to paraphrase it.

Original Text: Fenway Park is home to the beloved Boston Red Sox. The stadium opened on April 20, 1912. The stadium currently seats over 37,000 fans, many of whom travel from all over the country to experience the iconic team and nostalgia of Fenway Park.

Paraphrased: On April 20, 1912, Fenway Park opened. Home to the Boston Red Sox, the stadium now seats over 37,000 fans. Many spectators travel to watch the Red Sox and experience the spirit of Fenway Park.

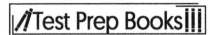
Paraphrasing, summarizing, and quoting can often cross paths with one another. The chart below shows the similarities and differences between the three strategies:

Paraphrasing	Summarizing	Quoting
Uses own words	Puts main ideas into own words	Uses words that are identical to text
References original source	References original source	Requires quotation marks
Uses own sentences	Shows important ideas of source	Uses author's words and ideas

Tone/Style/Figurative Language

Tone

An author's **tone** is the use of particular words, phrases, and writing style to convey an overall meaning. Tone expresses the author's attitude towards a particular topic. For example, a historical reading passage may begin like the following:

> The presidential election of 1960 ushered in a new era, a new Camelot, a new phase of forward thinking in U.S. politics that embraced brash action and unrest and responded with admirable leadership.

From this opening statement, a reader can draw some conclusions about the author's attitude towards President John F. Kennedy. Furthermore, the reader can make additional, educated guesses about the state of the Union during the 1960 presidential election. By close reading, the test taker can determine that the repeated use of the word *new* and words such as *admirable leadership* indicate the author's tone of admiration regarding President Kennedy's boldness. In addition, the author assesses that the era during President Kennedy's administration was problematic through the use of the words *brash action* and *unrest*. Therefore, if a test taker encountered a test question asking about the author's use of tone and their assessment of the Kennedy administration, the test taker should be able to identify an answer indicating admiration. Similarly, if asked about the state of the Union during the 1960s, a test taker should be able to correctly identify an answer indicating political unrest.

When identifying an author's tone, the following list of words may be helpful. This is not an inclusive list. Generally, parts of speech that indicate attitude will also indicate tone:

- Comical
- Angry
- Ambivalent
- Scary
- Lyrical
- Matter-of-fact
- Judgmental
- Sarcastic
- Malicious

- Objective
- Pessimistic
- Patronizing
- Gloomy
- Instructional
- Satirical
- Formal
- Casual

Style

Style can include any number of technical writing choices. A few examples of style choices include:

- Sentence Construction: When presenting facts, does the writer use shorter sentences to create a quicker sense of the supporting evidence, or do they use longer sentences to elaborate and explain the information?

- Technical Language: Does the writer use jargon to demonstrate their expertise in the subject, or do they use ordinary language to help the reader understand things in simple terms?

- Formal Language: Does the writer refrain from using contractions such as *won't* or *can't* to create a more formal tone, or do they use a colloquial, conversational style to connect to the reader?

- Formatting: Does the writer use a series of shorter paragraphs to help the reader follow a line of argument, or do they use longer paragraphs to examine an issue in great detail and demonstrate their knowledge of the topic?

Message

An author's **message** is the same as the overall meaning of a passage. It is the main idea, or the main concept the author wishes to convey. An author's message may be stated outright, or it may be implied. Regardless, the test taker will need to use careful reading skills to identify an author's message or purpose.

Often, the message of a particular passage can be determined by thinking about why the author wrote the information. Many historical passages are written to inform and to teach readers established, factual information. However, many historical works are also written to convey biased ideas to readers. Gleaning bias from an author's message in a historical passage can be difficult, especially if the reader is presented with a variety of established facts as well. Readers tend to accept historical writing as factual. This is not always the case. Any discerning reader who has tackled historical information on topics such as United States political party agendas can attest that two or more works on the same topic may have completely different messages supporting or refuting the value of the identical policies. Therefore, it is important to critically assess an author's message separate from factual information. One author, for example, may point to the rise of unorthodox political candidates in an election year based on the failures of the political party in office while another may point to the rise of the same candidates in the same election year based on the current party's successes. The historical facts of what has occurred leading up to an election year are not in refute. Labeling those facts as a failure or a success is a bias within an author's overall message, as is excluding factual information in order to further a particular point. In a standardized testing situation, a reader must be able to critically assess what the author is trying to say separate from the historical facts that surround their message.

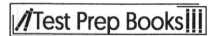

Using the example of Lincoln's Gettysburg Address, a test question may ask the following:

> What message is the speaker trying to convey through this address?

Then they will ask the test taker to select an answer that best expresses Lincoln's message to his audience. Based on the options given, a test taker should be able to select the answer expressing the idea that Lincoln's audience should recognize the efforts of those who died in the war as a sacrifice to preserving human equality and self-government.

Effect

An author may want to challenge a reader's intellect, inspire imagination, or spur emotion. An author may present information to appeal to a physical, aesthetic, or transformational sense.

Take the following text as an example:

> In 1963, Martin Luther King stated, "I have a dream." The gathering at the Lincoln Memorial was the beginning of the Civil Rights movement and, with its reference to the Emancipation Proclamation, electrified those who wanted freedom and equality while rising from hatred and slavery. It was the beginning of radical change.

The test taker may be asked about the effect this statement might have on King's audience. Through careful reading of the passage, the test taker should be able to choose an answer that best identifies an effect of grabbing the audience's attention. The historical facts are in place: King made the speech in 1963 at the Lincoln Memorial, kicked off the civil rights movement, and referenced the Emancipation Proclamation. The words *electrified* and *radical change* indicate the effect the author wants the reader to understand as a result of King's speech. In this historical passage, facts are facts. However, the author's message goes beyond the facts to indicate the effect the message had on the audience and, in addition, the effect the event should have on the reader.

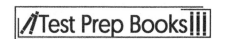
Figurative Language [ISEE]

Figurative language is a specific style of speaking or writing that uses tools for a variety of effects. It entertains readers, ignites imagination, and promotes creativity. Instead of writing in realistic terms or literal terms, figurative language plays with words and prompts readers to infer the underlying meaning.

There are seven types of figurative language:

Type	Definition	Example
Personification	Giving animate qualities to an inanimate object	The tree stood tall and still, staring up at the sky.
Simile	The comparison of two unlike things using connecting words	Your eyes are as blue as the ocean.
Metaphor	The comparison of two unlike things without the use of connecting words	Kayla is a walking encyclopedia!
Hyperbole	An over-exaggeration	I could eat a million of these cookies!
Alliteration	The patterned repetition of an initial consonant sound	The bunnies are bouncing in baskets.
Onomatopoeia	Words that are formed by using the very sound associated with the word itself	"Drip, drip, drip" went the kitchen faucet.
Idioms	Common sayings that carry a lesson or meaning that must be inferred	We were sure to turn back the hands of time.

Writing Devices [ISEE]

Authors use a variety of writing devices throughout texts. Below is a list of some of the stylistic writing devices authors use in their writing:

- Comparison and Contrast
- Cause and Effect
- Analogy
- Point of View
- Transitional Words and Phrases

Comparison and Contrast

One writing device authors use is comparison and contrast. When authors take two objects and show how they are alike or similar, a **comparison** is being made. When authors take the same two objects and show how they differ, they are **contrasting** them. Comparison and contrast essays are most commonly written in nonfiction form.

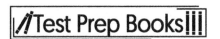

A review of the Venn diagram demonstrating common words or phrases used when comparing or contrasting objects appears below.

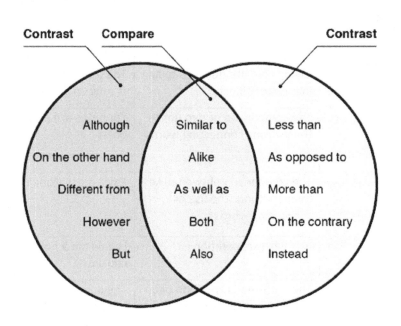

Compare and Contrast Venn Diagram

Cause and Effect

Cause and effect is one of the most common writing devices. A **cause** is why something happens, whereas an **effect** is the result that occurs because of the cause. Oftentimes, authors use key words to show cause and effect, such as *because, so, therefore, without, now, then,* and *since.* For example,

> *Because* of the sun shower, a rainbow appeared.

In this sentence, due to the sun shower (the cause), a rainbow appeared (the effect).

Analogy

An **analogy** is a comparison between two things that are quite different from one another. Authors commonly use analogies to add meaning and make ideas relatable in texts. Metaphors and similes are specific types of analogies. Metaphors compare two things that are not similar and directly connect them. Similes also compare two unlike items but connect them using the words *like* or *as.* For example,

> In the library, Alice was asked to be as quiet as a mouse.

Clearly, Alice and a mouse are very different. However, when Alice is asked to be as quiet as a mouse, readers understand that mice are small and therefore have small and soft voices—appropriate voice noise level for the library.

Point of View

Point of view is the perspective in which authors tell stories. Authors can tell stories in either the first or third person. When authors write in the first person, they are a character within a story telling about their own experiences. The pronouns *I* and *we* are used when writing in the first person. If an author writes in the third person, the narrator (the person telling the story) is telling the story from an outside perspective and is completely detached from the story. The author is not a character in the story, but rather tells about the characters' actions and dialogues. Pronouns such as *he, she, it,* and *they* are used in texts written in the third person.

Transitional Words and Phrases

There are approximately 200 transitional words and phrases that are commonly used in the English language. Below are lists of common transition words and phrases used throughout transitions:

Time

- After
- Before
- During
- In the middle

Example about to be Given

- For example
- In fact
- For instance

Compare

- Likewise
- Also

Contrast

- However
- Yet
- But

Addition

- And
- Also
- Furthermore
- Moreover

Logical Relationships

- If
- Then
- Therefore
- As a result
- Since

Steps in a Process

- First
- Second
- Last

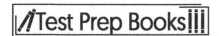
Transitional words and phrases are important writing devices because they connect sentences and paragraphs. Transitional words and phrases present logical order to writing and provide more coherent meaning to readers.

Author's Use of Evidence to Support Claims [ISEE]

Authors utilize a wide range of techniques to tell a story or communicate information. Readers should be familiar with the most common of these techniques. Techniques of writing are also commonly known as rhetorical devices, and they are some of the evidence that authors use to support claims.

In nonfiction writing, authors employ argumentative techniques to present their opinion to readers in the most convincing way. Persuasive writing usually includes at least one type of appeal: an appeal to logic (**logos**), emotion (**pathos**), or credibility and trustworthiness (**ethos**). When a writer appeals to logic, they are asking readers to agree with them based on research, evidence, and an established line of reasoning. An author's argument might also appeal to readers' emotions, perhaps by including personal stories and **anecdotes** (a short narrative of a specific event). A final type of appeal, appeal to authority, asks the reader to agree with the author's argument on the basis of their expertise or credentials. Consider three different approaches to arguing the same opinion:

Logic (Logos)

Below is an example of an appeal to logic. The author uses evidence to disprove the logic of the school's rule (the rule was supposed to reduce discipline problems, but the number of problems has not been reduced; therefore, the rule is not working) and call for its repeal.

> Our school should abolish its current ban on campus cell phone use. The ban was adopted last year as an attempt to reduce class disruptions and help students focus more on their lessons. However, since the rule was enacted, there has been no change in the number of disciplinary problems in class. Therefore, the rule is ineffective and should be done away with.

Emotion (Pathos)

An author's argument might also appeal to readers' emotions, perhaps by including personal stories and anecdotes.

The next example presents an appeal to emotion. By sharing the personal anecdote of one student and speaking about emotional topics like family relationships, the author invokes the reader's empathy in asking them to reconsider the school rule.

> Our school should abolish its current ban on campus cell phone use. If students aren't able to use their phones during the school day, many of them feel isolated from their loved ones. For example, last semester, one student's grandmother had a heart attack in the morning. However, because he couldn't use his cell phone, the student didn't know about his grandmother's accident until the end of the day—when she had already passed away, and it was too late to say goodbye. By preventing students from contacting their friends and family, our school is placing undue stress and anxiety on students.

Credibility (Ethos)

Finally, an appeal to authority includes a statement from a relevant expert. In this case, the author uses a doctor in the field of education to support the argument. All three examples begin from the same opinion—the school's phone ban needs to change—but rely on different argumentative styles to persuade the reader.

Our school should abolish its current ban on campus cell phone use. According to Dr. Bartholomew Everett, a leading educational expert, "Research studies show that cell phone usage has no real impact on student attentiveness. Rather, phones provide a valuable technological resource for learning. Schools need to learn how to integrate this new technology into their curriculum." Rather than banning phones altogether, our school should follow the advice of experts and allow students to use pho phones as part of their learning.

Practice Quiz

Questions 1-4 refer to the following passage, titled "Education is Essential to Civilization."

Early in my career, a master teacher shared this thought with me: "Education is the last bastion of civility." While I did not completely understand the scope of those words at the time, I have since come to realize the depth, breadth, truth, and significance of what he said. Education provides society with a vehicle for raising its children to be civil, decent human beings with something valuable to contribute to the world. It is really what makes us human and what distinguishes us as civilized creatures.

Being "civilized" humans means being "whole" humans. Education must address the minds, bodies, and souls of students. It would be detrimental to society if our schools were myopic in their focus, only meeting the needs of the mind. As humans, we are multidimensional, multifaceted beings who need more than head knowledge to survive. The human heart and psyche have to be fed in order for the mind to develop properly, and the body must be maintained and exercised to help fuel brain functioning.

Education is a basic human right, and it allows us to sustain a democratic society in which participation is fundamental to its success. It should inspire students to seek better solutions to world problems and to dream of a more equitable society. Education should never discriminate on any basis, and it should create individuals who are self-sufficient, patriotic, and tolerant of other's ideas.

All children can learn, although not all children learn in the same manner. All children learn best, however, when their basic physical needs are met, and they feel safe, secure, and loved. Students are much more responsive to a teacher who values them and shows them respect as individual people. Teachers must model at all times the way they expect students to treat them and their peers. If teachers set high expectations for their students, the students will rise to that high level. Teachers must make the well-being of their students their primary focus and must not be afraid to let their students learn from their own mistakes.

In the modern age of technology, a teacher's focus is no longer the "what" of the content, but more importantly, the "why." Students are bombarded with information and have access to any information they need right at their fingertips. Teachers have to work harder than ever before to help students identify salient information and to think critically about the information they encounter. Students have to read between the lines, identify bias, and determine who they can trust in the milieu of ads, data, and texts presented to them.

Schools must work in concert with families in this important mission. While children spend most of their time in school, they are dramatically and indelibly shaped by the influences of their family and culture. Teachers must respect this fact, strive to include parents in the education of their children, and work to keep parents informed of progress and problems. Communication between the classroom and home is essential for a child's success.

Humans have always aspired to be more, to do more, and to better ourselves and our communities. This is where education lies, right at the heart of humanity's desire to be all that we can be. Education helps us strive for higher goals and better treatment of ourselves and others. I shudder to think what would become of us if education ceased to be the "last bastion of civility." We must be unapologetic about expecting excellence from our students—our very existence depends upon it.

1. Which of the following best summarizes the author's main point?
   a. Education as we know it is overvalued in modern society, and we should find alternative solutions.
   b. The survival of the human race depends on the educational system, and it is worth fighting for to make it better.
   c. The government should do away with all public schools and require parents to home school their children instead.
   d. While education is important, some children simply are not capable of succeeding in a traditional classroom.
   e. Students are learning new ways to learn while teachers are learning to adapt to their needs.

2. Based on this passage, which of the following can be inferred about the author?
   a. The author feels passionately about education.
   b. The author does not feel strongly about their point.
   c. The author is angry at the educational system.
   d. The author is unsure about the importance of education.
   e. The author does not trust the government.

3. Based on this passage, which of the following conclusions could be drawn about the author?
   a. The author would not support raising taxes to help fund much-needed reforms in education.
   b. The author would support raising taxes to help fund much-needed reforms in education, as long as those reforms were implemented in higher socio-economic areas first.
   c. The author would support raising taxes to help fund much-needed reforms in education for all children in all schools.
   d. The author would support raising taxes only in certain states to help fund much-needed reforms in education.
   e. The author would not support raising taxes unless the people in the communities agreed to it.

4. According to the passage, which of the following is NOT mentioned as an important factor in education today?
   a. Parent involvement
   b. Communication between parents and teachers
   c. Impact of technology
   d. Cost of textbooks
   e. Safe and healthy children

Question 5 refers to the following paragraph:

The Brookside area is an older part of Kansas City, developed mainly in the 1920s and '30s, and is considered one of the nation's first "planned" communities with shops, restaurants, parks, and churches all within a quick walk. A stroll down any street reveals charming two-story Tudor and Colonial homes with smaller bungalows sprinkled throughout the beautiful tree-lined streets. It is common to see lemonade stands on the corners and baseball games in the numerous "pocket" parks tucked neatly behind rows of well-manicured houses. The Brookside shops on 63rd street between Wornall Road and Oak Street are a hub of commerce and entertainment where residents freely shop and dine with their pets (and children) in tow. This is also a common "hangout" spot for younger teenagers because it is easily accessible by bike for most. In short, it is an idyllic neighborhood just minutes from downtown Kansas City.

5. Which of the following states the main idea of this paragraph?
   a. The Brookside shops are a popular hangout for teenagers.
   b. There are a number of pocket parks in the Brookside neighborhood.
   c. Brookside is a great place to live.
   d. Brookside has a high crime rate.
   e. Everyone should move to Brookside.

See answers on the next page.

Answer Explanations

1. B: The author clearly states that education is crucial to the survival of the human race, and it can be easily inferred that if this is true, then improvements to our educational system are certainly worth fighting for. Choices *A* and *C* are incorrect because there is nothing in the passage that relates to these statements. Choice *D* is incorrect because it directly contradicts what the author states about all children's ability to learn. Choice *E* is mentioned in the passage, but it is not the main point.

2. A: Clearly, this author feels passionately about the importance of education. This is evident especially in the word choices.

3. C: Based on the author's passionate stance about the importance of education for all children, Choice *C* makes the most sense.

4. D: The author mentions the importance of parent involvement and communication between the school and home. He also devotes one full paragraph to the impact of technology on education. Nowhere in the passage does the author mention the cost of textbooks, so Choice *D* is correct.

5. C: All the details in this paragraph suggest that Brookside is a great place to live, plus the last sentence states that it is an *idyllic neighborhood*, meaning it is perfect, happy, and blissful. Choices *A* and *B* are incorrect, because although they do contain specific details from the paragraph that support the main idea, they are not the main idea. Choice *D* is incorrect because there is no reference in the paragraph to the crime rate in Brookside. Choice *E* is incorrect; the author does think Brookside is a great place, but they don't try and convince the audience to move there.

Verbal Section

Test takers encounter two parts in the verbal section of the Middle Level SSAT. In the first part, the vocabulary section, questions address the test taker's understanding of language and the meanings of different words. The second part is the analogy section, which assesses the test taker's ability to logically relate words to one another.

The vocabulary words are pulled from all areas of study and are of age-appropriate difficulty. Words may include those encountered specifically in science class, technology-related, social studies, mathematics, and language arts. Successful test takers should think about the parts of a word and the structure of the English language, including things like:

- Word origins
- Root words
- Prefixes
- Suffixes
- Words with multiple meanings

Synonyms

This portion of the exam is specifically constructed to test vocabulary skills and the ability to discern the best answer that matches the provided word. Unlike verbal analogies, which will test communication skills and problem-solving abilities along with vocabulary, these questions chiefly test vocabulary knowledge by asking test takers to select the best synonym for the provided word. While logic and reasoning come into play in this section, they are not as heavily emphasized as with the analogies. A prior knowledge of what the words mean is helpful in order to answer correctly. If the meaning of the words is unknown, that's fine, too. Strategies should be used to rule out false answers and choose the correct ones. Here are some study strategies for an optimum performance.

Format of the Questions

The synonyms questions are very simple in construction. Instead of a comparison of words with an underlying connection, like the verbal analogies, the prompt is just a single word. There are no special directions, alternate meanings, or analogies to work with. The objective is to analyze the given word and then choose the answer that means the same thing or is closest in meaning to the given word. Note the example below:

Blustery

- a. Hard
- b. Windy
- c. Mythical
- d. Stoney
- e. Corresponding

All of the questions on the Synonyms portion will appear exactly like the above sample. This is generally the standard layout throughout other exams, so some test-takers may already be familiar with the structure. The principle remains the same. At the top of the section, clear directions will be given to choose the answer that most precisely defines the given word. In this case, the answer is windy (B), since windy and blustery are synonymous.

Preparation

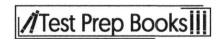

In truth, there is no set way to prepare for this portion of the exams that will guarantee a perfect score. This is simply because the words used on the test are unpredictable. There is no set list provided to study from. The definition of the provided word needs to be determined on the spot. This sounds challenging, but there are still ways to prepare mentally for the test. It may help to expand your vocabulary a little each day. Several resources are available, in books and online, that collect words and definitions that tend to show up frequently on standardized tests. Knowledge of words can increase the strength of your vocabulary.

Mindset is key. The meanings of challenging words can often be found by relying on the past experiences of the test-taker to help deduce the correct answer. How? Well, test-takers have been talking their entire lives—knowing words and how words work. It helps to have a positive mindset from the start. It's unlikely that all definitions of words will be known immediately, but the answer can still be found. There are aspects of words that are recognizable to help discern the correct answers and eliminate the incorrect ones. Here are some of the factors that contribute to word meanings!

Word Origins and Roots

Studying a foreign language in school, particularly Latin or any of the romance languages (Latin-influenced), is advantageous. English is a language highly influenced by Latin and Greek words. The **roots** of much of the English vocabulary have Latin origins; these roots can bind many words together and often allude to a shared definition. Here's an example:

Fervent

    a. Lame
    b. Joyful
    c. Thorough
    d. Boiling
    e. Cunning

Fervent descends from the Latin word, *fervere*, which means "to boil or glow" and figuratively means "impassioned." The Latin root present in the word is *ferv*, which is what gives fervent the definition: showing great warmth and spirit or spirited, hot, glowing. This provides a link to boiling (D) just by root word association, but there's more to analyze. Among the other choices, none relate to fervent. The word lame (A) means crippled, disabled, weak, or inadequate. None of these match with fervent. While being fervent can reflect joy, joyful (B) directly describes "a great state of happiness," while fervent is simply expressing the idea of having very strong feelings—not necessarily joy. Thorough (C) means complete, perfect, painstaking, or with mastery; while something can be done thoroughly and fervently, none of these words match fervent as closely as boiling does. Cunning (E) means crafty, deceiving or with ingenuity or dexterity. Doing something fervently does not necessarily mean it is done with dexterity. Not only does boiling connect in a linguistic way, but also in the way it is used in our language. While boiling can express being physically hot and undergoing a change, boiling is also used to reflect emotional states. People say they are "boiling over" when in heightened emotional states; "boiling mad" is another expression. Boiling, like fervent, also embodies a sense of heightened intensity. This makes boiling the best choice!

The Latin root *ferv* is seen in other words such as fervor, fervid, and even ferment. All of them are connected to and can be described by boil or glow, whether it is in a physical sense or in a metaphorical one. Such a pattern can be seen in other word sets! Here's another example:

145

Gracious

    a. Fruitful
    b. Angry
    c. Grateful
    d. Understood
    e. Overheard

This one's a little easier; the answer is grateful (*C*) because both words mean thankful! Even if the meanings of both words are known, there's a connection found by looking at the beginnings of both words: *gra/grat*. Once again, there is a root that stretches back to classical language. Both terms come from the Latin, *gratis*, which literally means "thanks."

Understanding root words can help identify the meaning in a lot of word choices, and help the test-taker grasp the nature of the given word. Many dictionaries, both in book form and online, offer information on the origins of words, which highlight these roots. When studying for the test, it helps to look up an unfamiliar word for its definition and then check to see if it has a root that can be connected to any of the other terms.

Pay Attention to Prefixes

The **prefix** of a word can actually reveal a lot about its definition. Many prefixes are actually Greco-Roman roots as well—but these are more familiar and a lot easier to recognize! When encountering any unfamiliar words, try looking at prefixes to discern the definition and then compare that with the choices. The prefix should be determined to help find the word's meaning. Here's an example question:

Premeditate

    a. Sporadic
    b. Calculated
    c. Interfere
    d. Determined
    e. Noble

With premeditate, there's the common prefix *pre*. This helps draw connections to other words like prepare or preassemble. *Pre* refers to "before, already being, or having already." Meditate means to think or plan. Premeditate means to think or plan beforehand with intent. Therefore, a term that deals with thinking or planning should be found, but also something done in preparation. Among the word choices, noble (E) and determined (D) are both adjectives with no hint of being related to something done before or in preparation. These choices are incorrect. Sporadic (A) refers to events happening in irregular patterns, so this is quite the opposite of premeditated. Interfere (C) also has nothing to do with premeditate; it goes counter to premeditate in a way similar to sporadic. Calculated (B), however, fits! A route and the cost of starting a plan can be calculated. Calculated refers to acting with a full awareness of consequences, so inherently planning is involved. In fact, calculated is synonymous with premeditated, thus making it the correct choice. Just by paying attention to a prefix, the doors to a meaning can open to help easily figure out which word would be the best choice. Here's another example.

Regain

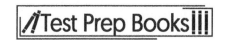

a. Erupt
b. Ponder
c. Seek
d. Recoup
e. Enamor

Recoup (D) is the right answer. The prefix *re* often appears in front of words to give them the meaning of occurring again. Regain means to repossess something that was lost. Recoup, which also has the *re* prefix, literally means to regain. In this example, both the given word and the answer share the *re* prefix, which makes the pair easy to connect. However, don't rely only on prefixes to choose an answer. Make sure to analyze all options before marking an answer. Going through the other words in this sample, none of them come close to meaning regain except recoup. After checking to make sure that recoup is the best matching word, then mark it!

Positive Versus Negative Sounding Words

Another tool for the mental toolbox is simply distinguishing whether a word has a positive or negative **connotation**. Like electrical wires, words carry energy; they are crafted to draw certain attention and to have certain strength to them. Words can be described as positive and uplifting (a stronger word) or they can be negative and scathing (a stronger word). Sometimes they are neutral—having no particular connotation. Distinguishing how a word is supposed to be interpreted will not only help learn its definition, but also draw parallels with word choices. While it's true that words must usually be taken in the context of how they are used, word definitions have inherent meanings as well. So, they have a distinct vibe to pick up on. Here is an example.

Excellent

a. Fair
b. Optimum
c. Reasonable
d. Negative
e. Agitation

As you know, excellent is a very positive word. It refers to something being better than good, above average. In this sample, negative (D) and agitation (E) can easily be eliminated because these are both words with negative connotations. Reasonable (C) is more or less a neutral word: it's not bad but it doesn't communicate the higher quality that excellent represents. It's just, well, reasonable. This leaves the possible choices of fair (A) and optimum (B). Or does it? Fair *is* a positive word; it's used to describe things that are good, even beautiful. But in the modern context, fair is defined as good, but somewhat average or just decent: "You did a fairly good job." or, "That was fair." On the other hand, optimum is positive and is a stronger word. Optimum describes the most favorable outcome. This makes optimum the best word choice that matches excellent in both strength and connotation. Not only are the two words positive, but they also express the same level of positivity! Here's another example:

Repulse

a. Draw
b. Encumber
c. Force
d. Disgust
e. Magnify

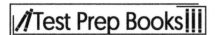

Repulse sounds negative when said. It is commonly used in the context of something being repulsive, disgusting, or that which is distasteful. It's also defined as an attack that drives people away. This tells us we need a word that also carries a negative meaning. Magnify (E) is positive, while draw (A) and force (C) are both neutral. Encumber (B) and disgust (D) are negative. Disgust is a stronger negative than encumber. Of all the words given, only disgust directly defines a feeling of distaste and aversion that is synonymous with repulse, and matches in both negativity and strength.

Parts of Speech

It is often very helpful to determine the **part of speech** of a word. Is it an adjective, adverb, noun, or verb, etc.? Often the correct answer will also be the same part of speech as the given word. Isolate the part of speech and what it describes and look for an answer choice that also describes the same part of speech. For example: if the given word is an adverb describing an action word, then look for another adverb describing an action word.

Swiftly

  a. Fast
  b. Quietly
  c. Angry
  d. Sudden
  e. Quickly

Swiftly is an adverb that describes the speed of an action. Angry (C), fast (A), and sudden (D) can be eliminated because they are not adverbs, and quietly (B) can be eliminated because it does not describe speed. This leaves quickly (E), which is the correct answer. Fast and sudden may throw off some test-takers because they both describe speed, but quickly matches more closely because it is an adverb, and swiftly is also an adverb.

Place the Word in a Sentence

Often it is easier to discern the meaning of a word if it is used in a sentence. If the given word can be used in a sentence, then try replacing it with some of the answer choices to see which words seem to make sense in the same sentence. Here's an example.

Remarkable

  a. Often
  b. Capable
  c. Outstanding
  d. Shining
  e. Excluding

A sentence can be formed with the word remarkable. "My grade point average is remarkable." None of the examples make sense when replacing the word remarkable in the sentence other than the word outstanding (C), so outstanding is the obvious answer. Shining (D) is also a word with a positive connotation, but outstanding fits better in the sentence.

Pick the Closest Answer

As the answer choices are reviewed, two scenarios might stand out. An exact definition match might not be found for the given word among the choices, or there are several word choices that can be considered synonymous to the

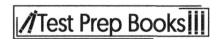

given word. This is intentionally done to test the ability to draw parallels between the words to produce an answer that best fits the prompt word. Again, the closest fitting word will be the answer. Even when facing these two circumstances, finding the one word that fits best is the proper strategy. Here's an example:

Insubordination

    a. Cooperative
    b. Disciplined
    c. Rebel
    d. Contagious
    e. Wild

Insubordination refers to a defiance or utter refusal of authority. Looking over the choices, none of these terms provide definite matches to insubordination like insolence, mutiny, or misconduct would. This is fine; the answer doesn't have to be a perfect synonym. The choices don't reflect insubordination in any way, except rebel (C). After all, when rebel is used as a verb, it means to act against authority. It's also used as a noun: someone who goes against authority. Therefore, rebel is the best choice.

As with the verbal analogies section, being a detective is a good course to take. Two or even three choices might be encountered that could be the answer. However, the answer that most perfectly fits the prompt word's meaning is the best answer. Choices should be narrowed one word at a time. The least-connected word should be eliminated first and then proceed until one word is left that is the closest synonym.

Sequence

    a. List
    b. Range
    c. Series
    d. Replicate
    e. Iconic

A sequence reflects a particular order in which events or objects follow. The two closest options are list (A) and series (C). Both involve grouping things together, but which fits better? Consider each word more carefully. A list is comprised of items that fit in the same category, but that's really it. A list doesn't have to follow any particular order; it's just a list. On the other hand, a series is defined by events happening in a set order. A series relies on sequence, and a sequence can be described as a series. Thus, series is the correct answer!

For both portions of the Verbal Section in the Middle Level, SSAT, the following information about English language usage can provide helpful background knowledge to successfully answer questions. While some of this information has previously been touched upon, test takers can benefit from further explanation for several of these concepts.

Verbal Analogies [SSAT]

What are Verbal Analogies?

Analogies compare two different things that have a relationship or some similarity. For example, a basic analogy is apple is to fruit as cucumber is to vegetable. This analogy points out the category under which each item falls. On the SSAT, the final term (vegetable, in this case) will be blank and must be filled in from the multiple choices, selecting the word that best demonstrates the relationship in the first pair of words. Other analogies include words that are *synonyms,* which are words that share similar meanings to one another. For example, big and large are

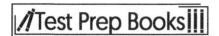

synonyms and tired and sleepy are also synonyms. Verbal analogy questions can be difficult because they require the test taker to demonstrate an understanding of small differences and similarities in both word meanings and word relationships.

Layout of the Questions

Verbal analogy sections are on other standardized tests such as the SAT. The format on the SSAT remains basically the same. First, two words are paired together that provide a frame for the analogy. Then, you are given a third word. You must find the relationship between the first two words, and then choose the fourth word to match the relationship to the third word. It may help to think of it like this: A is to B as C is to D. Examine the breakdown below:

Apple (A) is to fruit (B) as carrot (C) is to vegetable (D).

As shown above, there are four words: the first three are given and the fourth word is the answer that must be found. The first two words are given to set up the kind of analogy that is to be replicated for the next pair. We see that apple is paired with fruit. In the first pair, a specific food item, apple, is paired to the food group category it corresponds with, which is fruit. When presented with the third word in the verbal analogy, carrot, a word must be found that best matches carrot in the way that fruit matched with apple. Again, carrot is a specific food item, so a match should be found with the appropriate food group: vegetable! Here's a sample prompt:

Morbid is to dead as jovial is to

- a. Hate.
- b. Fear.
- c. Disgust.
- d. Happiness.
- e. Desperation.

As with the apple and carrot example, here is an analogy frame in the first two words: morbid and dead. Again, this will dictate how the next two words will correlate with one another. The word morbid can be defined as having a disturbing interest in unpleasant subjects, such as death and disease. In other words, morbid can mean ghastly or death-like, which is why the word dead is paired with it. Dead relates to morbid because it describes morbid. With this in mind, jovial becomes the focus. Jovial means joyful, so out of all the choices given, the closest answer describing jovial is happiness (D).

Prompts on the exam will be structured just like the one above. "A is to B as C is to ?" will be given, where the answer completes the second pair. Or sometimes, "A is to B as ? is to ?" is given, where the second pair of words must be found that replicate the relationship between the first pair. The only things that will change are the words and the relationships between the words provided.

Discerning the Correct Answer

While it wouldn't hurt in test preparation to expand vocabulary, verbal analogies are all about delving into the words themselves and finding the right connection, the right word that will fit an analogy. People preparing for the test shouldn't think of themselves as human dictionaries, but rather as detectives. Remember that the first two words that are connected dictates the second pair. From there, picking the correct answer or simply eliminating the ones that aren't correct is the best strategy.

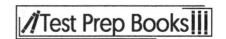

Just like a detective, a test-taker needs to carefully examine the first two words of the analogy for clues. It's good to get in the habit of asking the questions: What do the two words have in common? What makes them related or unrelated? How can a similar relationship be replicated with the word I'm given and the answer choices? Here's another example:

Pillage is to steal as meander is to

    a. Stroll.
    b. Burgle.
    c. Cascade.
    d. Accelerate.
    e. Pinnacle.

Why is pillage paired with steal? In this example, pillage and steal are synonymous: they both refer to the act of stealing. This means that the answer is a word that means the same as meander, which is stroll. In this case, the defining relationship in the whole analogy was a similar definition.

What if test-takers don't know what stroll or meander mean, though? Using logic helps to eliminate choices and pick the correct answer. Looking closer into the contexts of the words pillage and steal, here are a few facts: these are things that humans do; and while they are actions, these are not necessarily types of movement. Again, pick a word that will not only match the given word, but best completes the relationship. It wouldn't make sense that burgle (B) would be the correct choice because meander doesn't have anything to do with stealing, so that eliminates burgle. Pinnacle (E) also can be eliminated because this is not an action at all but a position or point of reference. Cascade (C) refers to pouring or falling, usually in the context of a waterfall and not in reference to people, which means we can eliminate cascade as well. While people do accelerate when they move, they usually do so under additional circumstances: they accelerate while running or driving a car. All three of the words we see in the analogy are actions that can be done independently of other factors. Therefore, accelerate (D) can be eliminated, and stroll (A) should be chosen. Stroll and meander both refer to walking or wandering, so this fits perfectly.

The *process of elimination* will help rule out wrong answers. However, the best way to find the correct answer is simply to differentiate the correct answer from the other choices. For this, test-takers should go back to asking questions, starting with the chief question: What's the connection? There are actually many ways that connections can be found between words. The trick is to look for the answer that is consistent with the relationship between the words given. What is the prevailing connection? Here are a few different ways verbal analogies can be formed.

Finding Connections in Word Analogies

Categories

One of the easiest ways to choose the correct answer in word analogies is simply to group the words. Ask if the words can be compartmentalized into *distinct categories*. Here are some examples:

Terrier is to dog as mystery is to

    a. Thriller.
    b. Murder.
    c. Detective.
    d. Novel.
    e. Investigation.

151

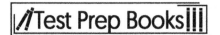

This one might have been a little confusing, but when looking at the first two words in the analogy, this is clearly one in which a category is the prevailing theme. Think about it: a terrier is a type of dog. While there are several breeds of dogs that can be categorized as a terrier, in the end, all terriers are still dogs. Therefore, mystery needs to be grouped into a category. Murders, detectives, and investigations can all be involved in a mystery plot, but a murder (B), a detective (C), or an investigation (E) is not necessarily a mystery. A thriller (A) is a purely fictional concept, a kind of story or film, just like a mystery. A thriller can describe a mystery, but the same issue appears as the other choices. What about novel (D)? For one thing, it's distinct from all the other terms. A novel isn't a component of a mystery, but a mystery can be a type of novel. The relationship fits: a terrier is a type of dog, just like a mystery is a type of novel.

Synonym/Antonym
Some analogies are based on words meaning the same thing or expressing the same idea. Sometimes it's the complete opposite!

Marauder is to brigand as

- a. King is to peasant.
- b. Juice is to orange.
- c. Soldier is to warrior.
- d. Engine is to engineer.
- e. Paper is to photocopier.

Here, soldier is to warrior (C) is the correct answer. Marauders and brigands are both thieves. They are synonyms. The only pair of words that fits this analogy is soldier and warrior because both terms describe combatants who fight.

Cap is to shoe as jacket is to

- a. Ring.
- b. T-shirt.
- c. Vest.
- d. Glasses.
- e. Pants.

Opposites are at play here because a cap is worn on the head/top of the person, while a shoe is worn on the foot/bottom. A jacket is worn on top of the body too, so the opposite of jacket would be pants (E) because these are worn on the bottom. Often the prompts on the test provide a synonym or antonym relationship. Just consider if the sets in the prompt reflect similarity or stark difference.

Parts of a Whole
Another thing to consider when first looking at an analogy prompt is whether the words presented come together in some way. Do they express parts of the same item? Does one word complete the other? Are they connected by process or function?

Tire is to car as

a. Wing is to bird.
b. Oar is to boat.
c. Box is to shelf.
d. Hat is to head.
e. Knife is to sheath.

We know that the tire fits onto the car's wheels and this is what enables the car to drive on roads. The tire is part of the car. This is the same relationship as oar is to boat (B). The oars are attached onto a boat and enable a person to move and navigate the boat on water. At first glance, wing is to bird (A) seems to fit too, since a wing is a part of a bird that enables it to move through the air. However, since a tire and car are not alive and transport people, oar and boat fit better because they are also not alive, and they transport people. Subtle differences between answer choices should be found.

Other Relationships

There are a number of other relationships to look for when solving verbal analogies. Some relationships focus on one word being a *characteristic/NOT a characteristic* of the other word. Sometimes the first word is the *source/comprised of* the second word. Still, other words are related by their *location*. Some analogies have *sequential* relationships, and some are *cause/effect* relationships. There are analogies that show *creator/provider* relationships with the *creation/provision*. Another relationship might compare an *object* with its *function* or a *user* with their *tool*. An analogy may focus on a *change of grammar* or a *translation of language*. Finally, one word of an analogy may have a relationship to the other word in its *intensity*.

The type of relationship between the first two words of the analogy should be determined before continuing to analyze the second set of words. One effective method of determining a relationship between two words is to form a comprehensible sentence using both words. Then plug the answer choices into the same sentence. For example in the analogy: *Bicycle is to handlebars as car is to steering wheel*, a sentence could be formed that says: A bicycle navigates using its handlebars; therefore, a car navigates using its steering wheel. If the second sentence makes sense, then the correct relationship likely is found. A sentence may be more complex depending on the relationship between the first two words in the analogy. An example of this may be: *food is to dishwasher as dirt is to carwash.* The formed sentence may be: A dishwasher cleans food off of dishes in the same way that a carwash cleans dirt off of a car.

Dealing with Multiple Connections

There are many other ways to draw connections between word sets. Several word choices might form an analogy that would fit the word set in your prompt. This is when an analogy from multiple angles needs to be explored. Several words might even fit in a relationship. If so, which one is an even closer match than the others? The framing word pair is another important point to consider. Can one or both words be interpreted as actions or ideas, or are they purely objects? Here's a question where words could have alternate meanings:

Hammer is to nail as saw is to

a. Electric.
b. Hack.
c. Cut.
d. Machete.
e. Groove.

Looking at the question above, it becomes clear that the topic of the analogy involves construction tools. Hammers and nails are used in concert since the hammer is used to pound the nail. The logical first thing to do is to look for an object that a saw would be used on. Seeing that there is no such object among the answer choices, a test-taker

153

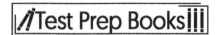

might begin to worry. After all, that seems to be the choice that would complete the analogy—but that doesn't mean it's the only choice that may fit. Encountering questions like this tests the ability to see multiple connections between words. Don't get stuck thinking that words have to be connected in a single way. The first two words given can be verbs instead of just objects. To hammer means to hit or beat; oftentimes it refers to beating something into place. This is also what nail means when it is used as a verb. Here are the word choices that reveal the answer.

First, it's known that a saw, well, saws. It uses a steady motion to cut an object, and indeed to saw means to cut! Cut (C) is one of our answer choices, but the other options should be reviewed. While some tools are electric (a), the use of power in the tools listed in the analogy isn't a factor. Again, it's been established that these word choices are not tools in this context. Therefore, machete (D) is also ruled out because machete is also not a verb. Another important thing to consider is that while a machete is a tool that accomplishes a similar purpose as a saw, the machete is used in a slicing motion rather than a sawing/cutting motion. The verb that describes machete is hack (B), another choice that can be ruled out. A machete is used to hack at foliage. However, a saw does not hack. Groove (E) is just a term that has nothing to do with the other words, so this choice can be eliminated easily. This leaves cut (C), which confirms that this is the word needed to complete the analogy!

Vocabulary

Parts of Speech

Also referred to as word classes, parts of speech refer to the various categories in which words are placed. Words can be placed in any one or a combination of the following categories:

- Nouns
- Determiners
- Pronouns
- Verbs
- Adjectives
- Adverbs
- Prepositions
- Conjunctions

Understanding the various parts of speech used in the English language helps readers to better understand the written language.

Nouns

Nouns are defined as any word that represents a person, place, animal, object, or idea. Nouns can identify a person's title or name, a person's gender, and a person's nationality, such as banker, commander-in-chief, female, male, or an American.

With animals, nouns identify the kingdom, phylum, class, etc. For example: animal is elephant; phylum is chordata; or class is mammalia.

When identifying places, nouns refer to a physical location, a general vicinity, or the proper name of a city, state, or country. Some examples include the desert, the East, Phoenix, Arizona, or the United States.

There are eight types of nouns: common, proper, countable, uncountable, concrete, abstract, compound, and collective.

Common nouns are used in general terms, without specific identification. Examples include girl, boy, country, or school. Proper nouns refer to the proper name given to people, places, animals, or entities, such as Melissa, Martin, Italy, or Harvard.

Countable nouns can be counted: one car, two cars, or three cars. Uncountable nouns cannot be counted, such as air, liquid, or gas.

To be abstract is to exist, but only in thought or as an idea. An abstract noun cannot be physically touched, seen, smelled, heard, or tasted. These include chivalry, day, fear, thought, truth, friendship, or freedom.

To be concrete is to be seen, touched, tasted, heard, and/or smelled. Examples include pie, snow, tree, bird, desk, hair, or dog.

A compound noun is another term for an open compound word. Any noun that is written as two nouns that together form a specific meaning is a compound noun, such as post office, ice cream, or swimming pool.

A collective noun is formed by grouping three or more words to create one meaning. Examples include bunch of flowers, herd of elephants, flock of birds, or school of fish.

Determiners

Determiners modify a noun and usually refer to something specific. Determiners fall into one of four categories: articles, demonstratives, quantifiers, or possessive determiners.

Articles can be both definite articles, as in *the*, and indefinite as in *a, an, some,* or *any*:

> *The* man with *the* red hat.

> *A* flower growing in *the* yard.

> *Any* person who visits *the* store.

There are four different types of demonstratives: this, that, these, and those.

True demonstrative words will not directly precede the noun of the sentence, but will *be* the noun. Some examples:

> *This* is the one.

> *That* is the place.

> *Those* are the files.

Once a demonstrative is placed directly in front of the noun, it becomes a demonstrative pronoun:

> *This* one is perfect.

> *That* place is lovely.

> *Those* boys are annoying.

Quantifiers proceed nouns to give additional information for how much or how many. They can be used with countable and uncountable nouns:

> She bought *plenty* of apples.

155

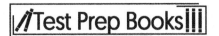

Few visitors came.

I got a *little* change.

Possessive determiners, sometimes called possessive adjectives, indicate possession. They are the possessive forms of personal pronouns, such as for my, your, hers, his, its, their, or our:

That is *my* car.

Tom rode *his* bike today.

Those papers are *hers.*

Pronouns

Pronouns are words that stand in place of nouns. There are three different types of pronouns: subjective pronouns (I, you, he, she, it, we, they), objective pronouns (me, you, him, her it, us, them), and possessive pronouns (mine, yours, his, hers, ours, theirs).

You'll see some words are found in more than one pronoun category. See examples and clarifications below:

You are going to the movies.

You is a subjective pronoun; it is the subject of the sentence and is performing the action.

I threw the ball to *you.*

You is an objective pronoun; it is receiving the action and is the object of the sentence.

We saw *her* at the movies.

Her is an objective pronoun; it is receiving the action and is the object of the sentence.

The house across the street from the park is *hers.*

Hers is a possessive pronoun; it shows possession of the house and is used as a possessive pronoun.

Verbs

Verbs are words in a sentence that show action or state. Just as there can be no sentence without a subject, there can be no sentence without a verb. In these sentences, notice verbs in the present, past, and future tenses. To form some tenses in the future and in the past requires auxiliary, or helping, verbs:

I *see* the neighbors across the street.

See is an action.

We *were eating* at the picnic.

Eating is the main action, and the verb *were* is the past tense of the verb *to be*, and is the helping or auxiliary verb that places the sentence in the past tense.

You *will turn* 20 years of age next month.

Turn is the main verb, but to show a future tense, *will* is the helping verb to show future tense of the verb *to be*.

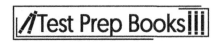

Adjectives

Adjectives are a special group of words used to modify, describe, or provide more information about a noun. For example:

The boy went to school. (There is no adjective.)

Rewrite the sentence, adding an adjective to further describe the boy and/or the school:

The *young* boy went to the *old* school. (The adjective *young* describes the boy, and the adjective *old* describes the school.)

Adverbs

Adverb can play one of two roles: to modify the adjective or to modify the verb. For example:

The young boy went to the old school.

We can further describe the adjectives *young* and *old* with adverbs placed directly in front of the adjectives:

The *very* young boy went to the *very* old school. (The adverb *very* further describes the adjectives *young* and *old*.)

Other examples of using adverbs to further describe verbs:

The boy *slowly* went to school.

The boy *quickly* went to school.

The adverbs *slowly* and *quickly* further modify the verbs.

Prepositions

Prepositions are special words that generally precede a noun. Prepositions clarify the relationship between the subject and another word or element in the sentence. They clarify time, place, and the positioning of subjects and objects in a sentence. Common prepositions in the English language include: near, far, under, over, on, in, between, beside, of, at, until, behind, across, after, before, for, from, to, by, and with.

Conjunctions

Conjunctions are a group of unique words that connect clauses or sentences. They also work to coordinate words in the same clause. It is important to choose an appropriate conjunction based on the meaning of the sentence. Consider these sentences:

I really like the flowers, *however* the smell is atrocious.

I really like the flowers, *besides* the smell is atrocious.

The conjunctions *however* and *besides* act as conjunctions, connecting the two ideas: *I really like the flowers,* and, *the smell is atrocious.* In the second sentence, the conjunction *besides* makes no sense and would confuse the reader. You must consider the message you wish to convey and choose conjunctions that clearly state that message without ambiguity.

Some conjunctions introduce an opposing opinion, thought, or fact. They can also reinforce an opinion, introduce an explanation, reinforce cause and effect, or indicate time. For example:

157

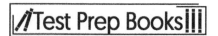
She wishes to go to the movies, *but* she doesn't have the money. (Opposition)

The professor became ill, *so* the class was postponed. (Cause and effect)

They visited Europe *before* winter came. (Time)

Each conjunction serves a specific purpose in uniting two separate ideas. Below are common conjunctions in the English language:

Opposition	Cause & Effect	Reinforcement	Time	Explanation
however	therefore	besides	afterward	for example
nevertheless	as a result	anyway	before	in other words
but	because of this	after all	firstly	for instance
although	consequently	furthermore	next	such as

Practice Quiz

Synonyms

1. GARISH
   a. Drab
   b. Flashy
   c. Gait
   d. Hardy
   e. Lithe

2. INANE
   a. Ratify
   b. Illicit
   c. Uncouth
   d. Senseless
   e. Wry

3. SOLACE
   a. Marred
   b. Induce
   c. Depose
   d. Inherent
   e. Comfort

4. COPIOUS
   a. Dire
   b. Adept
   c. Indignant
   d. Ample
   e. Nuance

5. SUPERCILIOUS
   a. Tenuous
   b. Waning
   c. Arrogant
   d. Placate
   e. Extol

Verbal Analogies

1. Begonia is to flower as
   a. Daisy is to pollen.
   b. Cat is to catnip.
   c. Cardiologist is to doctor.
   d. Radiology is to disease.
   e. Nutrition is to reproduction.

2. Malleable is to pliable as
 a. Corroborate is to invalidate.
 b. Avenue is to city.
 c. Blacksmith is to anvil.
 d. Hostile is to hospitable.
 e. Disparage is to criticize.

3. Cerebellum is to brain as
 a. Nurse is to medication.
 b. Nucleus is to cell.
 c. Bacteria is to spores.
 d. Refraction is to light.
 e. Painting is to sculpting.

4. Whisk is to baking as
 a. Glove is to boxing.
 b. Swimming is to water.
 c. Love is to romance.
 d. Azalea is to flower.
 e. Bench is to park.

5. Umpire is to officiate as
 a. Coaching is to coach.
 b. Baseball is to pastime.
 c. Counselor is to guide.
 d. Notary is to paper.
 e. Messenger is to letter.

See answers on the next page.

Answer Explanations

Synonyms

1. B: The word *garish* means excessively ornate or elaborate, which is most closely related to the word *flashy*. The word *drab* is the opposite of *garish*. The word *gait* means a particular manner of walking, *hardy* means robust or sturdy, and *lithe* means graceful and supple.

2. D: The word *inane* means senseless or absurd. The word *ratify* means to approve, *illicit* means illegal, *uncouth* means crude, and *wry* means clever.

3. E: The word *solace* most closely resembles the word *comfort*. *Marred* means scarred, *induce* means to cause something, *depose* means to dethrone, and *inherent* means natural.

4. D: *Copious* is synonymous with the word *ample*. *Dire* means urgent or dreadful, *adept* means skillful, *indignant* means angered by injustice, and *nuance* means subtle difference.

5. C: *Supercilious* means arrogant. *Tenuous* means weak or thin, *waning* means decreasing, *placate* means to appease, and *extol* means to praise or celebrate.

Verbal Analogies

1. C: This is a category analogy. Remember that we have to figure out the relationship between the first two words so that we can determine the relationship of the answer. Begonia is related to flower by type. Begonia is a type of flower, just as cardiologist is a type of doctor.

2. E: This is a synonym analogy. Notice that the word *malleable* is synonymous to the word *pliable*. Thus, in our answer, we should look for two words that have the same meaning. *Disparage* and *criticize* in Choice *E* have the same meaning, so this is the correct answer.

3. B: This is a part to whole analogy. The relationship between *cerebellum* and *brain* is that the cerebellum makes up part of the brain, while a *nucleus* makes up part of a *cell*.

4. A: Usually, a *whisk* is a cooking utensil used in the process of *baking*. As such, a *glove* is used in the sport of *boxing*. Both are objects used within a particular process.

5. C: This analogy relies on the logic of performer to related action. The original analogy says *umpires* (performer) *officiate* (action), which means to act as an official in a sporting event. In the same manner, a *counselor* (performer) *guides* (action) their clients toward well-being.

Essay [ISEE]

Parts of the Essay

The **introduction** has to do a few important things:

Establish the **topic** of the essay in original wording (i.e., not just repeating the prompt)

Clarify the significance/importance of the topic or purpose for writing. This should provide a brief overview rather than share too many details.

Offer a **thesis statement** that identifies the writer's own viewpoint on the topic. Typically, the thesis statement is one or two brief sentences that offer a clear, concise explanation of the main point on the topic.

Body paragraphs reflect the ideas developed in the outline. Three or four points is probably sufficient for a short essay, and they should include the following:

A **topic sentence** that identifies the sub-point (e.g., a reason why, a way how, a cause or effect)

A detailed **explanation** of each sub-point, explaining why the writer thinks this point is valid

Illustrative examples, such as personal examples or real-world examples, that support and validate the point (i.e., "prove" the point)

A **concluding sentence** that connects the examples, reasoning, and analysis to the point being made

The **conclusion,** or final paragraph, should be brief and should reiterate the focus, clarifying why the discussion is significant or important. It is important to avoid adding specific details or new ideas to this paragraph. The purpose of the conclusion is to sum up what has been said to bring the discussion to a close.

The Short Overview

The essay may seem challenging, but following these steps can help writers focus:

- Take one to two minutes to think about the topic.
- Generate some ideas through brainstorming (three to four minutes).
- Organize ideas into a brief outline, selecting just three to four main points to cover in the essay
- Develop essay in parts:
  - Introduction paragraph, with intro to topic and main points
  - Viewpoint on the subject at the end of the introduction
  - Body paragraphs, based on outline, each should make a main point, explain the viewpoint, and use examples to support the point
  - Brief conclusion highlighting the main points and closing
- Read over the essay (last five minutes).
- Look for any obvious errors, making sure that the writing makes sense.

Writing an essay can be overwhelming, and performance panic is a natural response. The outline serves as a basis for the writing and help writers keep focused. Getting stuck can also happen, and it's helpful to remember that brainstorming can be done at any time during the writing process. Following the steps of the writing process is the best defense against writer's block.

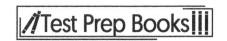

Timed essays can be particularly stressful, but assessors are trained to recognize the necessary planning and thinking for these timed efforts. Using the plan above and sticking to it helps with time management. Timing each part of the process helps writers stay on track. Sometimes writers try to cover too much in their essays. If time seems to be running out, this is an opportunity to determine whether all of the ideas in the outline are necessary. Three body paragraphs are sufficient, and more than that is probably too much to cover in a short essay.

More isn't always *better* in writing. A strong essay will be clear and concise. It will avoid unnecessary or repetitive details. It is better to have a concise, five-paragraph essay that makes a clear point, than a ten-paragraph essay that doesn't. The goal is to write one to two pages of quality writing. Paragraphs should also reflect balance; if the introduction goes to the bottom of the first page, the writing may be going off-track or may be repetitive. It's best to fall into the one to two-page range, but a complete, well-developed essay is the ultimate goal.

Applying Basic Knowledge of the Elements of the Writing Process

Practice Makes Prepared Writers

Like any other useful skill, writing only improves with practice. While writing may come more easily to some than others, it is still a skill to be honed and improved. Regardless of a person's natural abilities, there is always room for growth in writing. Practicing the basic skills of writing can aid in preparations for the ISEE.

One way to build vocabulary and enhance exposure to the written word is through reading. This can be through reading books, but reading of any materials such as newspapers, magazines, and even social media count towards practice with the written word. This also helps to enhance critical reading and thinking skills, through analysis of the ideas and concepts read. Think of each new reading experience as a chance to sharpen these skills.

Planning
Brainstorming

One of the most important steps in writing an essay is prewriting. Before drafting an essay, it's helpful to think about the topic for a moment or two, in order to gain a more solid understanding of the task. Then, spending about five minutes jotting down the immediate ideas that could work for the essay is recommended. Brainstorming is a way to get some words on the page and offer a reference for ideas when drafting. Scratch paper is provided for writers to use any prewriting techniques such as webbing, free writing, or listing. The goal is to get ideas out of the mind and onto the page.

In the planning stage, it's important to consider all aspects of the topic, including different viewpoints on the subject. There are more than two ways to look at a topic, and a strong argument considers those opposing viewpoints. Considering opposing viewpoints can help writers present a fair, balanced, and informed essay that shows consideration for all readers. This approach can also strengthen an argument by recognizing and potentially refuting opposing viewpoint(s).

Drawing from personal experience may help to support ideas. For example, if the goal for writing is a personal narrative, then the story should come from the writer's own life. Many writers find it helpful to draw from personal experience, even in an essay that is not strictly narrative. Personal anecdotes or short stories can help to illustrate a point in other types of essays as well.

Once the ideas are on the page, it's time to turn them into a solid plan for the essay. The best ideas from the brainstorming results can then be developed into a more formal outline.

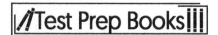

Outlining

An **outline** is a system used to organize writing. When reading texts, outlining is important because it helps readers organize important information in a logical pattern using Roman numerals. Usually, outlines start out with the main idea(s) and then branch out into subgroups or subsidiary thoughts or subjects. The outline should be methodical, with at least two main points followed each by at least two subpoints. Outlines provide a visual tool for readers to reflect on how events, characters, settings, or other key parts of the text or passage relate to one another. They can also lead readers to a stronger conclusion. The sample below demonstrates what a general outline looks like.

I. Main Topic 1

a. Subtopic 1

b. Subtopic 2

1. Detail 1

2. Detail 1

II. Main Topic 2

a. Subtopic 1

b. Subtopic 2

1. Detail 1

2. Detail 2

Free Writing

Like brainstorming, **free writing** is another prewriting activity to help the writer generate ideas. This method involves setting a timer for 2 or 3 minutes and writing down all ideas that come to mind about the topic using complete sentences. Once time is up, review the sentences to see what observations have been made and how these ideas might translate into a more coherent direction for the topic. Even if sentences lack sense as a whole, this is an excellent way to get ideas onto the page in the very beginning stages of writing. Using complete sentences can make this a bit more challenging than brainstorming, but overall, it is a worthwhile exercise, as it may force the writer to come up with more complete thoughts about the topic.

Writing

Now it comes time to actually write your essay. Follow the outline you developed in the brainstorming process and try to incorporate the sentences you wrote in the free writing exercise.

Basing the essay on the outline aids in both organization and coherence. The goal is to ensure that there is enough time to develop each sub-point in the essay, roughly spending an equal amount of time on each idea. Keeping an eye on the time will help. If there are fifteen minutes left to draft the essay, then it makes sense to spend about 5 minutes on each of the ideas. Staying on task is critical to success and timing out the parts of the essay can help writers avoid feeling overwhelmed.

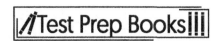

Remember that your work here does not have to be perfect. This process is often referred to as **drafting** because you're just creating a rough draft of your work.

Don't get bogged down on the small details. For instance, if you're not sure whether or not a word should be capitalized, mark it somehow and look up the capitalization rule while in the revision process if not in a testing situation. The same goes for referencing sources. That should not be focused on until after the writing process.

Referencing Sources

Anytime you quote or paraphrase another piece of writing you will need to include a citation. A **citation** is a short description of the work that your quote or information came from. The manual of style your teacher wants you to follow will dictate exactly how to format that citation. For example, this is how you would cite a book according to the APA manual of style:

Format: Last name, First initial, Middle initial. (Year Published) *Book Title*. City, State: Publisher.
Example: Sampson, M. R. (1989). *Diaries from an alien invasion*. Springfield, IL: Campbell Press.

Revising

Revising and proofreading offers an opportunity for writers to polish things up. Putting one's self in the reader's shoes and focusing on what the essay actually says helps writers identify problems—it's a movement from the mindset of writer to the mindset of editor. The goal is to have a clean, clear copy of the essay.

During the essay portion of a test, leaving a few minutes at the end to revise and proofread offers an opportunity for writers to polish things up. Putting one's self in the reader's shoes and focusing on what the essay actually says helps writers identify problems—it's a movement from the mindset of writer to the mindset of editor. The goal is to have a clean, clear copy of the essay. The following areas should be considered when proofreading:

- Sentence fragments
- Awkward sentence structure
- Run-on sentences
- Incorrect word choice
- Grammatical agreement errors
- Spelling errors
- Punctuation errors
- Capitalization errors

Recursive Writing Process

While the writing process may have specific steps, the good news is that the process is recursive, meaning the steps need not be completed in a particular order. Many writers find that they complete steps at the same time such as drafting and revising, where the writing and rearranging of ideas occur simultaneously or in very close order. Similarly, a writer may find that a particular section of a draft needs more development and will go back to the prewriting stage to generate new ideas. The steps can be repeated at any time, and the more these steps of the recursive writing process are employed, the better the final product will be.

Developing a Well-Organized Paragraph

Forming Paragraphs

A good **paragraph** should have the following characteristics:

- Be logical with organized sentences

165

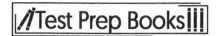

- Have a unified purpose within itself
- Use sentences as building blocks
- Be a distinct section of a piece of writing
- Present a single theme introduced by a topic sentence
- Maintain a consistent flow through subsequent, relevant, well-placed sentences
- Tell a story of its own or have its own purpose, yet connect with what is written before and after
- Enlighten, entertain, and/or inform

Though certainly not set in stone, the length should be a consideration for the reader's sake, not merely for the sake of the topic. When paragraphs are especially short, the reader might experience an irregular, uneven effect; when they're much longer than 250 words, the reader's attention span, and probably their retention, is challenged. While a paragraph can technically be a sentence long, a good rule of thumb is for paragraphs to be at least three sentences long and no more than ten sentence long. An optimal word length is 100 to 250 words.

Coherent Paragraphs

Coherence is simply defined as the quality of being logical and consistent. In order to have coherent paragraphs, therefore, authors must be logical and consistent in their writing, whatever the document might be. Two words are helpful to understanding coherence: flow and relationship. Earlier, transitions were referred to as being the "glue" to put organized thoughts together. Now, let's look at the topic sentence from which flow and relationship originate.

The **topic sentence**, usually the first in a paragraph, holds the essential features that will be brought forth in the paragraph. It is also here that authors either grab or lose readers. It may be the only writing that a reader encounters from that writer, so it is a good idea to summarize and represent ideas accurately.

The coherent paragraph has a logical order. It utilizes transitional words and phrases, parallel sentence structure, clear pronoun references, and reasonable repetition of key words and phrases. Use common sense for repetition. Consider synonyms for variety. Be consistent in verb tense whenever possible.

When writers have accomplished their paragraph's purpose, they prepare it to receive the next paragraph. While writing, read the paragraph over, edit, examine, evaluate, and make changes accordingly. Possibly, a paragraph has gone on too long. If that occurs, it needs to be broken up into other paragraphs, or the length should be reduced. If a paragraph didn't fully accomplish its purpose, consider revising it.

Main Point of a Paragraph

What is the main point of a paragraph? It is *the* point all of the other important and lesser important points should lead up to, and it should be summed up in the topic sentence.

Sometimes there is a fine line between a paragraph's topic sentence and its main point. In fact, they actually might be one and the same. Often, though, they are two separate, but closely related, aspects of the same paragraph.

Depending upon the writer's purpose, the topic sentence or the paragraph's main point might not be fully revealed until the paragraph's conclusion.

Sometimes, while developing paragraphs, authors deviate from the main point, which means they have to delete and rework their materials to stay on point.

Examining Paragraphs

While authors write, thoughts coalesce to form words on "paper." Authors strategically place those thoughts in sentences to give them "voice" in an orderly manner, and then they manipulate them into cohesive sentences for

166

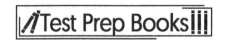

cohesion to express ideas. Like a hunk of modeling clay, sentences can be worked and reworked until they cooperate and say what was originally intended.

Before calling a paragraph complete, identify its main point, making sure that related sentences stay on point. Pose questions such as, "Did I sufficiently develop the main point? Did I say it succinctly enough? Did I give it time to develop? *Is* it developed?"

Let's examine the following two paragraphs, each an example of a movie review. Read them and form a critique.

Example 1: *Eddie the Eagle* is a movie about a struggling athlete. Eddie was crippled at birth. He had a lot of therapy and he had a dream. Eddie trained himself for the Olympics. He went far away to learn how to ski jump. It was hard for him, but he persevered. He got a coach and kept trying. He qualified for the Olympics. He was the only one from Britain who could jump. When he succeeded, they named him, "Eddie the Eagle."

Example 2: The last movie I saw in the theater was *Eddie the Eagle,* a story of extraordinary perseverance inspired by real life events. Eddie was born in England with a birth defect that he slowly but surely overcame, but not without trial and error (not the least of which was his father's perpetual *dis*couragement). In fact, the old man did everything to get him to give up, but Eddie was dogged beyond anyone in the neighborhood; in fact, maybe beyond anyone in the whole town or even the whole world! Eddie, simply, did not know to quit. As he grew up, so did his dream; a strange one, indeed, for someone so unaccomplished: to compete in the Winter Olympics as a ski jumper (which he knew absolutely nothing about). Eddie didn't just keep on dreaming about it. He actually went to Germany and *worked* at it, facing unbelievable odds, defeats, and put-downs by Dad and the other Men in Charge, aka the Olympic decision-makers. Did that stop him? No way! Eddie got a coach and persevered. Then, when he failed, he persevered some more, again and again. You should be able to open up a dictionary, look at the word "persevere," and see a picture of Eddie the Eagle because, when everybody told him he couldn't, he did. The result? He is forever dubbed, "Eddie the Eagle."

Both reviews tell something about the movie *Eddie the Eagle*. Does one motivate the reader to want to see the movie more than the other? Does one just provide a few facts while the other paints a virtual picture of the movie? Does one give a carrot and the other a rib eye steak, mashed potatoes, and chocolate silk pie?

Paragraphs sometimes only give facts. Sometimes that's appropriate and all that is needed. Sometimes, though, writers want to use the blank documents on their computer screens to paint a picture. Writers must "see" the painting come to life. To do so, pick a familiar topic, write a simple sentence, and add to it. Pretend, for instance, there's a lovely view. What does one see? Is it a lake? Try again—picture it as though it were the sea! Visualize a big ship sailing out there. Is it sailing away or approaching? Who is on it? Is it dangerous? Is it night and are there crazy pirates on board? Uh-oh! Did one just jump ship and start swimming toward shore?

Distinguishing Between Formal and Informal Language [ISEE]

It can be helpful to distinguish whether a writer or speaker is using formal or informal language because it can give the reader or listener clues to whether the text is informative, nonfiction, argumentative, or the intended tone or audience. Formal and informal language in written or verbal communication serve different purposes and are often intended for different audiences. Consequently, their tone, word choices, and grammatical structures vary. These differences can be used to identify which form of language is used in a given piece and to determine which type of language should be used for a certain context. Understanding the differences between formal and informal language will also allow a writer or speaker to implement the most appropriate and effective style for a given situation.

Formal language is less personal and more informative and pragmatic than informal language. It is more "buttoned-up" and business-like, adhering to proper grammatical rules. It is used in professional or academic contexts, to convey respect or authority. For example, one would use formal language to write an informative or argumentative essay for school and to address a superior or esteemed professional like a potential employer, a professor, or a manager. Formal language avoids contractions, slang, colloquialisms, and first-person pronouns. **Slang** refers to non-standard expressions that are not used in elevated speech and writing. Slang creates linguistic in-groups and out-groups of people, those who can understand the slang terms and those who can't. Slang is often tied to a specific time period. For example, "groovy" and "far out" are connected to the 1970s, and "as if!" and "4-1-1-" are connected to the 1990s. **Colloquial language** is language that is used conversationally or familiarly—e.g., "What's up?"—in contrast to formal, professional, or academic language—"How are you this evening?" Formal language uses sentences that are usually more complex and often in passive voice. Punctuation can differ as well. For example, **exclamations point (!)** are used to show strong emotion or can be used as an interjection but should be used sparingly in formal writing situations.

Informal language is often used when communicating with family members, friends, peers, and those known more personally. It is more casual, spontaneous, and forgiving in its conformity to grammatical rules and conventions. Informal language is used for personal emails, some light fiction stories, and some correspondence between coworkers or other familial relationships. The tone is more relaxed and slang, contractions, clichés, and the first and second person may be used in writing. The imperative voice may be used as well.

As a review, the perspectives from which something may be written or conveyed are detailed below:

- First-person point of view: The story is told from the writer's perspective. In fiction, this would mean that the main character is also the narrator. First-person point of view is easily recognized by the use of personal pronouns such as *I, me, we, us, our, my*, and *myself.*

- Second-person point of view: This point of view isn't commonly used in fiction or nonfiction writing because it directly addresses the reader using the pronouns *you, your*, and *yourself.* Second-person perspective is more appropriate in direct communication, such as business letters or emails.

- Third-person point of view: In a more formal essay, this would be an appropriate perspective because the focus should be on the subject matter, not the writer or the reader. Third-person point of view is recognized by the use of the pronouns *he, she, they*, and *it.* In fiction writing, third-person point of view has a few variations.

  o Third-person limited point of view refers to a story told by a narrator who has access to the thoughts and feelings of just one character.

  o In third-person omniscient point of view, the narrator has access to the thoughts and feelings of all the characters.

  o In third-person objective point of view, the narrator is like a fly on the wall and can see and hear what the characters do and say but does not have access to their thoughts and feelings.

Tips for the Essay [ISEE]

- Don't panic! This section isn't scored. It's just a great way to show teachers how smart you are and how well you can tell a story and write. You can do it!

- Use your time well. Fifteen minutes is quick! It is shorter than almost every TV show. Don't spend too much time doing any one thing. Try to brainstorm briefly and then get writing. Leave a few minutes to read it over and correct any spelling mistakes or confusing parts.

- Be yourself! You are smart and interesting, and teachers want to get to know you and your unique ideas. Don't feel pressured to use big vocabulary words if you aren't positive what they mean. You will be more understandable if you use the right word, not the fanciest word.

Practice Essay [ISEE]

You have 30 minutes to plan and write your essay. Do not worry too much about length; it's most important to focus on the content and quality of your writing. Choose one of the following three questions to answer in a coherent essay:

- What would you like to pursue as a career and why?
- Where in the world would you most like to have a pen pal and why?

If you were asked to mentor younger children in a skill or hobby you enjoy, what would you share with them? How has that activity influenced your life?

SSAT Practice Test

Practice Writing Sample

Select one of the following two-story starters and write a creative story in the space provided. Make sure that your story has a beginning, middle, and end and is interesting for readers.

- The wind whipped through the trees, and the windows began to rattle.

- Karen raced home from the bus stop, flung open the door, and yelled, "Mom!"

Quantitative Reasoning

1. Which of the following is equivalent to the value of the digit 3 in the number 792.134?
   a. 3×10
   b. 3×100
   c. $\frac{3}{10}$
   d. $\frac{3}{100}$
   e. $100 \div 3$

2. Write the following number in standard form: $(1 \times 10^4) + (3 \times 10^3) + (7 \times 10^1) + (8 \times 10^0)$
   a. 137
   b. 13,078
   c. 3,780
   d. 1,378
   e. 8,731

3. How would the number 847.89632 be written if rounded to the nearest hundredth?
   a. 850
   b. 900
   c. 847.89
   d. 847.896
   e. 847.90

4. What is the sum of $\frac{1}{3}$ and $\frac{2}{5}$?
   a. $\frac{3}{8}$
   b. $\frac{11}{15}$
   c. $\frac{11}{30}$
   d. $\frac{4}{5}$
   e. $\frac{2}{8}$

5. What is the value of the expression: $7^2 - 3 \times (4 + 2) + 15 \div 5$?
   a.   12.2
   b.   40.2
   c.   34
   d.   58.2
   e.   193

6. How will $\frac{4}{5}$ be written as a percent?
   a.   40%
   b.   125%
   c.   50%
   d.   80%
   e.   90%

7. If Danny takes 48 minutes to walk 3 miles, how long should it take him to walk 5 miles maintaining the same speed?
   a.   32 min
   b.   64 min
   c.   80 min
   d.   96 min
   e.   78 min

8. What are all the factors of 12?
   a.   12, 24, 36
   b.   1, 2, 4, 6, 12
   c.   12, 24, 36, 48
   d.   1, 2, 3, 4, 6, 12
   e.   0, 1, 12

9. A construction company is building a new housing development with the property of each house measuring 30 feet wide. If the length of the street is zoned off at 345 feet, how many houses can be built on the street?
   a.   10 houses
   b.   11 houses
   c.   115 houses
   d.   11.5 houses
   e.   12 houses

10. Simplify: $(5x^2 - 3x + 4) - (2x^2 - 7)$?
   a. x^5
   b. $3x^2 - 3x + 11$
   c. $3x^2 - 3x - 3$
   d. $x - 3$
   e. $7x^2 - 3x - 3$

172

11. Kassidy drove for 3 hours at a speed of 60 miles per hour. Using the distance formula, $d = r \times t$ ($distance = rate \times time$), calculate how far Kassidy traveled.
   a. 20 miles
   b. 90 miles
   c. 65 miles
   d. 120 miles
   e. 180 miles

12. If $-3(x + 4) \geq x + 8$, what is the value of x?
   a. $x = 4$
   b. $x \geq 2$
   c. $x \geq -5$
   d. $x \leq -5$
   e. $x \leq 10$

13. Karen gets paid a weekly salary and a commission for every sale that she makes. The table below shows the number of sales and her pay for different weeks.

Sales	2	7	4	8
Pay	$380	$580	$460	$620

Which of the following equations represents Karen's weekly pay?
   a. $y = 90x + 200$
   b. $y = 90x - 200$
   c. $y = 40x + 300$
   d. $y = 40x - 300$
   e. $y = 40x + 200$

14. Which inequality represents the values displayed on the number line?

   a. $x < 1$
   b. $x \leq 1$
   c. $x > 1$
   d. $x \geq 1$
   e. $x \geq 5$

15. What is the 42nd item in the pattern: ▲○○□ ▲○○□ ▲ ...?
   a. ○
   b. ▲
   c. □
   d. ○○
   e. None of the above

173

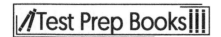
16. Which of the following statements is true about the two lines below?

    a. The two lines are parallel but not perpendicular.
    b. The two lines are perpendicular but not parallel.
    c. The two lines are both parallel and perpendicular.
    d. The two lines are neither parallel nor perpendicular.
    e. There is not enough information to determine their relationship.

17. Which of the following figures is NOT a polygon?
    a. Decagon
    b. Pentagon
    c. Triangle
    d. Rhombus
    e. Cone

18. What is the area of the regular hexagon shown below?

    a. 72
    b. 124.68
    c. 374.04
    d. 748.08
    e. 676.79

19. The area of a given rectangle is 24 cm^2. If the measure of each side is multiplied by 3, what is the area of the new figure?
    a. 48 cm^2
    b. 72 cm^2
    c. 111 cm^2
    d. 13,824 cm^2
    e. 216 cm^2

20. What are the coordinates of the point plotted on the grid?

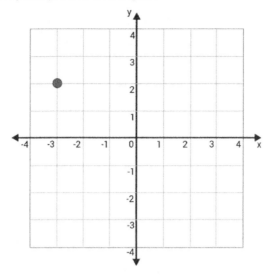

a. (-3, 2)
b. (2, -3)
c. (-3, -2)
d. (2, 3)
e. (3, 2)

21. The perimeter of a 6-sided polygon is 56 cm. The lengths of 3 sides are 9 cm each. The lengths of 2 other sides are 8 cm each. What is the length of the final side?

a. 11 cm
b. 12 cm
c. 13 cm
d. 10 cm
e. 9 cm

22. Katie works at a clothing company and sold 192 shirts over the weekend. One-third of the shirts that were sold were patterned, and the rest were solid. Which mathematical expression would calculate the number of solid shirts Katie sold over the weekend?

a. $192 \times \frac{1}{3}$

b. $192 \div \frac{1}{3}$

c. $192 \times (1 - \frac{1}{3})$

d. $192 \div 3$

e. $192 \div (1 - \frac{1}{3})$

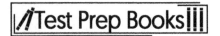

23. Which measure for the center of a small sample set is most affected by outliers?
    a. Mean
    b. Median
    c. Mode
    d. Range
    d. None of the above

24. Given the value of a particular stock at monthly intervals, which graph should be used to best represent the trend of the stock?
    a. Box plot
    b. Line plot
    c. Scatter plot
    d. Circle graph
    e. Line graph

25. Before a race of 4 horses, you make a random guess of which horse will get first place and which will get second place. What is the probability that both your guesses will be correct?
    a. $\frac{1}{4}$

    b. $\frac{1}{2}$

    c. $\frac{1}{16}$

    d. $\frac{1}{12}$

    e. $\frac{1}{3}$

26. Which of the following numbers has the greatest value?
    a. 1.43785
    b. 1.07548
    c. 1.43592
    d. 0.89409
    e. 0.94739

27. The value of 6×12 is the same as:
    a. $2 \times 4 \times 4 \times 2$
    b. $7 \times 4 \times 3$
    c. $6 \times 6 \times 3$
    d. $3 \times 3 \times 4 \times 2$
    e. $5 \times 9 \times 8$

28. This chart indicates how many sales of CDs, vinyl records, and MP3 downloads occurred over the last year. Approximately what percentage of the total sales was from CDs?

Total Sales of Vinyl Records, CDs, and MP3 Downloads (in millions)

Vinyl   ■ CD   ■ MP3

    a. 55%
    b. 25%
    c. 40%
    d. 5%
    e. 15%

29. After a 20% sale discount, Frank purchased a new refrigerator for $850. How much money did he save off of the original price?
    a. $170
    b. $212.50
    c. $105.75
    d. $200
    e. $187.50

30. Which of the following values is the largest?
    a. 0.45
    b. 0.096
    c. 0.3
    d. 0.313
    e. 0.25

31. What is the value of b in this equation?
$$5b - 4 = 2b + 17$$

    a. 13
    b. 24
    c. 7
    d. 21
    e. 15

32. A school's faculty consists of 15 teachers and 20 teaching assistants. They have 200 students. What is the ratio of faculty to students?
    a. $3:20$
    b. $4:17$
    c. $11:54$
    d. $3:2$
    e. $7:40$

33. Express the following in decimal form:

$$\frac{3}{5} \times \frac{7}{10} \div \frac{1}{2}$$

    a. 0.042
    b. 84%
    c. 0.84
    d. 0.42
    e. 0.084

34. A student gets an 85% on a test with 20 questions. How many questions did the student solve correctly?
    a. 15 questions
    b. 16 questions
    c. 17 questions
    d. 18 questions
    e. 19 questions

35. If Sarah reads at an average rate of 21 pages in 4 nights, how long will it take her to read 140 pages?
    a. 6 nights
    b. 26 nights
    c. 8 nights
    d. 27 nights
    e. 21 nights

36. Alan currently weighs 200 pounds, but he wants to lose weight to get down to 175 pounds. What is this difference in kilograms? (1 pound is approximately equal to 0.45 kilograms.)
    a. 9 kg
    b. 25 kg
    c. 78.75 kg
    d. 90 kg
    e. 11.25 kg

37. Johnny earns $2,334.50 from his job each month. He pays $1,437 for monthly expenses and saves the rest. Johnny is planning a vacation in 3 months that he estimates will cost $1,750 total. How much will Johnny have left over from 3 months of saving once he pays for his vacation?
    a. $948.50
    b. $584.50
    c. $852.50
    d. $942.50
    e. $742.50

38. What is $\frac{420}{98}$ rounded to the nearest integer?
   a. 6
   b. 4
   c. 3
   d. 5
   e. 2

39. Solve the following:

$$4 \times 7 + (25 - 21)^2 \div 2$$

   a. 512
   b. 36
   c. 60.5
   d. 22
   e. 16

40. The total perimeter of a rectangle is 36 cm. If the length is 12 cm, what is the width?
   a. 3 cm
   b. 12 cm
   c. 9 cm
   d. 8 cm
   e. 6 cm

41. Dwayne has received the following scores on his math tests: 78, 92, 83, 97. What score must Dwayne get on his next math test to have an overall average of 90?
   a. 89
   b. 98
   c. 95
   d. 94
   e. 100

42. What is the overall median of Dwayne's current scores: 78, 92, 83, 97?
   a. 80.5
   b. 85
   c. 83
   d. 87.5
   e. 86

43. Evaluate:

$$\left(\sqrt{36} \times \sqrt{16}\right) - 3^2$$

   a. 30
   b. 21
   c. 15
   d. 13
   e. 25

44. In Jim's school, there are a total of 650 students. There are three girls for every two boys. How many students are girls?
   a. 260 girls
   b. 130 girls
   c. 65 girls
   d. 390 girls
   e. 410 girls

45. Solve the following:

$$3 \times 8 - (2+1)^2 + 8$$

   a. 23
   b. 7
   c. 24
   d. 17
   e. 18

46. Kimberley earns $10 an hour babysitting, and after 10 p.m., she earns $12 an hour. The time she works is rounded to the nearest hour for pay purposes. On her last job, she worked from 5:30 p.m. to 11:00 p.m. In total, how much did Kimberley earn on her last job?
   a. $45
   b. $57
   c. $62
   d. $42
   e. $53

47. What value of x would solve the following equation?

$$9x + x - 7 = 16 + 2x$$

   a. $x = -4$
   b. $x = 3$
   c. $x = \frac{9}{8}$
   d. $x = \frac{23}{8}$
   e. $x = \frac{3}{4}$

48. Arrange the following numbers from least to greatest value:

$$0.85, \frac{4}{5}, \frac{2}{3}, \frac{91}{100}$$

   a. $0.85, \frac{4}{5}, \frac{2}{3}, \frac{91}{100}$
   b. $\frac{4}{5}, 0.85, \frac{91}{100}, \frac{2}{3}$
   c. $\frac{2}{3}, \frac{4}{5}, 0.85, \frac{91}{100}$
   d. $0.85, \frac{91}{100}, \frac{4}{5}, \frac{2}{3}$
   e. $\frac{4}{5}, \frac{91}{100}, \frac{2}{3}, 0.85$

180

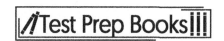

49. Keith's bakery had 252 customers go through its doors last week. This week, that number increased to 378. Express this increase as a percentage.
    a. 26%
    b. 50%
    c. 35%
    d. 12%
    e. 18%

50. If $4x - 3 = 5$, what is the value of x?
    a. 1
    b. 2
    c. 3
    d. 4
    e. 5

Reading Comprehension

Questions 1 – 5 are based on the following passage.

George Washington emerged out of the American Revolution as an unlikely champion of liberty. On June 14, 1775, the Second Continental Congress created the Continental Army, and John Adams, serving in the Congress, nominated Washington to be its first commander. Washington had fought under the British during the French and Indian War, and his experience and prestige proved instrumental to the American war effort. Washington provided invaluable leadership, training, and strategy during the Revolutionary War. He emerged from the war as the embodiment of liberty and freedom from tyranny.

After vanquishing the heavily favored British forces, Washington could have pronounced himself the autocratic leader of the former colonies without any opposition, but he famously refused and returned to his Mount Vernon plantation. His restraint proved his commitment to the fledgling state's republicanism. Washington was later unanimously elected as the first American president. But it is Washington's farewell address that cemented his legacy as a visionary worthy of study.

In 1796, President Washington issued his farewell address by public letter. Washington enlisted his good friend, Alexander Hamilton, in drafting his most famous address. The letter expressed Washington's faith in the Constitution and rule of law. He encouraged his fellow Americans to put aside partisan differences and establish a national union. Washington warned Americans against meddling in foreign affairs and entering military alliances. Additionally, he stated his opposition to national political parties, which he considered partisan and counterproductive.

Americans would be wise to remember Washington's farewell, especially during presidential elections, when politics hit a fever pitch. They might want to question the political institutions that were not planned by the Founding Fathers, such as the nomination process and political parties themselves.

1. Which of the following statements is based on the information in the passage above?
   a. George Washington's background as a wealthy landholder directly led to his faith in equality, liberty, and democracy.
   b. George Washington would have opposed America's involvement in the Second World War.
   c. George Washington would not have been able to write as great a farewell address without the assistance of Alexander Hamilton.
   d. George Washington would probably not approve of modern political parties.
   e. George Washington would likely befriend former President Barack Obama.

2. What is the purpose of this passage?
   a. To caution American voters about being too political during election times because George Washington would not have agreed with holding elections
   b. To introduce George Washington to readers as a historical figure worthy of study
   c. To note that George Washington was more than a famous military hero
   d. To convince readers that George Washington is a hero of republicanism and liberty
   e. To inform American voters about a Founding Father's sage advice on a contemporary issue and explain its applicability to modern times

3. What is the tone of the passage?
   a. Informative
   b. Excited
   c. Bitter
   d. Comic
   e. Somber

4. What does the word *meddling* mean in paragraph 3?
   a. Supporting
   b. Speaking against
   c. Interfering
   d. Gathering
   e. Avoiding

5. According to the passage, what did George Washington do when he was offered a role as leader of the former colonies?
   a. He refused the offer.
   b. He accepted the offer.
   c. He became angry at the offer.
   d. He accepted the offer then regretted it later.
   e. He ignored the offer.

Questions 6 – 10 are based on the following passage:

Christopher Columbus is often credited with discovering America. This is incorrect. First, it is impossible to "discover" something where people already live; however, Christopher Columbus did explore places in the New World that were previously untouched by Europe, so the term "explorer" would be more accurate. Another correction must be made, as well: Christopher Columbus was not the first European explorer to reach the Americas! Rather, it was Leif Erikson who first came to the New World and contacted the natives, nearly five hundred years before Christopher Columbus.

182

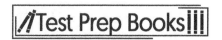

Leif Erikson, the son of Erik the Red (a famous Viking outlaw and explorer in his own right), was born in either 970 or 980, depending on which historian you read. His own family, though, did not raise Leif, which was a Viking tradition. Instead, one of Erik's prisoners taught Leif reading and writing, languages, sailing, and weaponry. At age 12, Leif was considered a man and returned to his family. He killed a man during a dispute shortly after his return, and the council banished the Erikson clan to Greenland.

In 999, Leif left Greenland and traveled to Norway, where he would serve as a guard to King Olaf Tryggvason. It was there that he became a convert to Christianity. Leif later tried to return home with the intention of taking supplies and spreading Christianity to Greenland, but his ship was blown off course and he arrived in a strange new land: present-day Newfoundland, Canada.

When he finally returned to his adopted homeland of Greenland, Leif consulted with a merchant who had also seen the shores of this previously unknown land. The son of the legendary Viking explorer then gathered a crew of 35 men and set sail. Leif became the first European to set foot in the New World as he explored present-day Baffin Island and Labrador, Canada. His crew called the land Vinland since it was plentiful with grapes.

During their time in present-day Newfoundland, Leif's expedition made contact with the natives, whom they referred to as Skraelings (which translates to "wretched ones" in Norse). There are several secondhand accounts of their meetings. Some contemporaries described trade between the peoples. Other accounts describe clashes where the Skraelings defeated the Viking explorers with long spears, while still others claim the Vikings dominated the natives. Regardless of the circumstances, it seems that the Vikings made contact of some kind. This happened around 1000, nearly 500 years before Columbus famously sailed the ocean blue.

Eventually, in 1003, Leif set sail for home and arrived at Greenland with a ship full of timber.

In 1020, 17 years later, the legendary Viking died. Many believe that Leif Erikson should receive more credit for his contributions in exploring the New World.

6. Which of the following best describes how the author generally presents the information?
   a. Chronological order
   b. Comparison-contrast
   c. Cause-effect
   d. Conclusion-premises
   e. Spatial order

7. Which of the following is an opinion, rather than a historical fact, expressed by the author?
   a. Leif Erikson was definitely the son of Erik the Red; however, historians debate the year of his birth.
   b. Leif Erikson's crew called the land Vinland since it was plentiful with grapes.
   c. Leif Erikson deserves more credit for his contributions in exploring the New World.
   d. Leif Erikson explored the Americas nearly 500 years before Christopher Columbus.
   e. Leif's expedition made contact with the natives whom they referred to as Skraelings.

8. Which of the following most accurately describes the author's main conclusion?
   a. Leif Erikson is a legendary Viking explorer.
   b. Leif Erikson deserves more credit for exploring America hundreds of years before Columbus.
   c. Spreading Christianity motivated Leif Erikson's expeditions more than any other factor.
   d. Leif Erikson contacted the natives nearly five hundred years before Columbus.
   e. Leif Erikson discovered the Americas.

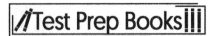

9. Which of the following best describes the author's intent in the passage?
   a. To entertain
   b. To inform
   c. To alert
   d. To suggest
   e. To share

10. Which of the following can be logically inferred from the passage?
    a. The Vikings disliked exploring the New World.
    b. Leif Erikson's banishment from Iceland led to his exploration of present-day Canada.
    c. Leif Erikson never shared his stories of exploration with the King of Norway.
    d. Historians have difficulty definitively pinpointing events in the Vikings' history.
    e. Christopher Columbus knew of Leif Erikson's explorations.

Questions 11 – 15 are based on the following passage:

Smoking is Terrible

Smoking tobacco products is terribly destructive. A single cigarette contains over 4,000 chemicals, including 43 known carcinogens and 400 deadly toxins. Some of the most dangerous ingredients include tar, carbon monoxide, formaldehyde, ammonia, arsenic, and DDT. Smoking can cause numerous types of cancer, including throat, mouth, nasal cavity, esophageal, gastric, pancreatic, renal, bladder, and cervical cancer.

Cigarettes contain a drug called nicotine, one of the most addictive substances known. Addiction is defined as a compulsion to seek the substance despite negative consequences. According to the National Institute on Drug Abuse, nearly 35 million smokers expressed a desire to quit smoking in 2015; however, more than 85 percent of those who struggle with addiction will not achieve their goal. Almost all smokers regret picking up that first cigarette. You would be wise to learn from their mistake if you have not yet started smoking.

According to the US Department of Health and Human Services, 16 million people in the United States presently suffer from a smoking-related condition, and nearly nine million suffer from a serious smoking-related illness. According to the Centers for Disease Control and Prevention (CDC), tobacco products cause nearly six million deaths per year. This number is projected to rise to over eight million deaths by 2030. Smokers, on average, die ten years earlier than their nonsmoking peers.

In the United States, local, state, and federal governments typically tax tobacco products, which leads to high prices. Nicotine users who struggle with addiction sometimes pay more for a pack of cigarettes than for a few gallons of gas. Additionally, smokers tend to stink. The smell of smoke is all-consuming and creates a pervasive nastiness. Smokers also risk staining their teeth and fingers with yellow residue from the tar.

Smoking is deadly, expensive, and socially unappealing. Clearly, smoking is not worth the risks.

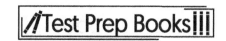

11. Which of the following statements most accurately summarizes the passage?
    a. Almost all smokers regret picking up that first cigarette.
    b. Tobacco is deadly, expensive, and socially unappealing, and smokers would be much better off kicking the addiction.
    c. In the United States, local, state, and federal governments typically tax tobacco products, which leads to high prices.
    d. Tobacco products shorten smokers' lives by ten years and kill more than six million people per year.
    e. Tobacco is less healthy than many alternatives.

12. The author would be most likely to agree with which of the following statements?
    a. Nicotine users who struggle with addiction sometimes pay more for a pack of cigarettes than for a few gallons of gas.
    b. Other substances are more addictive than tobacco.
    c. Smokers should quit for whatever reason gets them to stop smoking.
    d. People who want to continue smoking should advocate for a reduction in tobacco product taxes.
    e. Smokers don't have the desire to quit and often don't see their smoking as a bad habit.

13. Which of the following is the author's opinion?
    a. According to the Centers for Disease Control and Prevention (CDC), tobacco products cause nearly six million deaths per year.
    b. Nicotine users who struggle with addiction sometimes pay more for a pack of cigarettes than a few gallons of gas.
    c. Smokers also risk staining their teeth and fingers with yellow residue from the tar.
    d. Additionally, smokers tend to stink. The smell of smoke is all-consuming and creates a pervasive nastiness.
    e. Smokers, on average, die ten years earlier than their nonsmoking peers.

14. What is the tone of this passage?
    a. Objective
    b. Cautionary
    c. Indifferent
    d. Admiring
    e. Philosophical

15. What does the word *pervasive* mean in paragraph 4?
    a. Pleasantly appealing
    b. A floral scent
    c. To convince someone
    d. Difficult to sense
    e. All over the place

Questions 16 – 20 are based on the following passage.

The Myth of Head Heat Loss

It has recently been brought to my attention that most people believe that 75% of your body heat is lost through your head. I had certainly heard this before, and I'm not going to attempt to say I didn't believe it when I first heard it. It is natural to be gullible to anything said with enough authority. But the "fact" that the majority of your body heat is lost through your head is a lie.

Let me explain. Heat loss is proportional to surface area exposed. An elephant loses a great deal more heat than an anteater because it has a much greater surface area than an anteater. Each cell has mitochondria that produce energy in the form of heat, and it takes a lot more energy to run an elephant than an anteater.

So, each part of your body loses its proportional amount of heat in accordance with its surface area. The human torso probably loses the most heat, though the legs lose a significant amount as well. Some people have asked, "Why does it feel so much warmer when you cover your head than when you don't?" Well, that's because your head loses a lot of heat when it is not clothed, while the clothing on the rest of your body provides insulation. If you went outside with a hat and pants but no shirt, not only would you look silly, but your heat loss would be significantly greater because so much more of you would be exposed. So, if given the choice to cover your chest or your head in the cold, choose the chest. It could save your life.

16. Why does the author compare elephants and anteaters?
    a. To express an opinion
    b. To give an example that helps clarify the main point
    c. To show the differences between the two
    d. To persuade why one is better than the other
    e. To educate about animals

17. Which of the following best describes the tone of the passage?
    a. Harsh
    b. Angry
    c. Casual
    d. Indifferent
    e. Comical

18. The author appeals to which branch of rhetoric to prove their case?
    a. Expert testimony
    b. Emotion
    c. Ethics and morals
    d. Author qualification
    e. Factual evidence

19. What does the word *gullible* mean in paragraph 1?
    a. To be angry toward
    b. To distrust something
    c. To believe something easily
    d. To be happy toward
    e. To be frightened

20. What is the main idea of the passage?
    a. To illustrate how people can easily believe anything they are told
    b. To prove that you have to have a hat to survive in the cold
    c. To persuade the audience that anteaters are better than elephants
    d. To convince the audience that heat loss comes mostly from the head
    e. To debunk the myth that heat loss comes mostly from the head

This article discusses the famous poet and playwright William Shakespeare. Read it and answer questions 21 – 25.

People who argue that William Shakespeare is not responsible for the plays attributed to his name are known as anti-Stratfordians (from the name of Shakespeare's birthplace, Stratford-upon-Avon). The most

186

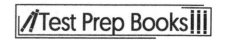

common anti-Stratfordian claim is that William Shakespeare simply was not educated enough or from a high enough social class to have written plays overflowing with references to such a wide range of subjects like history, the classics, religion, and international culture. William Shakespeare was the son of a glove-maker, he only had a basic grade-school education, and he never set foot outside of England—so how could he have produced plays of such sophistication and imagination? How could he have written in such detail about historical figures and events, or about different cultures and locations around Europe? According to anti-Stratfordians, the depth of knowledge contained in Shakespeare's plays suggests a well-traveled writer from a wealthy background with a university education, not a countryside writer like Shakespeare. But in fact, there is not much substance to such speculation, and most anti-Stratfordian arguments can be refuted with a little background about Shakespeare's time and upbringing.

First of all, those who doubt Shakespeare's authorship often point to his common birth and brief education as stumbling blocks to his writerly genius. Although it is true that Shakespeare did not come from a noble class, his father was a very *successful* glove-maker and his mother was from a very wealthy landowning family—so while Shakespeare may have had a country upbringing, he was certainly from a well-off family and would have been educated accordingly. Also, even though he did not attend university, grade-school education in Shakespeare's time was actually quite rigorous and exposed students to classic drama through writers like Seneca and Ovid. It is not unreasonable to believe that Shakespeare received a very solid foundation in poetry and literature from his early schooling.

Next, anti-Stratfordians tend to question how Shakespeare could write so extensively about countries and cultures he had never visited before. For instance, several of his most famous works like *Romeo and Juliet* and *The Merchant of Venice* were set in Italy, which is located on the opposite side of Europe from England. But again, this criticism does not hold up under scrutiny. For one thing, Shakespeare was living in London, a bustling metropolis of international trade, the most populous city in England, and a political and cultural hub of Europe. In the daily crowds of people, Shakespeare would certainly have been able to meet travelers from other countries and hear firsthand accounts of life in their home country. And, in addition to the influx of information from world travelers, this was also the age of the printing press. This jump in technology made it possible to print and circulate books much more easily than in the past. This also facilitated a freer flow of information across different countries, allowing people to read about life and ideas from all over Europe. One needn't travel the continent in order to learn and write about its different cultures.

21. Which sentence contains the author's thesis?
   a. People who argue that William Shakespeare is not responsible for the plays attributed to his name are known as anti-Stratfordians.
   b. First of all, those who doubt Shakespeare's authorship often point to his common birth and brief education as stumbling blocks to his writerly genius.
   c. It is not unreasonable to believe that Shakespeare received a very solid foundation in poetry and literature from his early schooling.
   d. Next, anti-Stratfordians tend to question how Shakespeare could write so extensively about countries and cultures he had never visited before.
   e. But in fact, there is not much substance to such speculation, and most anti-Stratfordian arguments can be refuted with a little background about Shakespeare's time and upbringing.

22. In the first paragraph, "How could he have written in such detail about historical figures and events, or about different cultures and locations around Europe?" is an example of which of the following?
    a. Hyperbole
    b. Onomatopoeia
    c. Rhetorical question
    d. Appeal to authority
    e. Figurative language

23. How does the author respond to the claim that Shakespeare was not well-educated because he did not attend university?
    a. By insisting upon Shakespeare's natural genius
    b. By explaining grade-school curriculum in Shakespeare's time
    c. By comparing Shakespeare with other uneducated writers of his time
    d. By pointing out that Shakespeare's wealthy parents probably paid for private tutors
    e. By discussing Shakespeare's upbringing in London which was a political and cultural hub of Europe

24. The word *bustling* in the third paragraph most nearly means which of the following?
    a. Busy
    b. Foreign
    c. Expensive
    d. Undeveloped
    e. Quiet

25. According to the passage, what did Shakespeare's father do to make a living?
    a. He was a king's guard.
    b. He acted in plays.
    c. He was a glove-maker.
    d. He was a cobbler.
    e. He was a musician.

Questions 26 – 30 are based on the following passage:

Do you want to vacation at a Caribbean island destination? We chose to go to St. Lucia, and it was the best vacation we ever had. We lounged in crystal blue waters, swam with dolphins, and enjoyed a family-friendly resort and activities. One of the activities we did was free diving in the ocean. We put our snorkels on, waded into the ocean, and swam down to the ocean floor. The water was clear all the way down—the greens and blues were so beautiful. We saw a stingray, some conches, and a Caribbean Reef Shark. The shark was so scary, I came up to the surface after that! But the rest of the day was spent lying on the beach, getting massages, and watching other kids play with a Frisbee in front of the water.

Towards the end of our vacation, I was reluctant to go home. We started to pack our things, and then I realized I wanted to take one more walk with my mom and dad. Our resort was between the ocean and some mountains, so we decided to hike up a mountain and enjoy the view of the beach from way up high! We trekked for what seemed like miles, observing the vegetation along the way; it was so lush with reds and greens and blues. Finally, we got up to the top of the mountain and observed the wonderful ocean that stretched on for hundreds of miles. On our way back down, I felt totally at peace to be leaving the island, although I would miss it very much and would want to visit the island again soon. You should visit St. Lucia, or pick another island in the Caribbean! Every island offers a unique and dazzling vacation destination.

26. What island did the family stay on?
    a. St. Lucia
    b. Barbados
    c. Antigua
    d. Saint Kitts
    e. Aruba

27. What is/are the supporting detail(s) of this passage?
    a. Cruising to the Caribbean
    b. Local events
    c. Family activities
    d. Exotic cuisine
    e. All of the above

28. What was the last activity the speaker did?
    a. Swam with the sharks
    b. Went for a hike up a mountain
    c. Lounged on the beach
    d. Surfed in the waves
    e. Received a massage

29. Which of the following is the best definition for the word *trekked* in the second paragraph?
    a. Drove
    b. Ran
    c. Swam
    d. Sang
    e. Walked

30. Which of the following words best describes the author's attitude toward the topic?
    a. Worried
    b. Resigned
    c. Objective
    d. Enthusiastic
    e. Apathetic

Questions 31 – 35 are based on the following passage:

Even though the rain can put a damper on the day, it can be helpful and fun, too. For one, the rain helps plants grow. Without rain, grass, flowers, and trees would be deprived of vital nutrients they need to develop. It's like how humans need water to survive; plants also need water to survive and flourish and keep that wonderful green color instead of turning brown.

Not only does the rain help plants grow, but on days where there are brief spurts of sunshine, rainbows can appear. The rain reflects and refracts the light, creating beautiful rainbows in the sky. One time I was on a trip with my brother across the United States. Before the trip, we said that we wanted to see a rainbow in every state we went through. We ended up driving through eleven states, and guess what? We saw fifteen rainbows, at least one in each state. What an incredible trip!

Finally, puddle jumping is another fun activity that can be done in or after the rain. Whenever there are heavy thunderstorms, I always look forward to when the storm lifts. I usually go outside right after, because there are a lot of families in my neighborhood, and I love to watch all the children jump, skip, and splash in

189

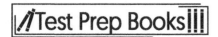

the puddles. The bigger kids create huge torrents of water and the smaller kids create little splashes. Thinking about all the positive things rain brings to us, I know that rain can be helpful and fun.

31. What is the *cause* in this passage?
    a. Plants growing
    b. Rainbows
    c. Puddle jumping
    d. Rain
    e. Interstate trip

32. In the following sentence, the author is using what literary device regarding the grass, flowers, and trees? "Without rain, grass, flowers, and trees would be deprived of vital nutrients they need to develop."

    a. Comparing
    b. Contrasting
    c. Describing
    d. Transitioning
    e. Imagery

33. In the same sentence from above, what is most likely the meaning of *vital?*
    a. Energetic
    b. Truthful
    c. Lively
    d. Dangerous
    e. Necessary

34. What is an *effect* in this passage?
    a. Rain
    b. Brief spurts of sunshine
    c. Rainbows
    d. Weather
    e. Thunderstorms

35. What kind of evidence does the author use most in this passage?
    a. Interviews
    b. Personal testimonies
    c. Journal articles
    d. Statistics
    e. Analogical comparison

Questions 36 – 40 are based on the following passage.

Sylvia's father was a beekeeper and Sylvia loved watching him take care of bees. When he was gone to work, Sylvia would stealthily try to find bees in her garden and pretend like she was her father on a magnificent mission to save all the bees she came into contact with. She really just wanted to be helpful. So, she started to pick out all the bees (she wasn't afraid of the stingers, though she had been stung several times in the past), and put them in jars in her house so that they could all be safe from harm.

One day Sylvia's mother walked into her bedroom and noticed that Sylvia had a large container that her mother had never seen before. When Sylvia's mother opened the container, a swarm of bees flew out and started to buzz around her mother's head! Sylvia's mother screamed and ran out of the room, her face scrunched in

190

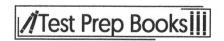

terror. Sylvia was outside playing, and when she saw her mother run out of the house, Sylvia knew immediately what had happened. Her mother found the bee jar! She quickly helped her mother swat away the bees and told her mother that she just wanted to help the bees stay safe from the outside harms that could come to them. "Sylvia," her mother said, "Do you feel afraid when you are outside?" "No," Sylvia replied. "I feel safe, and I have lots of fun out here." "Well," her mother said, "the bees are just like you! They love the sunlight, and the flowers are so important to them they fly around them all day and never get tired. Leave the bees outside, and they will thank you for it." Sylvia laughed at her own thoughts and knew that the bees would be safer outside, away from her terrified mother and into the hands of nature.

36. What does the word *stealthily* mean in the first paragraph?
    a. Hurriedly
    b. Begrudgingly
    c. Confidently
    d. Secretly
    e. Efficiently

37. What point of view is the story written in?
    a. First person
    b. Second person
    c. Third person
    d. No person
    e. None of the above

38. According to the passage, why did Sylvia want to keep the bees inside a jar?
    a. She wanted to conduct a science experiment with them.
    b. She wanted to learn how to work as a beekeeper.
    c. She wanted to bring them as a gift to her father.
    d. She wanted to use them to scare her mother.
    e. She wanted to keep them away from harm.

39. What organization does this passage use?
    a. Chronological
    b. Cause and effect
    c. Problem to solution
    d. Sequential
    e. Order of importance

40. Which of the following most closely matches the theme of the passage?
    a. Loss/Grief
    b. Friendship
    c. Freedom
    d. Suffering
    e. Growth

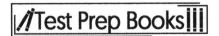

Verbal Section

Synonyms

1. DEDUCE
   a. Explain
   b. Win
   c. Reason
   d. Gamble
   e. Undo

2. ELUCIDATE
   a. Learn
   b. Enlighten
   c. Plan
   d. Corroborate
   e. Conscious

3. VERIFY
   a. Criticize
   b. Change
   c. Teach
   d. Substantiate
   e. Resolve

4. INSPIRE
   a. Motivate
   b. Impale
   c. Exercise
   d. Patronize
   e. Collaborate

5. PERCEIVE
   a. Sustain
   b. Collect
   c. Prove
   d. Lead
   e. Comprehend

6. NOMAD
   a. Munching
   b. Propose
   c. Wanderer
   d. Conscientious
   e. Blissful

7. PERPLEXED
   a. Annoyed
   b. Vengeful
   c. Injured
   d. Confused
   e. Prepared

8. LYRICAL
   a. Whimsical
   b. Vague
   c. Fruitful
   d. Expressive
   e. Playful

9. BREVITY
   a. Dullness
   b. Dangerous
   c. Brief
   d. Ancient
   e. Calamity

10. IRATE
   a. Anger
   b. Knowledge
   c. Tired
   d. Confused
   e. Taciturn

11. LUXURIOUS
   a. Faded
   b. Bright
   c. Lavish
   d. Inconsiderate
   e. Overwhelming

12. IMMOBILE
   a. Fast
   b. Slow
   c. Eloquent
   d. Vivacious
   e. Sedentary

13. OVERBEARING
   a. Neglect
   b. Domineering
   c. Clandestine
   d. Formidable
   e. Amicable

14. PREVENT
   a. Avert
   b. Rejoice
   c. Endow
   d. Fulfill
   e. Ensure

15. REPLENISH
   a. Falsify
   b. Hindsight
   c. Dwell
   d. Refresh
   e. Nominate

16. REGALE
   a. Remember
   b. Grow
   c. Outnumber
   d. Entertain
   e. Bore

17. WEARY
   a. tired
   b. clothing
   c. happy
   d. hot
   e. whiny

18. VAST
   a. Rapid
   b. Expansive
   c. Small
   d. Ocean
   e. Uniform

19. DEMONSTRATE
   a. Tell
   b. Show
   c. Build
   d. Complete
   e. Make

20. ORCHARD
   a. Flower
   b. Fruit
   c. Grove
   d. Peach
   e. Farm

21. TEXTILE
    a. Fabric
    b. Document
    c. Mural
    d. Ornament
    e. Knit

22. OFFSPRING
    a. Bounce
    b. Parent
    c. Music
    d. Child
    e. Skip

23. PERMIT
    a. Law
    b. Parking
    c. Crab
    d. Jail
    e. Allow

24. WOMAN
    a. Man
    b. Lady
    c. Women
    d. Girl
    e. Mother

25. ROTATION
    a. Wheel
    b. Year
    c. Spin
    d. Flip
    e. Orbit

26. CONSISTENT
    a. Stubborn
    b. Contains
    c. Sticky
    d. Texture
    e. Steady

27. PRINCIPLE
    a. Principal
    b. Leader
    c. President
    d. Foundation
    e. Royal

28. PERIMETER
    a. Outline
    b. Area
    c. Side
    d. Volume
    e. Inside

29. SYMBOL
    a. Drum
    b. Music
    c. Clang
    d. Emblem
    e. Text

30. GERMINATE
    a. Doctor
    b. Sick
    c. Infect
    d. Plants
    e. Grow

Verbal Analogies

1. Cat is to paws as
    a. giraffe is to neck.
    b. elephant is to ears.
    c. horse is to hooves.
    d. snake is to skin.
    e. turtle is to shell.

2. *Dancing* is to *rhythm* as *singing* is to
    a. pitch.
    b. mouth.
    c. sound.
    d. volume.
    e. words.

3. *Towel* is to *dry* as *hat* is to
    a. cold.
    b. warm.
    c. expose.
    d. cover.
    e. top.

4. *Sand* is to *glass* as
    a. protons are to atoms.
    b. ice is to snow.
    c. seeds are to plants.
    d. water is to steam.
    e. air is to wind.

5. Design is to create as allocate is to
   a. finish.
   b. manage.
   c. multiply.
   d. find.
   e. distribute.

6. *Books* are to *reading* as
   a. movies are to making.
   b. shows are to watching.
   c. poetry is to writing.
   d. scenes are to performing.
   e. concerts are to music.

7. *Cool* is to *frigid* as *warm* is to
   a. toasty.
   b. summer.
   c. sweltering.
   d. hot.
   e. mild.

8. Cereal boxes are to rectangular prisms as globes are to
   a. circles.
   b. maps.
   c. wheels.
   d. spheres.
   e. movement.

9. Backpacks are to textbooks as
   a. houses are to people.
   b. fences are to trees.
   c. plates are to food.
   d. chalkboards are to chalk.
   e. computers are to mice.

10. *Storm* is to *rainbow* as *sunset* is to
    a. clouds.
    b. sunrise.
    c. breakfast.
    d. bedtime.
    e. stars.

11. *Falcon* is to *mice* as *giraffe* is to
    a. leaves.
    b. rocks.
    c. antelope.
    d. grasslands.
    e. hamsters.

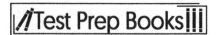

12. Car is to motorcycle as speedboat is to
    a. raft.
    b. jet-ski.
    c. sailboat.
    d. plane.
    e. canoe.

13. *Arid* is to *damp* as *anxious* is to
    a. happy.
    b. petrified.
    c. ireful.
    d. confident.
    e. sorrowful.

14. *Mechanic* is to *repair* as
    a. mongoose is to cobra.
    b. rider is to bicycle.
    c. tree is to grow.
    d. food is to eaten.
    e. doctor is to heal.

15. Whistle is to blow horn as painting is to
    a. view.
    b. criticize.
    c. sculpture.
    d. painter.
    e. paintbrush.

16. *Paddle* is to *boat* as *keys* are to
    a. unlock.
    b. success.
    c. illuminate.
    d. piano.
    e. keychain.

17. *Mountain* is to *peak* as *wave* is to
    a. ocean.
    b. surf.
    c. fountain.
    d. wavelength.
    e. crest.

18. Fluent is to communication as
    a. crater is to catastrophe.
    b. gourmet is to cooking.
    c. ink is to pen.
    d. crow is to raven.
    e. whistle is to whistler.

19. Validate is to verify as conquer is to
    a. withdraw.
    b. subjugate.
    c. expand.
    d. surrender.
    e. expose.

20. *Winter* is to *autumn* as *summer* is to
    a. vacation.
    b. fall.
    c. spring.
    d. march.
    e. weather.

21. Fiberglass is to surfboard as
    a. bamboo is to panda.
    b. capital is to D.C.
    c. copper is to penny.
    d. flint is to knapping.
    e. wind is to windmill.

22. *Myth* is to *explain* as *joke* is to
    a. enlighten.
    b. inspire.
    c. collect.
    d. laughter.
    e. amuse.

23. *Cow* is to *milk* as
    a. horse is to cow
    b. egg is to chicken
    c. chicken is to egg
    d. glass is to milk
    e. milk is to glass

24. *Web* is to *spider* as *den* is to
    a. living room
    b. eagle
    c. fox
    d. dog
    e. turtle

25. *Sad* is to *blue* as *happy* is to
    a. glad
    b. yellow
    c. smiling
    d. laugh
    e. calm

26. *Door* is to *store* as *deal* is to
    a. money
    b. purchase
    c. sell
    d. wheel
    e. market

27. *Dog* is to *veterinarian* as *baby* is to
    a. daycare
    b. mother
    c. puppy
    d. babysitter
    e. pediatrician

28. *Clock* is to *time* as
    a. ruler is to length
    b. jet is to speed
    c. alarm is to sleep
    d. drum is to beat
    e. watch is to wrist

29. *Wire* is to *electricity* as
    a. power is to lamp
    b. pipe is to water
    c. fire is to heat
    d. heat is to fire
    e. water is to pipe

30. President is to Executive Branch as _____ is to Judicial Branch.
    a. Supreme Court Justice
    b. Judge
    c. Senator
    d. Lawyer
    e. Congressmen

SSAT Answer Explanations

Quantitative Reasoning

1. D: Digits to the left of the decimal point represent the digit value times increasing multiples of 10 (first 1, then 10, 100, 1,000, and so on). Digits to the right of the decimal point represent the digit value divided by increasing multiples of 10 (first $\frac{1}{10}$, then $\frac{1}{100}$, $\frac{1}{1000}$, and so on). So, the second digit to the right of the decimal point equals the digit value divided by 100.

2. B: The power of 10 by which a digit is multiplied corresponds with the number of zeros following the digit when expressing its value in standard form. Therefore:

$$(1 \times 10^4) + (3 \times 10^3) + (7 \times 10^1) + (8 \times 10^0)$$

$$10,000 + 3,000 + 70 + 8$$

$$13,078$$

3. E: The hundredths place value is located two digits to the right of the decimal point (the digit 9 in the original number). To decide whether to round up or keep the digit, examine the digit to the right, and if it is 5 or greater, round up. In this case, the digit to the right is 6, so the hundredths place is rounded up. When rounding up, if the digit to be increased is a 9, the digit to its left is increased by one and the digit in the desired place value is made a zero. Therefore, the number is rounded to 847.90.

4. B: Fractions must have like denominators to be added. The common denominator is the least common multiple (LCM) of the two original denominators. In this case, the LCM is 15, so both fractions should be changed to equivalent fractions with a denominator of 15. Multiply the bottom of each fraction by whatever number is needed to produce 15, and multiply the top of each fraction by that same number:

$$\frac{1 \times 5}{3 \times 5} = \frac{5}{15} \text{ and } \frac{2 \times 3}{5 \times 3} = \frac{6}{15}$$

Now, add the numerators and keep the denominator the same:

$$\frac{5}{15} + \frac{6}{15} = \frac{11}{15}$$

5. C: When performing calculations consisting of more than one operation, the order of operations should be followed: parentheses, exponents, multiplication & division, addition & subtraction.

Parentheses:

$$7^2 - 3 \times (4 + 2) + 15 \div 5$$

$$7^2 - 3 \times (6) + 15 \div 5$$

Exponents:

$$49 - 3 \times 6 + 15 \div 5$$

201

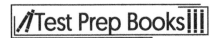

Multiplication & division (from left to right):

$$49 - 18 + 3$$

Addition & subtraction (from left to right):

$$49 - 18 + 3 = 34$$

6. D: To convert a fraction to a percent, the fraction is first converted to a decimal. To do so, the numerator is divided by the denominator:

$$4 \div 5 = 0.8$$

To convert a decimal to a percent, the number is multiplied by 100:

$$0.8 \times 100 = 80\%$$

7. C: To solve the problem, we can write a proportion consisting of ratios comparing distance and time. One way to set up the proportion is: $\frac{3}{48} = \frac{5}{x}$. x represents the unknown value of time. To solve this proportion, we can cross-multiply:

$$(3)(x) = (5)(48) \text{ or } 3x = 240$$

To isolate the variable, we divide by 3 on both sides, getting $x = 80$.

8. D: A given number divides evenly by each of its factors to produce an integer (no decimals). To find the factors of 12, determine what whole numbers when multiplied equal 12. 1×12, 2×6, and 3×4 are all the ways to multiply to 12 using whole numbers, so the factors of 12 are: 1, 2, 3, 4, 6, 12.

9. B: To determine the number of houses that can fit on the street, we can divide the length of the street by the width of each house's property:

$$345 \div 30 = 11.5$$

However, the construction company is not going to build half a house, so they will need to build either 11 or 12 houses. Since the width of 12 houses (360 feet) would extend past the length of the street, only 11 houses can be built.

10. B: By distributing the implied 1 in front of the first set of parentheses and the negative one in front of the second set of parentheses, the parentheses can be eliminated:

$$1(5x^2 - 3x + 4) - 1(2x^2 - 7)$$

$$5x^2 - 3x + 4 - 2x^2 + 7$$

Next, like terms are combined by adding the coefficients of the same variables with the same exponents, while keeping the variables and their powers unchanged:

$$5x^2 - 3x + 4 - 2x^2 + 7$$

$$3x^2 - 3x + 11$$

11. E: We are given $t = 3$ and $r = 60$, so using the formula $d = r \times t$, we get $d = 60 \times 3 = 180$.

12. D: When solving a linear inequality, distribution is performed first, if necessary:

$$-3(x + 4)$$

$$-3x - 12 \geq x + 8$$

The inequality is manipulated to get the variable on one side by combining any like terms.

$$-4x - 12 \geq 8$$

The variable is isolated using inverse operations to undo subtraction. Adding 12 to both sides produces:

$$-4x \geq 20$$

The variable is isolated using inverse operations to undo multiplication. Remember, if dividing by a negative number, the relationship of the inequality reverses, so the sign is flipped. In this case, dividing by -4 on both sides produces $x \leq -5$.

13. C: In this scenario, the variables are the number of sales and Karen's weekly pay. The weekly pay depends on the number of sales. Therefore, weekly pay is the dependent variable (y), and the number of sales is the independent variable (x). All four answer choices are in slope-intercept form, $y = mx + b$, so we just need to find m (the slope) and b (the y-intercept). We can calculate both by picking any two points, for example, (2, 380) and (4, 460).

The slope is given by $m = \frac{y_2 - y_1}{x_2 - x_1}$, so $m = \frac{460 - 380}{4 - 2} = 40$. This gives us the equation $y = 40x + b$. Now we can plug in the x and y values from our first point to find b. Since $380 = 40(2) + b$, we find $b = 300$. This means the equation is $y = 40x + 300$.

14. D: The closed dot on 1 indicates that the value is included in the set. The arrow pointing right indicates that numbers greater than 1 (numbers get larger to the right) are included in the set. Therefore, the set includes numbers greater than or equal to 1, which can be written as $x \geq 1$.

15. A: The core of the pattern consists of 4 items: ▲○○□. Therefore, the core repeats in multiples of 4, with the pattern starting over on the next step. The highest multiple of 4 that's below 42 is 40. Step 40 is the end of the core (□), so step 41 will start the core over (▲) and step 42 is ○.

16. D: Parallel lines will never intersect. Therefore, the lines are not parallel. Perpendicular lines intersect to form a right angle (90°). Although the lines intersect, they do not form a right angle, which is usually indicated with a box at the intersection point. Therefore, the lines are not perpendicular.

17. E: A polygon is a closed two-dimensional figure consisting of three or more sides. A decagon is a polygon with 10 sides. A pentagon is a polygon with five sides. A triangle is a polygon with three sides. A rhombus is a type of polygon with 4 sides. A cone is a three-dimensional figure and is classified as a solid.

18. C: The formula for finding the area of a regular polygon is $A = \frac{1}{2} \times a \times P$ where a is the length of the apothem (the distance from the center to any side at a right angle), and P is the perimeter of the figure. The apothem a is given as 10.39, and the perimeter can be found by multiplying the length of one side by the number of sides (since the polygon is regular):

$$P = 12 \times 6 \rightarrow P = 72$$

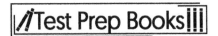

To find the area, substitute the values for a and P into the formula:

$$A = \frac{1}{2} \times a \times P$$

$$A = \frac{1}{2} \times (10.39) \times (72)$$

$$A = 374.04$$

19. E: The area of a rectangle is $A = lw$. We don't know the length or width of this rectangle, but the area is 24, so we can say that $lw = 24$. Length and width are each multiplied by 3, so the area of our new rectangle is $3l \times 3w$, or $9lw$. Since we know that $lw = 24$, the area of the new rectangle is $9lw = 9 \times 24 = 216$ cm^2.

20. A: The coordinates of a point are written as an ordered pair (x, y). To determine the x-coordinate, a line is traced directly above or below the point until reaching the x-axis. This step notes the value on the x-axis. In this case, the x-coordinate is -3. To determine the y-coordinate, a line is traced directly to the right or left of the point until reaching the y-axis, which notes the value on the y-axis. In this case, the y-coordinate is 2. Therefore, the ordered pair is written (-3, 2).

21. C: The perimeter is found by calculating the sum of all sides of the polygon:

$$9 + 9 + 9 + 8 + 8 + s = 56$$

Let s be the missing side length.

Therefore, $43 + s = 56$.

The missing side length is 13 cm.

22. C: $\frac{1}{3}$ of the shirts sold were patterned. Therefore, $1 - \frac{1}{3}$ (that is, $\frac{2}{3}$) of the shirts sold were solid. A fraction of something is calculated with multiplication, so $192 \times (1 - \frac{1}{3})$ solid shirts were sold. (We could calculate that this equals 128, but that's not necessary for this question.)

23. A: An outlier is a data value that is either far above or far below the majority of values in a sample set. The mean is the average of all the values in the set. In a small sample set, a very high or very low number could drastically change the average of the data points. Outliers will have no more of an effect on the median (the middle value when arranged from lowest to highest) than any other value above or below the median. The range is not a measure of the center of a data set, it merely gives the highest and lowest values. If the same outlier does not repeat, outliers will have no effect on the mode (value that repeats most often).

24. E: The scenario involves data consisting of two variables: month and stock value. Box plots display data consisting of values for one variable. Therefore, a box plot is not an appropriate choice. Both line plots and circle graphs are used to display frequencies within categorical data. Neither can be used for the given scenario. Scatter plots compare the values of two variables to see if there are any patterns present. Line graphs display two numerical variables on a coordinate grid and show trends among the variables.

25. D: The probability of picking the winner of the race is $\frac{1}{4}$, or $\left(\frac{\text{number of favorable outcomes}}{\text{number of total outcomes}}\right)$. Assuming the winner was picked on the first selection, three horses remain from which to choose the runner-up (these are dependent

204

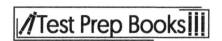

events). Therefore, the probability of picking the runner-up is $\frac{1}{3}$. To determine the probability that multiple events all happen, multiply the probabilities of the events:

$$\frac{1}{4} \times \frac{1}{3} = \frac{1}{12}$$

26. A: Compare each number after the decimal point to figure out which overall number is greatest. In Choices *A* (1.43785) and *C* (1.43592), both have the same tenths place (4) and hundredths place (3). However, the thousandths place is greater in Choice *A* (7), so *A* has the greatest value overall.

27. D: By rearranging and grouping the factors in Choice *D*, we can notice that $3 \times 3 \times 4 \times 2 = (3 \times 2) \times (4 \times 3) = 6 \times 12$, which is what we were looking for. Alternatively, each of the answer choices could be prime-factored or multiplied out and compared to the original value. 6×12 has a value of 72 and a prime factorization of $2^3 \times 3^2$. The answer choices respectively have values of 64, 84, 108, 72, and 360 and prime factorizations of 2^6, $2^2 \times 3 \times 7$, $2^2 \times 3^3$, $2^3 \times 3^2$, and $5 \times 3^2 \times 2^3$, so Choice *D* is correct.

28. C: The total percentage of a pie chart equals 100%. We can see that CD sales make up less than half of the chart (50%) but more than a quarter (25%), and the only answer choice that meets these criteria is Choice *C*, 40%.

29. B: Since $850 is the price after a 20% discount, $850 represents 80% (or 0.8) of the original price. In other words, $850 = 0.8x$ (where x is the original price). Solving this, we find $x = \frac{850}{0.8} = 1,062.5$. Now, to find the savings, calculate the original price minus the sale price: $1,062.50 - $850 = $212.50.

30. A: Figure out which is largest by looking at the first non-zero digits. Choice *B*'s first non-zero digit is in the hundredths place. The other three all have non-zero digits in the tenths place, so it must be *A*, *C*, *D*, or *E*. Of these, *A* has the largest first non-zero digit, a 4.

31. C: To solve for the value of b, both sides of the equation need to be equalized.

Start by cancelling out the lower value of -4 by adding 4 to both sides:

$$5b - 4 = 2b + 17$$

$$5b - 4 + 4 = 2b + 17 + 4$$

$$5b = 2b + 21$$

The variable b is the same on each side, so subtract the lower $2b$ from each side:

$$5b = 2b + 21$$

$$5b - 2b = 2b + 21 - 2b$$

$$3b = 21$$

Then divide both sides by 3 to get the value of b:

$$3b = 21$$

$$\frac{3b}{3} = \frac{21}{3}$$

$$b = 7$$

205

32. E: The total faculty is $15 + 20 = 35$. So, the ratio is 35:200. Then, divide both of these numbers by 5, since 5 is a common factor to both, with a result of 7:40.

33. C: The first step in solving this problem is expressing the result in fraction form. Multiplication and division are typically performed in order from left to right, but they can be performed in any order. For this problem, let's start with the division operation between the last two fractions. When dividing one fraction by another, invert—or flip—the second fraction and then multiply the numerators and denominators.

$$\frac{7}{10} \times \frac{2}{1} = \frac{14}{10}$$

Next, multiply the first fraction by this value:

$$\frac{3}{5} \times \frac{14}{10} = \frac{42}{50}$$

In this instance, to find the decimal form, we can multiply the numerator and denominator by 2 to get 100 in the denominator.

$$\frac{42}{50} \times \frac{2}{2} = \frac{84}{100}$$

In decimal form, this would be expressed as 0.84.

34. C: To find what 85% of 20 questions is, multiply 20 by .85:

$$20 \times .85 = 17 \text{ questions}$$

35. D: This problem can be solved by setting up a proportion involving the given information and the unknown value. The proportion is:

$$\frac{21 \text{ pages}}{4 \text{ nights}} = \frac{140 \text{ pages}}{x \text{ nights}}$$

We can cross-multiply to get $21x = 4 \times 140$. Solving this, we find $x \approx 26.67$. Since this is not an integer, we round up to 27 nights because 26 nights would not give Sarah enough time to finish.

36. E: Using the conversion rate, multiply the projected weight loss of 25 lb by $0.45 \frac{\text{kg}}{\text{lb}}$ to get the amount in kilograms (11.25 kg).

37. D: First, subtract $1,437 from $2,334.50 to find Johnny's monthly savings; this equals $897.50. Then, multiply this amount by 3 to find out how much he will have in three months before he pays for his vacation; this equals $2,692.50. Finally, subtract the cost of the vacation ($1750) from this amount to find how much Johnny will have left: $942.50.

38. B: Dividing by 98 can be approximated by dividing by 100, which would mean shifting the decimal point of the numerator to the left by 2. The result is 4.2, which rounds to 4.

39. B: To solve this correctly, keep in mind the order of operations with the mnemonic PEMDAS (Please Excuse My Dear Aunt Sally). This stands for Parentheses, Exponents, Multiplication & Division, Addition & Subtraction. Taking it step by step, start with the parentheses:

$$4 \times 7 + (4)^2 \div 2$$

206

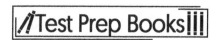

Then, apply the exponent:

$$4 \times 7 + 16 \div 2$$

Multiplication and division are both performed next:

$$28 + 8$$

Addition and subtraction are done last.

$$28 + 8 = 36$$

The solution is 36.

40. E: The formula for the perimeter of a rectangle is $P = 2L + 2W$, where P is the perimeter, L is the length, and W is the width. The first step is to substitute all of the data into the formula:

$$36 = 2(12) + 2W$$

Simplify by multiplying 2×12:

$$36 = 24 + 2W$$

Simplifying this further by subtracting 24 on each side, which gives:

$$36 - 24 = 24 - 24 + 2W$$

$$12 = 2W$$

Divide by 2:

$$6 = W$$

The width is 6 cm. Remember to test this answer by substituting this value into the original formula:

$$36 = 2(12) + 2(6)$$

41. E: To find the average of a set of values, add the values together and then divide by the total number of values. In this case, include the unknown value, x, of what Dwayne needs to score on his next test. The average must equal 90. Set up the equation and solve:

First, combine like terms:

$$\frac{78 + 92 + 83 + 97 + x}{5} = 90$$

Next, divide both sides by 5:

$$\frac{350 + x}{5} = 90$$

Lastly, subtract 350 from both sides:

$$350 + x = 450$$

$$x = 100$$

207

42. D: For an even number of total values, the median is calculated by finding the mean, or average, of the two middle values once all values have been arranged in ascending order from least to greatest. In this case, $(83 + 92) \div 2$ would equal the median 87.5, Choice *D*. Choice *A* is the lowest two values divided by 2, $\frac{78+83}{2} = 80.5$. Choice *B* is the first and third values divided by 2, $\frac{78+92}{2} = 85$. Choice *C* is the second and fourth values divided by 2, $\frac{83+97}{2} = 90$.

43. C: Follow the order of operations in order to solve this problem. Evaluate inside the parentheses first, being sure to follow the order of operations inside the parentheses as well. First, simplify the square roots:

$$(6 \times 4) - 3^2$$

Then, multiply inside the parentheses:

$$24 - 3^2$$

Next, simplify the exponents:

$$24 - 9$$

Finally, subtract to get 15, Choice *C*.

44. D: Three girls for every two boys can be expressed as a ratio: $3:2$. This can be visualized as splitting the school into five groups: three girl groups and two boy groups. The number of students that are in each group can be found by dividing the total number of students by five:

$$\frac{650 \text{ students}}{5 \text{ groups}} = \frac{130 \text{ students}}{\text{group}}$$

To find the total number of girls, multiply the number of students per group (130) by the number of girl groups in the school (3). This equals 390, Choice *D*.

45. A: To solve this correctly, keep in mind the order of operations with the mnemonic PEMDAS (Please Excuse My Dear Aunt Sally). This stands for Parentheses, Exponents, Multiplication & Division, Addition & Subtraction. Taking it step by step, solve inside the parentheses first:

$$3 \times 8 - (3)^2 + 8$$

Then, apply the exponent:

$$3 \times 8 - 9 + 8$$

Multiplication is performed next:

$$24 - 9 + 8$$

Subtraction and addition are performed after that:

$$15 + 8 = 23$$

46. C: Kimberley worked 4.5 hours at the rate of \$10/h and 1 hour at the rate of \$12/h. The problem states that her time is rounded to the nearest hour, so the 4.5 hours would round up to 5 hours at the rate of \$10/h.

$$(5 \text{ h}) \times \left(\frac{\$10}{\text{h}}\right) + (1 \text{ h}) \times \left(\frac{\$12}{\text{h}}\right) = \$50 + \$12 = \$62$$

47. D:

$9x + x - 7 = 16 + 2x$	Combine $9x$ and x.
$10x - 7 = 16 + 2x$	
$10x - 7 + 7 = 16 + 2x + 7$	Add 7 to both sides to remove (-7).
$10x = 23 + 2x$	
$10x - 2x = 23 + 2x - 2x$	Subtract $2x$ from both sides to move it to the other side of the equation.
$8x = 23$	
$\dfrac{8x}{8} = \dfrac{23}{8}$	Divide by 8 to get x by itself.
$x = \dfrac{23}{8}$	

48. C: For each fraction, we can divide the numerator by the denominator to find a decimal value. $\frac{4}{5} = 0.8, \frac{2}{3} \approx 0.67$, and $\frac{91}{100} = 0.91$. Ordering these from least to greatest gives us 0.67, 0.8, 0.85, and 0.91, which matches Choice *C*.

49. B: First, calculate the difference between the larger value and the smaller value.

$$378 - 252 = 126$$

To calculate this difference as a percentage of the original value, and thus calculate the percentage *increase*, divide 126 by 252 to get 0.5, then multiply by 100 to reach the percentage 50%, Choice *B*.

50. B: When solving for x, add 3 to both sides to get $4x = 8$. Then, divide both sides by 4 to get $x = 2$.

Reading Comprehension

1. D: Although Washington was from a wealthy background, the passage does not say that his wealth led to his republican ideals, so Choice *A* is not supported. Choice *B* also does not follow from the passage. Washington's warning against meddling in foreign affairs does not mean that he would oppose wars of every kind, so Choice *B* is incorrect. Choice *C* is also unjustified since the author does not indicate that Alexander Hamilton's assistance was absolutely necessary. Choice *E* is incorrect because we don't know which particular presidents Washington would befriend. Choice *D* is correct because the passage states that Washington's farewell address clearly opposes political parties and partisanship. The author then notes that presidential elections often hit a fever pitch of partisanship. Thus, it follows that George Washington would probably not approve of modern political parties and their involvement in presidential elections.

2. E: The author finishes the passage by applying Washington's farewell address to modern politics, so the purpose probably includes this application. Choice *B* is incorrect because George Washington is already a well-established historical figure; furthermore, the passage does not seek to introduce him. Choice *C* is incorrect because the author is not fighting a common perception that Washington was merely a military hero. Choice *D* is incorrect because the author is not convincing readers. Persuasion does not correspond to the passage. Choice *E* states the primary purpose.

3. A: The tone in this passage is informative. Choice *B*, excited, is incorrect, because there are not many word choices used that would indicate excitement from the author. Choice *C*, bitter, is incorrect. Although the author does make a suggestion in the last paragraph to Americans, the statement is not necessarily bitter, but based on the preceding information. Choice *D*, comic, is incorrect, as the author does not try to make the audience laugh, nor do they make light of the situation in any way. Choice *E*, somber, is incorrect since the passage isn't sad or mournful.

4. C: Interfering. Meddling means to interfere in something. Choice *A* is incorrect. One helpful thing would be to use the word in the sentence: "Washington warned Americans against 'supporting' in foreign affairs" does not make that much sense, so we can mark it off. Choice *B*, *speaking against*, is incorrect. This phrase would make sense in the sentence, but it goes against the meaning that is intended. George Washington warned against interference in foreign affairs, not speaking *against* foreign affairs. Choice *D* is also incorrect, because "gathering in foreign affairs" does not sound quite right. Choice *E*, *avoiding*, is incorrect because it is nearly the opposite of meddling. Choice *C*, *interfering*, is therefore the best choice for this question.

5. A: When Washington was offered a role as leader of the former colonies, he refused the offer. This is explained in the first sentence of the second paragraph. He did not simply ignore the offer, as he "famously" refused it. All of the other answer choices are incorrect and not mentioned in the passage.

6. D: The passage does not proceed in chronological order since it begins by pointing out Christopher Columbus's explorations in America, so Choice *A* does not work. Although the author compares and contrasts Erikson with Columbus, this is not the main way the information is presented; therefore, Choice *B* does not work. Choice *C* is also incorrect because there is no mention of or reference to cause and effect in the passage. However, the passage does offer a conclusion (Leif Erikson deserves more credit) and premises (first European to set foot in the New World and first to contact the natives) to substantiate Erikson's historical importance. Thus, Choice *D* is correct. Choice *E* is incorrect because spatial order refers to the space and location of something or where things are located in relation to each other.

7. C: Choice *A* is incorrect because it describes facts: Leif Erikson was the son of Erik the Red and historians debate Leif's date of birth. These are not opinions. Choice *B* is incorrect; Erikson calling the land Vinland is a verifiable fact, as is Choice *D*, because he did contact the natives almost 500 years before Columbus. Choice *E* is also a fact and the passage mentions that there are several secondhand accounts (evidence) of their meetings. Choice *C* is the correct answer because it is the author's opinion that Erikson deserves more credit. Choice *C* is the correct answer because it is the author's opinion that Erikson deserves more credit. Another person could argue that Columbus or another explorer deserves more credit, which makes it an opinion rather than a historical fact.

8. B: Choice *A* is incorrect because the author aims to go beyond describing Erikson as merely a legendary Viking. Choice *C* is incorrect because the author does not focus on Erikson's motivations, let alone name the spreading of Christianity as his primary objective. Choice *D* is incorrect because it is a premise that Erikson contacted the natives 500 years before Columbus, which is simply a part of supporting the author's conclusion. Choice *E* is incorrect because the author states at the beginning that he or she believes it can't be considered "discovering" if people already lived there. Choice *B* is correct because it accurately identifies the author's statement that Erikson deserves more credit than he has received for being the first European to explore the New World.

9. B: Choice *B* is correct because the author wants the reader to be informed about Leif Erikson's contribution to exploring the new world. While several other answers are possible options, Choice *B* is the strongest. Choice *A* is incorrect because the author is not in any way trying to entertain the reader. Choice *C* is incorrect because the nature of the writing does not indicate the author would be satisfied with the reader merely being alerted to Erikson's exploration; instead, the author is making an argument about the credit he should receive. Choice *D* is incorrect because the author goes beyond merely a suggestion; "suggest" is too vague.

10. D: Choice *A* is incorrect because the author never addresses the Vikings' state of mind or emotions. Choice *B* is incorrect because the author does not elaborate on Erikson's exile and whether he would have become an explorer if not for his banishment. Choice *C* is incorrect because there is not enough information to support this premise. It is unclear whether Erikson informed the King of Norway of his findings. Although it is true that the king did not send a follow-up expedition, he could have simply chosen not to expend the resources after receiving Erikson's news. It is not possible to logically infer whether Erikson told him. Choice *E* is incorrect because the passage does not mention anything about Columbus' awareness of Erikson's travels. Choice *D* is correct because the uncertainty about Leif Erikson's birth year is an example of how historians have trouble pinning down important details in Viking history.

11. B: The author is opposed to tobacco. The author cites disease and deaths associated with smoking, and points to the monetary expense and aesthetic costs. Choices *A* and *C* are incorrect because they do not summarize the passage but rather are just premises. Choice *D* is incorrect because, while these statistics are a premise in the argument, they do not represent a summary of the piece. Choice *E* is incorrect because alternatives to smoking are not addressed in the passage. Choice *B* is the correct answer because it states the three critiques offered against tobacco and expresses the author's conclusion.

12. C: We are looking for something the author would agree with, so it should be anti-smoking or an argument in favor of quitting smoking. Choice *A* is incorrect because the author does not speak against means of cessation. Choice *B* is incorrect because the author does not reference other substances but does speak of how addictive nicotine, a drug in tobacco, is. Choice *D* is incorrect because the author would not encourage reducing taxes to encourage a reduction of smoking costs, thereby helping smokers to continue the habit. Choice *E* is incorrect because the author states that According to the National Institute on Drug Abuse, nearly 35 million smokers expressed a desire to quit smoking in 2015. If the author had used the word "only" instead of "nearly" (and perhaps if the number was a lot lower) that would have changed the argument. Choice *C* is correct because the author is attempting to persuade smokers to quit smoking.

13. D: Here, look for an opinion of the author rather than a fact or statistic. Choice *A* is incorrect because quoting statistics from the CDC is stating facts, not opinions. Choice *B* is incorrect because it expresses the fact that cigarettes sometimes cost more than a few gallons of gas. It would be an opinion if the author said that cigarettes were not affordable. Choice *C* is incorrect because yellow stains are a known possible adverse effect of smoking. Choice *E* is incorrect because decreased life expectancy for smokers is a known fact because of the health problems

211

it can create. Choice *D* is correct as an opinion because smell is subjective. Some people might like the smell of smoke, they might not have working olfactory senses, or some people might not find the smell of smoke akin to "pervasive nastiness," so this is the expression of an opinion. Thus, Choice *D* is the correct answer.

14. B: The passage is cautionary, because the author warns about the hazards of smoking and uses the second-person *you* to offer suggestions, like "You would be wise to learn from their mistake." Choice *A*, objective, means that the passage would be totally without persuasion or suggestions, so this answer choice is incorrect. Choice *C*, indifferent, is incorrect because the author expresses an opinion and makes it clear they dislike smoking. Choice *D* is also incorrect; the passage is the opposite of admiring towards the subject of smoking. Choice *D* is also incorrect; the passage is opposite of admiring towards the subject of smoking. Finally, Choice *E*, philosophical, is incorrect, because this is a down-to-earth passage that presents facts and gives suggestions based on those facts, and there are no philosophical underpinnings here.

15. E: The word *pervasive* means "all over the place." The passage says that "The smell of smoke is all-consuming and creates a pervasive nastiness," which means a smell that is everywhere or all over. Choices *A* and *B*, *pleasantly appealing* and a *floral scent*, are too pleasant for the context of the passage. Choice *C* doesn't make sense in the sentence, as "to convince someone" wouldn't really describe the word *nastiness* like pervasive does. Choice *D* is also incorrect because that's the opposite of what the author is describing.

16. B: Choice *B* is correct because the author is trying to demonstrate the main idea, which is that heat loss is proportional to surface area, so they compare two animals with different surface areas to clarify the main point. Choice *A* is incorrect because the author uses elephants and anteaters to prove a point, that heat loss is proportional to surface area, not to express an opinion. Choice *C* is incorrect because though the author does use them to show differences, they do so in order to give examples that prove the above points. Choice *D* is incorrect because there is no language to indicate favoritism between the two animals. Choice *E* is incorrect because the passage is not about animals and only uses the elephant and the anteater to make a point.

17. C: Because of the way the author addresses the reader and the colloquial language the author uses (e.g., "let me explain," "so," "well," "didn't," "you would look stupid"), Choice *C* is the best answer because it has a much more casual tone than the usual informative article. Choice *A* may be a tempting choice because the author says the "fact" that most of one's heat is lost through their head is a "lie" and that someone who does not wear a shirt in the cold looks stupid. However, this only happens twice within the passage, and the passage does not give an overall tone of harshness. Choice *B* is incorrect because again, while not necessarily nice, the language does not carry an angry charge. The author is clearly not indifferent to the subject because of the passionate language that they use, so Choice *D* is incorrect. Choice *E* is incorrect because the author is not trying to show or use humor in the passage.

18. E: The author gives logical examples and reasons in order to prove that most of one's heat is not lost through their head; therefore, Choice *E* is correct. Choice *A* is incorrect because the author never mentions any specific experts as references. Choice *B* is incorrect because there is not much emotionally charged language in this selection, and even the small amount present is greatly outnumbered by the facts and evidence. Choice *C* is incorrect because there is no mention of ethics or morals in this selection. Choice *D* is incorrect because the author never qualifies himself as someone who has the authority to be writing on this topic.

19. C: *Gullible* means to believe something easily. The other answer choices could fit easily within the context of the passage: you can be angry toward, distrustful toward, frightened by, or happy toward authority. For this answer choice and the surrounding context, however, the author talks about a myth that people believe easily, so *gullible* would be the word that fits best in this context.

20. E: The whole passage is dedicated to debunking the head heat loss myth. The whole passage is dedicated to debunking the head heat loss myth. The passage says that "each part of your body loses its proportional amount of

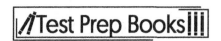

heat in accordance with its surface area," which means an area such as the chest would lose more heat than the head because it's bigger.

21. E: The thesis is a statement that contains the author's topic and main idea. The main purpose of this article is to use historical evidence to provide counterarguments to anti-Stratfordians. Choice *A* is simply a definition; Choice *B* states part of the reasoning of the anti-Stratfordians; Choice *C* is a supporting detail, not a main idea; and Choice *D* represents an idea of anti-Stratfordians, not the author's opinion.

22. C: This requires readers to be familiar with different types of rhetorical devices. A rhetorical question is a question that is asked not to obtain an answer but to encourage readers to more deeply consider an issue.

23. B: This question asks readers to refer to the organizational structure of the article and demonstrate understanding of how the author provides details to support their argument. This particular detail can be found in the second paragraph where the author says, "even though he did not attend university, grade-school education in Shakespeare's time was actually quite rigorous."

24. A: This is a vocabulary question that can be answered using context clues. Other sentences in the paragraph describe London as "the most populous city in England" filled with "crowds of people," giving an image of a busy city full of people. Choice *B* is incorrect because London was in Shakespeare's home country, not a foreign one. Choice *C* is not mentioned in the passage. Choice *D* is not a good answer choice because the passage describes how London was a popular and important city, not an undeveloped one. Choice *E* is incorrect because quiet would be the opposite of how the city of London is described.

25. C: The passage states this fact in paragraph two, where it says "his father was a very successful glove-maker."

26. A: The author mentions St. Lucia a couple times throughout the passage.

27. C: Remember that supporting details help readers find out the main idea by answering questions like *who, what, where, when, why,* and *how.* In this question, cruises, local events, and cuisine are not talked about in the passage. However, family resorts and activities are talked about.

28. B: The last activity the speaker did was go for a hike up a mountain. We know this because the speaker "wanted to take one more walk" before the family left. The speaker did do Choices *A, C,* and *E*—swam with the sharks, lounged on the beach, and had a massage—but those weren't the last activities the speaker did. The speaker never said anything about surfing in the waves, so Choice *D* is incorrect.

29. E: To trek means to hike or walk, so Choice *E* is the best answer here. The other choices (ran, swam, sang, and drove) are incorrect because they do not reflect the hike mentioned earlier in the passage.

30. D: The author's attitude towards the topic is enthusiastic. We see the author's enthusiasm through the word choice such as *best vacation, enjoyed, beautiful,* and *peace.* We also see the author using multiple exclamation marks, which denotes excitement. Therefore, our best answer is Choice *D.* The author doesn't demonstrate any worry or resignation, except maybe a bit in the part where they have to go home soon, but the enthusiasm overrides these feelings in the rest of the passage. Choice *C,* objective, means to be fair and based in fact, and the author is far too enthusiastic toward St. Lucia, which creates some bias towards the topic. Choice *E* is incorrect because the author's apparent enthusiasm is the opposite of apathy, or a lack of interest.

31. D: Rain is the cause in this passage because it is why something happened. The effects of the rain are plants growing, rainbows, and puddle jumping. The author's trip was an element of the story but not what caused the listed effects.

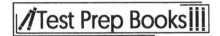

32. A: The author is comparing the plants, trees, and flowers. The author is showing how these things react the same to rain. They all get important nutrients from rain. If the author described the differences, then it would be contrasting, Choice *B*.

33. E: *Vital* can mean different things depending on the context or how it is used. In one sense, the word *vital* means full of life and energy. However, in this sentence, the word *vital* means necessary. Choices *A*, *B*, and *C* do not make sense in this context. Choice *D*, *dangerous,* is nearly an antonym of the word we are looking for, since the sentence says the nutrients are needed for growing. Something needed would not be dangerous. The best context clue is that it says the vital nutrients are needed, which tells us they are necessary.

34. C: Rainbows. This passage mentions several effects. Effects are the outcome of a certain cause. Remember that the cause here is rain, so Choice *A* is incorrect. Since the cause is rain, Choice *B*—brief spurts of sunshine—doesn't make sense because rain doesn't *cause* brief spurts of sunshine. Choice *C* makes the most sense because the effects of the rain in the passage are plants growing, rainbows, and puddle jumping. Choice *D*, weather, is not an effect of rain but describes rain in a general sense. Lastly, Choice *E*, thunderstorms, often accompany rain, but are not necessarily a cause or effect of it.

35. B: The author uses personal testimonies in this passage. We see this in the second and third paragraphs. The first time the author gives a personal testimony is when they talk about going on a trip across the United States and seeing all the rainbows. The second personal testimony we see is when the author goes outside after a storm to watch everyone play in the puddles. The other answer choices are not represented in the passage.

36. D: *Stealthily* means secretly, Choice *D*. Given the context of the passage, we probably can assume that Sylvia was trying her best to be secretive, since she was gathering bees while her father was away at work. *Hurriedly* might fit, Choice *A*, but it is not the best answer. *Begrudgingly*, Choice *B*, is incorrect, because if Sylvia was begrudging, or resentful, that she had to gather bees, she probably wouldn't have done it. Choice *C*, *confidently*, although it could fit in this context, is not the best choice for this definition. Finally, Choice *E*, *efficiently*, would mean Syliva collected them quickly or with little waste of effort, but this does not fit as well as *stealthily*.

37. C: The story is written in third-person point of view, which tells the story using *he, she, they*, etc. First-person narrative is used when the narrator is an *I* in the story, so it'll use language such as *I, we*, etc. There are no instances of *I* or *we* in the story, so Choice *A* is incorrect. Second person uses *you* to talk directly to the audience. However, *you* is not used in this manner in the narrative, so Choice *B* is incorrect. Finally, all stories have some kind of point of view, so Choices *D* and *E* are incorrect.

38. E: She wanted to keep them away from harm. Choice *A* is incorrect; the passage mentions nothing about a science experiment. Choice *B* is incorrect because doesn't indicate Sylvia is gathering the bees to learn beekeeping. Choice *C* is incorrect; the passage does not mention Sylvia wanting to give the bees to her father. Finally, Choice *D* is incorrect; although Sylvia's mother *is* terrified of the bees, this isn't her motivation for putting them inside a jar.

39. A: This passage is chronologically ordered, which means it goes from a beginning to an end in a logical way. Cause and effect order is when a topic goes from talking about a specific cause to its effects, and this is incorrect. Problem to solution is more of a formal paper where the narrative depicts a problem and then offers a solution at the end, so Choice *C* is incorrect. Sequential order is similar to chronological order, but it is more like step-by-step instructions, so Choice *D* is incorrect. Order of importance places the most important information first to give it emphasis, so Choice *E* is incorrect.

40. C: If we had to choose one theme, it would probably be freedom. The theme is posed at the end of the passage, when Sylvia's mother basically asks her if she enjoys her own freedom playing outside. Sylvia realizes that she does and that the bees would probably enjoy that freedom as well, despite the dangers of being outdoors.

Verbal Section

Synonyms

1. C: To *deduce* something is to figure it out using reasoning. While you can explain something you've *deduced*, *explain* is not a synonym for *deduce*.

2. B: To *elucidate* is to figuratively shine a light on a previously unknown or confusing subject. This Latin root, "lux" meaning "light," prominently figures into the solution. *Enlighten* means to educate or bring to light.

3. D: Looking at the Latin word "veritas," meaning "truth," will yield a clue as to the meaning of *verify*. To *verify* is the act of finding or assessing the truthfulness of something. This usually means amassing evidence to substantiate a claim. *Substantiate*, of course, means to provide evidence to prove a point.

4. A: If someone is *inspired*, they are *motivated* to do something. Someone who is an inspiration motivates others to follow their example.

5. E: All the connotations of *perceive* involve the concept of seeing. Whether figuratively or literally, *perceiving* implies the act of understanding what is presented. *Comprehending* is synonymous with *understanding*.

6. C: *Nomadic* tribes are those who, throughout history and even today, prefer to wander their lands instead of settling in any specific place. *Wanderer* best describes these people.

7. D: Perplexed means *baffled* or *puzzled*, which are synonymous with *confused*.

8. D: *Lyrical* is used to refer to something being poetic or song-like, characterized by showing enormous imagination and description. While the context of *lyrical* can be playful or even whimsical, the best choice is *expressive*, since whatever emotion *lyrical* may be used to convey in its context will be expressive in nature.

9. C: *Brevity* literally means *brief* or *concise*. Note the similar beginnings of *brevity* and *brief*—from the Latin "brevis," meaning *brief*.

10. A: *Irate* means being in a state of anger. Clearly this is a negative word that can be paired with another word in kind. The closest word to match this is obviously *anger*. Research would also reveal that *irate* comes from the Latin "ira," which means *anger*.

11. C: *Lavish* is a synonym for *luxurious*. Both words describe elaborate, elegant lifestyles and/or settings.

12. E: *Immobile* means "not able to move." The two best selections are *B* and *E*—but *slow* still implies some form of motion, whereas *sedentary* has the connotation of being seated and/or inactive for a significant portion of time and/or as a natural tendency.

13. B: *Overbearing* refers to *domineering* or being *oppressive*. This is emphasized in the "over" prefix, which emphasizes an excess in definitions.

14. A: The "pre" prefix describes something that occurs before an event. *Prevent* means to stop something before it happens. This leads to a word that relates to something occurring beforehand and, in a way, is preventive—wanting to stop something. *Avert* literally means to turn away or ward off an impending circumstance, making it the best fit.

15. D: *Refresh* is synonymous with *replenish*. Both words mean to restore or refill. Additionally, these terms do share the "re" prefix as well.

215

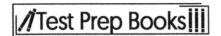

16. D: *Regale* literally means to *amuse* someone with a story. This is a very positive word; the best way to eliminate choices is to look for a term that matches *regale* in both positive context/sound and definition. *Entertain* is both a positive word and a synonym of *regale*.

17. A: *Weary* most closely means tired. Someone who is *weary* and *tired* may be *whiny*, but they do not necessarily mean the same thing.

18. B: Something that is *vast* is far-reaching and expansive. Choice *D, ocean,* may be described as *vast,* but the word alone doesn't mean *vast*. The *heavens* or *skies* may also be described as *vast*, but those things do not mean *vast* either. Someone's *imagination* or *vocabulary* can also be vast.

19. B: To *demonstrate* something means to show it. The word *demonstration* comes from *demonstrate,* and a *demonstration* is a modeling or show-and-tell type of example that is usually visual.

20. C: An *orchard* is most like a *grove* because both are areas like plantations that grow different kinds of fruit. Peach is a type of fruit that may be grown in an *orchard,* but it is not a synonym for *orchard*. Many citrus fruits are grown in groves, but either word can be used to describe many fruit-bearing trees in one area. Choice *E, farm,* may have an *orchard* or *grove* on the property, but they are not the same thing, and many farms do not grow fruit trees.

21. A: *Textile* is another word for *fabric*. The most confusing alternative choice in this case is *knit,* because some *textiles* are *knit* but *textile* and *knit* are not synonyms, and plenty of textiles are not knit.

22. D: *Offspring* are the *children* of parents. The other answer choice, *parent,* may be somewhat tricky because *parents* have *offspring*, but they are not synonyms.

23. E: *Permit* can be a verb or a noun. As a verb, it means to *allow* or *give authorization* for something. As a noun, it generally refers to a document or something that has been authorized like a parking permit or driving permit, allowing the authorized individual to park or drive under the rules of the document.

24. B: A *woman* is a *lady*. Test takers must read carefully and remember the difference between *woman* and *women*. *Woman* refers to an individual lady or one person who is female, while *women* is the plural form and refers to more than one, or a group, of ladies. A woman may be a mother but not necessarily, and these words are not synonyms. A *girl* is a child and not yet a woman.

25. C: *Rotation* means to spin or turn, such as a *wheel* rotating on a car, although *wheel* does not mean rotation.

26. E: Something that is *consistent* is *steady, predictable, reliable,* or *constant*. The tricky one here is that the word *consistency* comes from the word *consistent*, and may describe something that is sticky. *Consistent* also comes from the word *consist,* which means to contain, Choice *B*. Test takers must be discerning readers and knowledgeable about vocabulary to recognize the difference in these words and look for the true synonym of *consistent*.

27. D: A *principle* is a *foundation* or a *guiding idea* or *belief*. Someone with good moral character is described as having strong *principles*. Test takers must be careful not to get confused with the homonym's *principle* and *principal,* because these words have very different meanings. A principal is the leader of a school, and the word *principal* also refers to the main or most important idea or thing.

28. A: *Perimeter* refers to the outline or borders of an object. Test takers may recognize that word from math class, where *perimeter* refers to the edges or distance around an enclosed shape. Some of the other answer choices refer to other math vocabulary encountered in geometry lessons, but they do not have the same meaning as *perimeter*.

29. D: A *symbol* is an *object*, *picture*, or *sign* that is used to represent something. For example, a pink ribbon is a *symbol* for breast-cancer awareness, and a flag can be a *symbol* for a country. The tricky part of this question was also knowing the meaning of *emblem,* which typically describes a design that represents a group or concept, much like a *symbol. Emblems* often appear on flags or a coat of arms.

30. E: *Germinate* means to *develop* or *grow* and most often refers to sprouting seeds as a new plant first breaks through the seed coat. It can also refer to the development of an idea. Choice *D* may be an attractive choice since plants germinate, but *germinate* does not mean *plant.*

Verbal Analogies

1. C: This is a part/whole analogy. The common thread is what animals walk on. *A, B,* and *E* all describe signature parts of animals, but paws are not the defining feature of cats. Snakes travel by crawling on their skinned bellies. They do not walk because they do not have the correct limbs to do so.

2. A: This is a characteristic analogy. The connection lies in what observers will judge a performance on. While the other choices are also important, an off-key singer is as unpleasant as a dancer with no rhythm.

3. D: This is a use/tool analogy. The analogy focuses on an item's use. While hats are worn when it's cold with the goal of making the top of your head warm, this is not always guaranteed—their primary use is to provide cover. There is also the fact that not all hats are used to keep warm, but all hats cover the head.

4. D: This is a source/comprised of analogy. The common thread is addition of fire. Protons contribute to atoms and seeds grow into plants, but these are simple matters of building and growing without necessarily involving fire. Choices *B* and *E* relate objects that already have similar properties.

5. E: This is a synonym analogy. The determining factor is synonymous definition. Design and create are synonyms, as are allocate and distribute. One could argue that an item could be found and then allocated or that management sometimes requires allocation of items. However, allocate is not a synonym for find or manage like it is for distribute. Allocation generally refers to the division of commodities instead of multiplication.

6. B: This is a tool/use analogy. The common thread is audience response to an art form. Choices *A, C,* and *D* deal with the creation of artwork instead of its consumption. Choice *E* describes a form of art instead of the audience engagement with the art.

7. C: This is an intensity analogy. The common thread is degree of severity. While *A, D,* and *E* can all describe warmth, they don't convey the harshness of sweltering. Choice *B* simply describes a time when people may be more likely to think of warmth.

8. D: This is a characteristic analogy and is based on matching objects to their geometric shapes. Choice *A* is not correct because globes are three-dimensional, whereas circles exist in two dimensions. While wheels are three-dimensional, they are not always solid or perfectly round.

9. A: This is a tool/use analogy. The key detail of this analogy is the idea of enclosing or sealing items/people. When plates are filled with food, there is no way to enclose the item. While trees can be inside a fence, they can also be specifically outside of one.

10. E: This is a sequence of events analogy. The common thread is celestial cause-and-effect. Not everyone has breakfast or goes to bed after sunset. Sunrise is not typically thought of as the next interesting celestial event after sunsets. While clouds can develop after sunsets, they are also present before and during this activity. Stars, however, can be seen after dark, just like rainbows can be seen after storms.

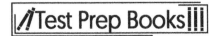
11. A: This is a consumer/food analogy. The theme of this analogy is pairing a specific animal to their food source. Falcons prey on mice. Giraffes are herbivores and only eat one of the choices: leaves. Grasslands describe a type of landscape, not a food source for animals.

12. B: This is a category analogy. The common thread is motorized vehicles. While *A, C*, and *E* also describe vehicles that move on water, they are not motorized. Although relying on engines, planes are not a form of water transportation.

13. D: This is an antonym analogy. The prevailing connection is opposite meanings. While happy can be an opposite of anxious, it's also possible for someone to experience both emotions at once. Choices *B, C,* and *E* are also concurrent with anxious, not opposite.

14. E: This is a consumer/food analogy. This analogy looks at professionals and what their job is. Just as a mechanic's job is to repair machinery, a doctor works to heal patients.

15. C: This is a category analogy. Both whistles and blow horns are devices used to project/produce sound. Therefore, the analogy is based on finding something of a categorical nature. While Choices *A, B, D,* and *E* involve or describe painting, they do not pertain to a distinct discipline alongside painting. Sculpture, however, is another form of art and expression, just like painting.

16. D: This is a part/whole analogy. This analogy examines the relationship between two objects. Specifically, this analogy examines how one object connects to another object, with the first object(s) being the means by which people use the corresponding object to produce a result directly. People use a paddle to steer a boat, just as pressing keys on a piano produces music. Choices *B* and *C* can be metaphorically linked to keys but are unrelated. Choice *A* is related to keys but is a verb, not another object. Choice *E* is the trickiest alternative, but what's important to remember is that while keys are connected to key chains, there is no result just by having the key on a key chain.

17. E: This is a part/whole analogy. This analogy focuses on natural formations and their highest points. The peak of a mountain is its highest point, just as the crest is the highest rise in a wave.

18. B: This is an intensity analogy. Fluent refers to how well one can communicate, while gourmet describes a standard of cooking. The analogy draws on degrees of a concept.

19. B: This is a synonym analogy, which relies on matching terms that are most closely connected. Validate and verify both mean to confirm that something is accurate or true. Therefore, finding the term that best fits conquer is a good strategy. While nations have conquered others to expand their territory, they are ultimately subjugating those lands and people to their will. Therefore, subjugate is the best-fitting answer.

20. C: This is a sequence of events analogy. This analogy pairs one season with the season that precedes it. Winter is paired with autumn because autumn actually comes before winter. Out of all the answers only Choices *B* and *C* are actual seasons. Fall is another name for autumn, which comes after summer, not before. Spring, of course, is the season that comes before summer, making it the correct answer.

21. C: This is a source/comprised of analogy. This analogy focuses on pairing a raw material with an object that it's used to create. Fiberglass is used to build surfboards, just as copper is used in the creation of pennies. While wind powers a windmill, there is no physical object produced, like with the fiberglass/surfboards pair.

22. E: This is an object/function analogy. The common thread between these words is that one word describes a kind of story and it is paired with the purpose of the story. Myth are/were told in order to explain fundamental beliefs and natural phenomena. While laughter can result from a joke, the purpose of telling a joke is to amuse the audience, thus making Choice *E* the right choice.

23. C: Cows produce milk, so the question is looking for another pair that has a producer and their product. Horses don't produce cows, Choice *A*, glasses don't produce milk, Choice *D*, and milk doesn't produce a glass, Choice *E*. The correct choice is *C*: chicken is to egg. The tricky one here is Choice *B*, egg is to chicken, because it has the correct words but the wrong order, and therefore it reverses the relationship. Eggs don't produce chickens, so it doesn't work with the first part of the analogy: cow is to milk.

24. C: The first part of the analogy—web is to spider—describes the home (web) and who lives in it (spider), so the question is looking for what animal lives in a den. The best choice is *C*, fox. Living room is another word or a synonym for a den.

25. A: Sad and blue are synonyms because they are both describing the same type of mood. The word *blue* in this case is not referring to the color; therefore, although yellow is sometimes considered a "happy" color, the question isn't referring to blue as a color (or any color for that matter) and yellow and happy are not synonyms. Someone who is happy may laugh or smile, but these words are not synonyms for happy. Lastly, someone who is happy may be calm, although he or she could also be excited, and calm and happy are not synonyms. The best choice is glad.

26. D: The key to answering this question correctly is to recognize that the relationship between door and store are that the words rhyme. One may at first consider the fact that stores have doors, but after reviewing the other word choices and the given word *deal*, he or she should notice that none of the other words have this relationship. Instead, the answer choice should be one that rhymes with *deal*. Wheel and deal, although spelled differently, are rhyming words, and therefore the correct answer is *D*.

27. E: This question relies on the test takers' knowledge of occupations. Dogs are taken care of by veterinarians so the solution is looking for who takes care of babies. However, this level of detail is not yet specific enough because mothers and babysitters can also take care of babies. Veterinarians take care of sick dogs and act as a medical doctor for pets. Therefore, with this higher level of specificity and detail, test takers should select pediatrician, because pediatricians are doctors for babies and children.

28. A: The relationship in the first half of the analogy is that clocks are used to measure time, so the second half of the analogy should have a tool that is used to measure something followed by what it measures. Rulers can be used to measure length, so that is the best choice. Remember that the key to solving analogies is to be a good detective. Some of the other answer choices are related to clocks and time but not to the relationship between clocks and time.

29. B: Wires are the medium that carry electricity, allowing the current to flow in a circuit. Pipes carry water in a similar fashion, so the best choice is Choice *B*. Test takers must be careful to not select Choice *E*, which reverses the relationship between the components. Choices *A, C,* and *D* contain words that are related to one another but not in the same manner as wires and electricity.

30. A: This question pulls from social studies knowledge and the understanding of the basic roles and positions of the three branches of the government. The president serves in the executive branch, and the Supreme Court justices serve in the judicial branch.

Scoring comes with a raw score and a scaled score. Raw scores might be something like 35/40 for the Verbal Reasoning section, showing the number of questions guessed correctly. Scaled scores have been converted to a higher number and show a range from 760 to 940.

ISEE Practice Test

Quantitative Reasoning

Word Problems

1. A shuffled deck of 52 cards contains 4 kings. One card is drawn and is not put back in the deck. Then, a second card is drawn. What's the probability that both cards are kings?
   a. $\frac{1}{169}$
   b. $\frac{1}{221}$
   c. $\frac{1}{13}$
   d. $\frac{4}{13}$

2. The hospital has a nurse-to-patient ratio of 1 : 25. If there are a maximum of 325 patients admitted at a time, how many nurses are there?
   a. 13 nurses
   b. 25 nurses
   c. 325 nurses
   d. 12 nurses

3. A truck is carrying three cylindrical barrels. Each barrel has a diameter of 2 feet and a height of 3 feet. What is the total volume of the three barrels in cubic feet?
   a. 3π
   b. 9π
   c. 12π
   d. 15π

4. Greg buys a $10 lunch with 5% sales tax. He leaves a $2 tip after paying his bill. How much money does he spend?
   a. $12.50
   b. $12.00
   c. $13.00
   d. $13.25

5. Taylor works two jobs. The first pays $20,000 per year. The second pays $10,000 per year. She donates 15% of her income to charity. How much does she donate each year?
   a. $4,500
   b. $5,000
   c. $5,500
   d. $6,000

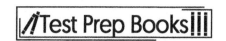

6. Suppose an investor deposits $1,200 into a bank account that accrues 1 percent interest per month. Assuming x represents the number of months since the deposit and y represents the money in the account, which of the following exponential functions models the scenario?
    a. $y = (0.01)(1,200^x)$
    b. $y = (1,200)(0.01^x)$
    c. $y = (1.01)(1,200^x)$
    d. $y = (1,200)(1.01^x)$

7. Mom's car drove 72 miles in 90 minutes. There are 5,280 feet per mile. How fast did she drive in feet per second?
    a. 0.8 feet per second
    b. 48.9 feet per second
    c. 0.009 feet per second
    d. 70.4 feet per second

8. A family purchases a vehicle in 2005 for $20,000. In 2010, they decide to sell it for a newer model. They are able to sell the car for $8,000. By what percentage did the value of the family's car drop?
    a. 40%
    b. 68%
    c. 60%
    d. 33%

9. On May 1, 2010, a couple purchased a house for $100,000. On September 1, 2016, the couple sold the house for $93,000 so they could purchase a bigger one to start a family. How many months did they own the house?
    a. 76 months
    b. 54 months
    c. 85 months
    d. 93 months

10. A shipping box has a length of 8 inches, a width of 14 inches, and a height of 4 inches. If all three dimensions are doubled, what is the relationship between the volume of the new box and the volume of the original box?
    a. The volume of the new box is double the volume of the original box.
    b. The volume of the new box is four times as large as the volume of the original box.
    c. The volume of the new box is six times as large as the volume of the original box.
    d. The volume of the new box is eight times as large as the volume of the original box.

11. A pizzeria owner regularly creates jumbo pizzas, each with a radius of 9 inches. She is mathematically inclined, and wants to know the area of the pizza to purchase the correct boxes and know how much she is feeding her customers. What is the area of a circle with a radius of 9 inches, in terms of π?
    a. $81\pi \text{ in}^2$
    b. $18\pi \text{ in}^2$
    c. $90\pi \text{ in}^2$
    d. $9\pi \text{ in}^2$

12. The phone bill is calculated each month using the equation $c = 50g + 75$. The cost of the phone bill per month is represented by c, and g represents the gigabytes of data used that month. What is the value and interpretation of the slope of this equation?
    a. 75 dollars per day
    b. 75 gigabytes per day
    c. 50 dollars per day
    d. 50 dollars per gigabyte

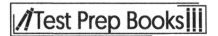

13. Which of the following equations best represents the problem below?
The width of a rectangle is 2 centimeters less than the length. If the perimeter of the rectangle is 44 centimeters, then what are the dimensions of the rectangle?

    a. $2l + 2(l - 2) = 44$
    b. $(l + 2) + (l + 2) + l = 48$
    c. $l \times (l - 2) = 44$
    d. $(l + 2) + (l + 2) + l = 44$

14. A company invests $50,000 in a building where they can produce saws. If the cost of producing one saw is $40, then which function expresses the total amount of money the company spends on producing saws? The variable y is the money paid, and x is the number of saws produced.
    a. $y = 50,000x + 40$
    b. $y + 40 = x - 50,000$
    c. $y = 40x - 50,000$
    d. $y = 40x + 50,000$

15. A piggy bank contains 12 dollars' worth of nickels. A nickel weighs 5 grams, and the empty piggy bank weighs 1,050 grams. What is the total weight of the full piggy bank?
    a. 1,110 grams
    b. 1,200 grams
    c. 2,250 grams
    d. 2,200 grams

The following stem-and-leaf plot shows plant growth in cm for a group of tomato plants.

Stem	Leaf
2	0 2 3 6 8 8 9
3	2 6 7 7
4	7 9
5	4 6 9

16. What is the range of measurements for the tomato plants' growth?
    a. 29 cm
    b. 37 cm
    c. 39 cm
    d. 59 cm

17. How many plants grew more than 35 cm?
    a. 4 plants
    b. 5 plants
    c. 8 plants
    d. 9 plants

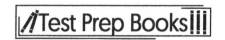

18. It costs Shea $12 to produce 3 necklaces. If he can sell each necklace for $20, how much profit would he make if he sold 60 necklaces?
   a. $240
   b. $360
   c. $960
   d. $1200

19. Five students took a test. Jenny scored the highest with a 94. James scored the lowest with a 79. Hector scored lower than Jenny, but higher than Sam. Sam scored lower than Mary who scored an 84. Which of the following statements must be true?
   a. There were 3 people who scored higher than Sam.
   b. The median test score was an 84.
   c. Jenny is the only student who scored above 90.
   d. Hector scored lower than Mary.

20. The width of a rectangular house is 22 feet. What is the perimeter of this house if it has the same area as a house that is 33 feet wide and 50 feet long?
   a. 184 feet
   b. 200 feet
   c. 194 feet
   d. 206 feet

21. Because of an increase in demand, the price of a designer purse has increased 25% from the original price of $128. What is the new price of the purse?
   a. $32
   b. $160
   c. $192
   d. $96

22. Carly purchased 84 bulbs for her flower garden. Tulips came in trays containing six bulbs and daffodils came in trays containing 8 bulbs. Carly bought an equal number of tulip and daffodil trays. How many of each type of flower bulb were purchased?
   a. 3 trays
   b. 4 trays
   c. 6 trays
   d. 8 trays

Quantitative Comparison

For each of questions 23–37, compare Quantity A to Quantity B, using additional information presented above the two quantities.

23. h is an integer in the following mathematical series: 4, h, 19, 39, 79

Quantity A	Quantity B
The value of h	9

   a. Quantity A is greater.
   b. Quantity B is greater.
   c. The two quantities are equal.
   d. The relationship cannot be determined from the information given.

223

24.

g inches

Area = 56 square inches   **4 inches**

Quantity A	Quantity B
The value of g	13

a. Quantity A is greater.
b. Quantity B is greater.
c. The two quantities are equal.
d. The relationship cannot be determined from the information given.

25. $4x - 12 = -2x$

Quantity A	Quantity B
The value of x	3

a. Quantity A is greater.
b. Quantity B is greater.
c. The two quantities are equal.
d. The relationship cannot be determined from the information given.

26.

Jimmy	Steve
7 red marbles	6 green marbles
8 blue marbles	4 blue marbles

Quantity A	Quantity B
All of Jimmy's marbles divided marbles	Jimmy's blue marbles divided by all of Steve's Steve's green marbles

a. Quantity A is greater.
b. Quantity B is greater.
c. The two quantities are equal.
d. The relationship cannot be determined from the information given.

27.

Quantity A	Quantity B
7 times the area of the triangle	2 times the area of the rectangle

a. Quantity A is greater.
b. Quantity B is greater.
c. The two quantities are equal.
d. The relationship cannot be determined from the information given.

28. Truck A drives 1,236 yards and truck B drives 3,680 feet.

Quantity A	Quantity B
The distance that truck A drove	The distance that truck B drove

a. Quantity A is greater.
b. Quantity B is greater.
c. The two quantities are equal.
d. The relationship cannot be determined from the information given.

29. $x > 6 > z$

Quantity A	Quantity B
$x + z$	$x - 6$

a. Quantity A is greater.
b. Quantity B is greater.
c. The two quantities are equal.
d. The relationship cannot be determined from the information given.

30. There are 16 rocks in a bag. 12 of them are smooth and 4 of them are rough.

Quantity A	Quantity B
The probability of choosing a rough rock	$\frac{2}{8}$

   a. Quantity A is greater.
   b. Quantity B is greater.
   c. The two quantities are equal.
   d. The relationship cannot be determined from the information given.

31. Bill is four years older than Jim.

Quantity A	Quantity B
Twice Jim's age	Bill's age

   a. Quantity A is greater.
   b. Quantity B is greater.
   c. The two quantities are equal.
   d. The relationship cannot be determined from the information given.

32. Angie has more cats than Janet.

Quantity A	Quantity B
Angie's number of cats	4 more than Janet's number of cats

   a. Quantity A is greater.
   b. Quantity B is greater.
   c. The two quantities are equal.
   d. The relationship cannot be determined from the information given.

33. Gage is twice as old as Cam.

Quantity A	Quantity B
Cam's age	Half of Gage's age

   a. Quantity A is greater.
   b. Quantity B is greater.
   c. The two quantities are equal.
   d. The relationship cannot be determined from the information given.

34.

Quantity A	Quantity B
Largest prime number less than 35	Smallest prime number greater than 25

   a. Quantity A is greater.
   b. Quantity B is greater.
   c. The two quantities are equal.
   d. The relationship cannot be determined from the information given.

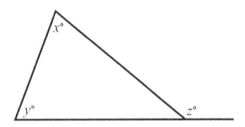
35.

Quantity A	Quantity B
28% of 345	$\frac{1}{5}$ of 300

   a.   Quantity A is greater.
   b.   Quantity B is greater.
   c.   The two quantities are equal.
   d.   The relationship cannot be determined from the information given.

36.

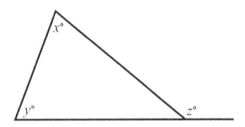

Quantity A	Quantity B
$x + y$	z

   a.   Quantity A is greater.
   b.   Quantity B is greater.
   c.   The two quantities are equal.
   d.   The relationship cannot be determined from the information given.

37.

Quantity A	Quantity B
Circumference of a circle with radius 4 cm	Perimeter of a rectangle with sides 5 cm and 7 cm

a. Quantity A is greater.
b. Quantity B is greater.
c. The two quantities are equal.
d. The relationship cannot be determined from the information given.

Mathematics Achievement

1. Which of the following inequalities is equivalent to $3 - \frac{1}{2}x \geq 2$?
   a. $x \geq 2$
   b. $x \leq 2$
   c. $x \geq 1$
   d. $x \leq 1$

2. $(2x - 4y)^2$ can be expanded to which of the following?
   a. $4x^2 - 16xy + 16y^2$
   b. $4x^2 - 8xy + 16y^2$
   c. $4x^2 - 16xy - 16y^2$
   d. $2x^2 - 8xy + 8y^2$

3. What is the simplified form of the expression $(7n + 3n^3 + 3) + (8n + 5n^3 + 2n^4)$?
   a. $9n^4 + 15n - 2$
   b. $2n^4 + 5n^3 + 15n - 2$
   c. $9n^4 + 8n^3 + 15n$
   d. $2n^4 + 8n^3 + 15n + 3$

4. Multiply and reduce $\frac{15}{23} \times \frac{54}{127}$.
   a. $\frac{810}{2,921}$

   b. $\frac{81}{292}$

   c. $\frac{69}{150}$

   d. $\frac{810}{2929}$

5. What is the product of the following expressions?
$$(4x - 8)(5x^2 + x + 6)$$
   a. $20x^3 - 36x^2 + 16x - 48$
   b. $6x^3 - 41x^2 + 12x + 15$
   c. $20x^3 + 11x^2 - 37x - 12$
   d. $2x^3 - 11x^2 - 32x + 20$

6. What is the solution for the following equation?
$$\frac{x^2 + x - 30}{x - 5} = 11$$
   a. $x = -6$
   b. There is no solution.
   c. $x = 16$
   d. $x = 5$

7. Which of the following formulas would correctly calculate the perimeter of a legal-sized piece of paper that is 14 inches long and $8\frac{1}{2}$ inches wide?

   a. $P = 14 + 8\frac{1}{2}$
   b. $P = 14 + 8\frac{1}{2} + 14 + 8\frac{1}{2}$
   c. $P = 14 \times 8\frac{1}{2}$
   d. $P = 14 \times \frac{17}{2}$

8. Which of the ordered pairs below is a solution to the following system of inequalities?

$$\begin{cases} y > 2x - 3 \\ y < -4x + 8 \end{cases}$$

    a. $(4, 5)$
    b. $(-3, -2)$
    c. $(3, -1)$
    d. $(5, 2)$

9. Convert $\frac{2}{9}$ to a percentage.

    a. 22.22%
    b. 4.5%
    c. 450%
    d. 0.22%

10. What is the volume of a cone, in terms of π, with a radius of 10 centimeters and height of 12 centimeters?

    a. $400 \pi \text{ cm}^3$
    b. $200 \pi \text{ cm}^3$
    c. $120 \pi \text{ cm}^3$
    d. $140 \pi \text{ cm}^3$

11. What is 3 out of 8 expressed as a percent?

    a. 37.5%
    b. 37%
    c. 26.7%
    d. 2.67%

12. If a car can travel 300 miles in four hours, how far can it go in an hour and a half?

    a. 100 miles
    b. 112.5 miles
    c. 135.5 miles
    d. 150 miles

13. Marty wishes to save $150 over a 4-day period. How much must Marty save each day on average?

    a. $37.50
    b. $35.00
    c. $45.50
    d. $41.00

14. Which of the following is NOT a way to write 40 percent of N?

    a. $(0.4)N$

    b. $\frac{2}{5}N$

    c. $40N$

    d. $\frac{4N}{10}$

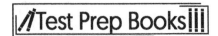

15. The graph of which function has an x-intercept of -2?
   a. $y = 2x - 3$
   b. $y = 4x + 2$
   c. $y = x^2 + 5x + 6$
   d. $y = 2x^2 + 3x - 1$

16. A closet is filled with red, blue, and green shirts. If $\frac{1}{3}$ of the shirts are green and $\frac{2}{5}$ are red, what fraction of the shirts are blue?
   a. $\frac{4}{15}$
   b. $\frac{1}{5}$
   c. $\frac{7}{15}$
   d. $\frac{1}{2}$

17. Shawna buys $2\frac{1}{2}$ gallons of paint. If she uses $\frac{1}{3}$ of it on the first day, how much does she have left?
   a. $1\frac{5}{6}$ gallons
   b. $1\frac{1}{2}$ gallons
   c. $1\frac{2}{3}$ gallons
   d. 2 gallons

18. Solve this equation:
$$9x + x - 7 = 16 + 2x$$
   a. $x = -4$
   b. $x = 3$
   c. $x = \frac{9}{8}$
   d. $x = \frac{23}{8}$

19. Which graph will be a line parallel to the graph of $y = 3x - 2$?
   a. $6x - 2y = -2$
   b. $4x - y = -4$
   c. $3y = x - 2$
   d. $2x - 2y = 2$

20. What is the equation for the line passing through the origin and the point $(2,1)$?
   a. $y = 2x$
   b. $y = \frac{1}{2}x$
   c. $y = x - 2$
   d. $2y = x + 1$

21. A line goes through the point $(-4, 0)$ and the point $(0, 2)$. What is the slope of the line?

    a. 2

    b. 4

    c. $\frac{3}{2}$

    d. $\frac{1}{2}$

22. Write the expression for three times the sum of twice a number and one, minus six.

    a. $2x + 1 - 6$
    b. $3x + 1 - 6$
    c. $3(x + 1) - 6$
    d. $3(2x + 1) - 6$

23. What would be the coordinates if the point plotted on the grid was reflected over the x-axis?

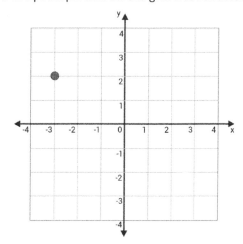

    a. $(-3, 2)$
    b. $(2, -3)$
    c. $(-3, -2)$
    d. $(2, 3)$

24. Jessica buys 10 cans of paint. Red paint costs $1 per can, and blue paint costs $2 per can. In total, she spends $16. How many red cans did she buy?

    a. 2
    b. 3
    c. 4
    d. 5

25. The variable y is directly proportional to x. If $y = 3$ when $x = 5$, then what is y when $x = 20$?

    a. 10
    b. 12
    c. 14
    d. 16

26. If $-3(x + 4) \geq x + 8$, what is the value of x?
 a. $x = 4$
 b. $x \geq 2$
 c. $x \geq -5$
 d. $x \leq -5$

27. Simplify the following fraction:

$$\frac{\left(\frac{5}{7}\right)}{\left(\frac{9}{11}\right)}$$

 a. $\frac{55}{63}$

 b. $\frac{7}{1,000}$

 c. $\frac{13}{15}$

 d. $\frac{5}{11}$

28. What is the slope of this line?

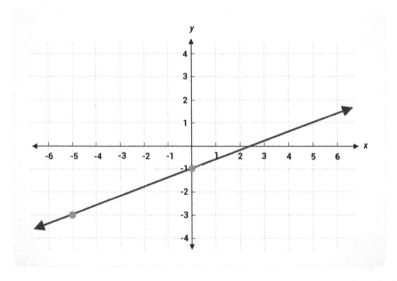

 a. 2

 b. $\frac{5}{2}$

 c. $\frac{1}{2}$

 d. $\frac{2}{5}$

29. What is the perimeter of the figure below? Note that the solid outer line is the perimeter.

8 in.

8 in.

4 in.   4 in.

a. 48.565 in
b. 36.565 in
c. 39.78 in
d. 39.565 in

30. Which four-sided shape is always a rectangle?
a. Rhombus
b. Square
c. Parallelogram
d. Quadrilateral

31. Of the numbers -1, 17, -13, or -6, which is farthest from 5 on the number line?
a. -1
b. 17
c. -13
d. -6

32. If $\sqrt{1+x} = 4$, what is x?
a. 10
b. 15
c. 20
d. 25

33. Five students take a test. The scores of the first four students are 80, 85, 75, and 60. If the median score is 80, which of the following could NOT be the score of the fifth student?
a. 60
b. 80
c. 85
d. 100

34. What is the volume of a rectangular prism with a height of 2 inches, a width of 4 inches, and a depth of 6 inches?
a. 12 in^3
b. 24 in^3
c. 48 in^3
d. 96 in^3

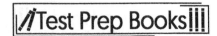

35. What is the volume of a cylinder, in terms of π, with a radius of 5 inches and a height of 10 inches?
    a. $250\pi \text{ in}^3$
    b. $50\pi \text{ in}^3$
    c. $100\pi \text{ in}^3$
    d. $200\pi \text{ in}^3$

36. Ten students take a test. Five students get a 50. Four students get a 70. If the average score is 55, what was the last student's score?
    a. 20
    b. 40
    c. 50
    d. 60

37. An equilateral triangle has a perimeter of 18 feet. The sides of a square have the same length as the triangle's sides. What is the area of the square?
    a. 6 square feet
    b. 36 square feet
    c. 256 square feet
    d. 1,000 square feet

38. What is $(2 \times 20) \div (7 + 1) + (6 \times 0.01) + (4 \times 0.001)$?
    a. 5.064
    b. 5.64
    c. 5.0064
    d. 48.064

39. Last year, the New York City area received approximately $27\frac{3}{4}$ inches of snow. The Denver area received approximately three times as much snow as New York City. How much snow fell in Denver?
    a. 60 inches
    b. $27\frac{1}{4}$ inches
    c. $9\frac{1}{4}$ inches
    d. $83\frac{1}{4}$ inches

40. Solve for x: $\frac{2x}{5} - 1 = 59$.
    a. 60
    b. 145
    c. 150
    d. 115

41. A National Hockey League store in the state of Michigan advertises 50% off all items. Sales tax in Michigan is 6%. How much would a hat originally priced at $32.99 and a jersey originally priced at $64.99 cost during this sale? Round to the nearest penny.
    a. $97.98
    b. $103.86
    c. $51.93
    d. $48.99

234

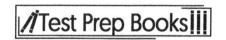

42. Store-brand coffee beans cost $1.23 per pound. A local coffee bean roaster charges $1.98 per $1\frac{1}{2}$ pounds. How much more would 5 pounds from the local roaster cost than 5 pounds of the store-brand?
    a. $0.55
    b. $1.55
    c. $1.45
    d. $0.45

43. Paint Inc. charges $2,000 for painting the first 1,800 feet of trim on a house and an additional $1.00 per foot for each foot beyond that. How much would it cost to paint a house with 3,125 feet of trim?
    a. $3,125
    b. $2,000
    c. $5,125
    d. $3,325

44. A train traveling 50 miles per hour takes a trip lasting 3 hours. If a map has a scale of 1 inch per 10 miles, how many inches apart are the train's starting point and ending point on the map?
    a. 14 inches
    b. 12 inches
    c. 13 inches
    d. 15 inches

45. A traveler takes an hour to drive to a museum, spends three hours and 30 minutes there, and takes half an hour to drive home. What percentage of their time was spent driving?
    a. 15%
    b. 30%
    c. 40%
    d. 60%

46. A couple buys a house for $150,000. They sell it for $165,000. By what percentage did the house's value increase?
    a. 10%
    b. 13%
    c. 15%
    d. 17%

47. A map has a scale of 1 inch per 5 miles. A car can travel 60 miles per hour. If the distance from the start to the destination is 3 inches on the map, how long will it take the car to make the trip?
    a. 12 minutes
    b. 15 minutes
    c. 17 minutes
    d. 20 minutes

Reading Comprehension

Passage 1

[1]In recent years, some modern approaches to public transportation have made significant additions to conventional modes, such as city buses, subways, and taxis. [2]Private transportation has become convenient and affordable to anyone with access to the Internet.

[3]One of the most well-known modern transportation companies is Uber. [4]Uber employs individuals to pick up and drop off riders with the touch of a button. [5]When a rider needs to be picked up, they simply log into the Uber app and request a car. [6]Once the app verifies the rider's location, a driver arrives for pick-up within minutes. [7]Payment for the ride is done through the app, so riders don't need to worry about carrying cash in order to catch a ride.

[8]Uber is a great resource; it is commonly used by adult commuters. [9]Smaller cities have launched their own versions of Uber. For example, Deer Park, Texas, created DeerHaul. [10]DeerHaul operates under the same idea as Uber, only it caters to kids. [11]Many working parents find it difficult to transport their children themselves during work hours, and DeerHaul is a viable alternative. [12]If a child needs to be picked up from school and dropped off at Little League baseball practice, but his or her parents can't leave work, a ride with DeerHaul can be arranged. [13]All DeerHaul drivers are previous or current teachers who have passed a battery of fingerprint background checks. [14]Like Uber, DeerHaul rides are arranged through an Internet app, and all payments are handled electronically, so no cash is exchanged between the child and the driver.

1. The main purpose of this passage is to
   a. Advertise for private transportation companies such as Uber and DeerHaul
   b. Inform readers about new modes of private transportation
   c. Persuade readers to schedule a ride with DeerHaul for their children
   d. Convince readers to consider conventional methods of transportation

2. Which statement about DeerHaul is best supported by the passage?
   a. DeerHaul is a convenient way for parents to transport their kids.
   b. DeerHaul takes no special safety measures to ensure safe rides for kids.
   c. DeerHaul is a better transportation option than Uber.
   d. Anyone can apply to be a driver for DeerHaul.

3. According to the passage, how are payments handled for private transportation?
   a. Bus or subway tickets are purchased.
   b. Riders pay the driver at the end of each ride.
   c. Tipping drivers with cash is always appreciated.
   d. Rides are paid for electronically when the ride is requested.

4. In sentence 13, the word **battery** most nearly means
   a. Cell
   b. Artillery
   c. Series
   d. Violence

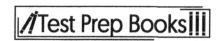

5. Which sentence contains the main idea of this passage?
   a. Sentence 1
   b. Sentence 2
   c. Sentence 3
   d. Sentence 8

6. Which of the following best describes the subject matter of the passage?
   a. Two modes of private transportation are explained.
   b. The best method of private transportation is discussed.
   c. The analysis of one transportation company is refuted by the analysis of a second company.
   d. Conventional transportation methods are compared to more modern transportation.

Passage 2

[1]Rudolph the Red-Nosed Reindeer hasn't always been an iconic staple in the tradition of Christmas. [2] In 1939, Montgomery Ward department stores gave Robert L. May an assignment that would change the tradition of Christmas around the world. [3]May, a copywriter for Montgomery Ward, was asked to create a promotional Christmas coloring book. [4]The coloring book was to be a gift for children from the store Santa. [5]Montgomery Ward hoped the gift would increase store traffic.

[6]The poem, "A Visit from St. Nicholas," published in 1823, originally depicted eight flying reindeer as members of Santa's team. [7] In 1939, May added Rudolph. [8]May's story depicts Rudolph as a **misfit** among the other reindeer because of his red nose. [9]Rudolph has the opportunity to prove his worth as he leads Santa's team through a blizzard on Christmas Eve. [10]For this, Rudolph becomes known as "the most famous reindeer of all". [11]At the time, Montgomery Ward officials were unsure of Rudolph's red nose because this was also known as a symptom of drunkenness. [12]However, after May and coworker Denver Gillan created a sketch of the red-nosed reindeer, officials approved the story.

[13] Montgomery Ward's promotion was a great success during the Christmas season, with 2.4 million copies of "Rudolph the Red-Nosed Reindeer" gifted from Santas in their stores. [14] In 1947, "Rudolph the Red-Nosed Reindeer" was commercially printed as a children's literature book available for purchase in bookstores.

7. Which of the following best describes the subject matter in the passage?
   a. A Montgomery Ward advertising project made Rudolph a famous Christmas tradition.
   b. Denver Gillan first created the character of Rudolph for Montgomery Ward.
   c. Robert L. May's work helped him climb the ranks at Montgomery Ward.
   d. Without Montgomery Ward's Rudolph, Christmas would have been canceled in many countries.

8. Which statement is best supported by the passage?
   a. When first presented to the public, the character of Rudolph was associated with drunkenness.
   b. Rudolph became *the most famous reindeer of all* because he saved Christmas.
   c. Gillan is responsible for turning Way's story into a poem.
   d. The Rudolph Christmas promotional saved Montgomery Ward from having to close many stores.

9. According to the passage, *Rudolph the Red-Nosed Reindeer* was
   a. Commercially printed in 1949
   b. Originally a promotional coloring book
   c. Part of an earlier poem called "A Visit from St. Nicholas"
   d. Written by Denver Gillan

10. In sentence 8, the word **misfit** most nearly means
   a. member.
   b. conformist.
   c. insider.
   d. oddball.

11. Which of the following best describes the author's tone in this passage?
   a. Humorous
   b. Apologetic
   c. Informative
   d. Sad

12. The phrase *Rudolph the Red-Nosed Reindeer* is what type of figurative language?
   a. Simile
   b. Metaphor
   c. Alliteration
   d. Onomatopoeia

Passage 3

[1]Water is the only substance on Earth that can occur in three states: liquid, gas, and solid. [2]The liquid state of water is the type of water you drink, cook with, or find in streams and rivers. [3]The gas form is called *water vapor,* or *steam,* and the solid, or frozen, form of water is known as *ice*.
[4]Water, also known as H_2O, is made up of hydrogen and oxygen atoms. [5]These atoms join together to form water **molecules**.

[6]Water molecules move at various rates of speed and distances from each other depending on the state of water. [7]When the temperature of water reaches its boiling point at 212°F, water molecules move more rapidly and spread farther apart, allowing some of them to escape into the air. [8]This turns liquid water into water vapor, or steam.

[9]On the other hand, when the temperature of liquid water becomes cooler, the water molecules begin to slow down and move closer together. [10]Eventually, the water molecules stop moving and stick together to form a solid called ice. [11]**Conversely**, when the temperature of ice becomes warmer, water molecules begin to spread apart, causing the ice to melt and return to a liquid state.

13. According to the passage, the water molecules of boiling water
   a. Move rapidly and spread farther apart
   b. Move more slowly and spread farther apart
   c. Move closer together and slow down
   d. Move rapidly and get closer together

14. If water vapor is formed when the temperature of water reaches 212°F, what happens to water vapor when it rises into the air and cools?
   a. As the water vapor cools, the molecules will return to a liquid state.
   b. The water molecules will move closer together to form a solid.
   c. The water molecules will disappear into the atmosphere.
   d. Once water becomes a gas, it always remains a gas.

15. Which sentence best represents the main idea of this passage?
   a.   Sentence 1
   b.   Sentence 4
   c.   Sentence 6
   d.   Sentence 9

16. In sentence 4, the word **molecules** most nearly means
   a.   Masses
   b.   Bundles
   c.   Vast amounts
   d.   Particles

17. According to this passage, what state of water is steam?
   a.   Liquid
   b.   Gas
   c.   Solid
   d.   Molecule

18. In sentence 11, the term **conversely** most nearly means
   a.   Identically
   b.   Comparably
   c.   Similarly
   d.   The other way around

Passage 4

[1]My friend Alyssa and I had spent most of the day getting ready. [2]Our moms had treated us to manicures and pedicures, followed by a fancy lunch at Burgdorf's Tea Room and then a trip to the hair salon for some curls and up-dos. [3]Alyssa and I had smiled and giggled all day in disbelief that the big day had finally arrived.

[4]At seven o'clock sharp, Ricky and Bobby came to pick us up. [5]There was an exchange of corsages and boutonnieres as our moms took an abundance of pictures to remember the night. [6]The four of us giggled and laughed as the limo driver whisked us off to the eighth-grade dance.
[7]We blared the radio and sang our favorite songs as the limo hustled into town. [8]It was all fun and games until the car suddenly swerved and we tumbled over each other in the back seat like rag dolls. [9]The tires *screeched like an alley cat* just before everything went black.

[10]It's been three months since everything went dark that night, although it feels like a lifetime. [11]The driver swerved to avoid a deer in the road. [12]He might have seen it sooner if he hadn't been texting while he was driving. [13]We never made it to the eighth-grade dance. [14]The only dancing lights I got to see that night were those of ambulances and police cars. [15]Ricky, Bobby, and Alyssa never even got to see those.

19. What is the main purpose of this passage?
   a.   To persuade readers to attend their eighth-grade dance
   b.   To inform readers about the availability of limo rides
   c.   To illustrate the impact of texting and driving
   d.   To explain how girls get ready for a dance

20. The phrase *screeched like an alley cat* in sentence 9 is an example of a
    a. Metaphor
    b. Simile
    c. Alliteration
    d. Cliché

21. This story is told in which point of view?
    a. First person
    b. Second person
    c. Third person
    d. Fourth person

22. According to the last sentence in the passage, readers can conclude that
    a. Ricky, Bobby, and Alyssa did not survive the accident.
    b. Ricky, Bobby, and Alyssa did not have to ride in an ambulance.
    c. Ricky, Bobby, and Alyssa had never planned to attend the dance.
    d. Ricky, Bobby, and Alyssa were blinded in the accident.

23. What is the overall message of this passage?
    a. Limo drivers are not required to take driving safety courses.
    b. Don't text and drive.
    c. Car accidents are common occurrences on special nights.
    d. Friends should not travel together in a limo.

24. Which statement can best be supported by this passage?
    a. The girls had been best friends since kindergarten.
    b. Ricky and Bobby came to pick up the girls in a limo.
    c. The girls' mothers were very supportive of their decision to go to the dance.
    d. The town has a great emergency response team.

Passage 5

[1]Princess Diana, born Diana Spencer on July 1, 1961 in Sandringham, England, left this world on August 31, 1997, at the age of thirty-six.

[2]Princess Diana was a graduate of Riddlesworth Hall School and West Heath School. [3]After completing further schooling at Institut Alpin Videmanette in Switzerland, she worked as a teacher's assistant so she could pursue her passion for working with children.

[4]Princess Diana was known for her big heart and support of various charities. [5]Some of her most influential work included helping the homeless and children in need. [6]She also worked to provide support to people living with HIV and AIDS. [7]Princess Diana also partnered with her sons, working diligently to raise awareness in Angola about the dangers of landmines left behind after war.

[8]Princess Diana is survived by son, Prince William Arthur Philip Louis; son, Prince Henry Charles Albert David; and ex-husband, Prince Charles of Wales.

[9]Funeral services will be held September 6 at Westminster Abbey. [10]A family-only graveside ceremony will be held at the Spencer family estate, Althorp.

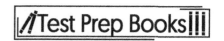

[11]*In lieu of* flowers, the family requests donations be made to the Diana, Princess of Wales Memorial Fund in an effort to continue the valuable charity work Princess Diana cherished.

25. What type of article is this passage?
    a. News article
    b. Preface
    c. Obituary
    d. Short story

26. In sentence 11, the phrase *in lieu of* most nearly means
    a. Because of
    b. Instead of
    c. Preferably
    d. Do not send

27. With the information in this passage, readers can conclude Princess Diana was passionate about
    a. Having children
    b. Doing charity work
    c. Getting an education
    d. Funding charities

28. After Princess Diana completed school, she
    a. Moved to Sandringham, England
    b. Had children
    c. Became a teacher's assistant
    d. Did charity work

29. With the information in the passage, readers can infer donations to the Diana, Princess of Wales Memorial Fund will
    a. Pay for her funeral at the family estate
    b. Buy clothes and school supplies for less fortunate children
    c. Be transferred to the family trust
    d. Send her sons to college

30. How is this passage organized?
    a. Biographical information is followed by current events.
    b. An opinion is offered about an individual.
    c. Evidence is presented to refute an individual's popularity.
    d. A thesis statement is followed by supporting paragraphs.

Passage 6

[1]Mr. Walter lived here in Vinson, Oklahoma, for his entire life. [2]He owned the little green house in town where he and his wife, Hilda, raised four boys. [3]Mr. Walter worked at the paper mill as a welder for forty-eight years.

[4]When he retired, he became the school crossing guard. [5]Every day, Mr. Walter stood on that corner and helped kids safely cross the street. [6]He knew the name of every kid who stopped at his corner, and he was always happy to see each one. [7]In the wintertime, he handed out hats and gloves to kids who'd left theirs at home. [8]Mr. Walter was always smiling as he waved to every driver that passed his corner.

241

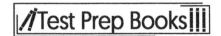
[9]After he got too old to be the crossing guard, Mr. Walter bought himself a bicycle. [10]It was a three-wheeled bike, metallic red with a basket on the front. [11]At eighty years old, Mr. Walter put on his helmet and started running the roads.

[12]Mr. Walter rode that red bike around town picking up cans and trash. [13]He said it was his job to look out for his city. [14]It wasn't uncommon to see his bike parked at the McDonald's on Main. [15]He'd be standing out near the street waving at every car that passed.

[16]The whole town showed up at Mr. Walter's funeral. [17]In eighty-four years, there wasn't a day that had gone by where Mr. Walter hadn't touched one of our lives. [18]Mr. Walter had been a hero to us. [19]He'd never saved anyone from a burning house or leapt tall buildings in a single bound, but he had loved our town and each of us in it, wholeheartedly. [20]That is what made him our hero.

31. In sentence 11, the phrase *running the roads* is an example of a(an)
    a. Simile
    b. Personification
    c. Idiom
    d. Metaphor

32. What can readers conclude from this passage?
    a. Mr. Walter retired from the paper mill and started riding his bike around town.
    b. Mr. Walter could never remember the names of the children he crossed at his corner.
    c. Mr. Walter picked up cans and trash when he worked at the paper mill.
    d. Mr. Walter touched the lives of everyone in the town of Vinson.

33. This passage can be categorized as a(n)
    a. Informational text
    b. Short story
    c. News article
    d. Persuasive letter

34. According to the passage, it was common for Mr. Walter to
    a. Give kids hats and gloves in the winter
    b. Forget to wear his safety helmet
    c. Encourage kids to pick up their trash
    d. Take his cans to the McDonald's

35. What is the overall message of this passage?
    a. Heroes should save people from burning buildings.
    b. Sometimes it's the little things that make you a hero.
    c. Kids think all adults like Mr. Walter are heroes.
    d. All school crossing guards are special people.

36. In sentence 19, the phrase *leapt tall buildings in a single bound* is an example of a(n)
    a. Hyperbole
    b. Simile
    c. Onomatopoeia
    d. Allusion

ISEE Answer Explanations

Quantitative Reasoning

Word Problems

1. B: For the first card drawn, the probability of a king being pulled is $\frac{4}{52}$. Since this card isn't replaced, if a king is drawn first, the probability of a king being drawn second is $\frac{3}{51}$. The probability of a king being drawn in both the first and second draw is the product of the two probabilities:

$$\frac{4}{52} \times \frac{3}{51} = \frac{12}{2,652}$$

To reduce this fraction, divide the top and bottom by 12 to get $\frac{1}{221}$.

2. A: Using the given information of one nurse to 25 patients and 325 total patients, set up an equation to solve for the number of nurses (N):

$$\frac{N}{325} = \frac{1}{25}$$

Multiply both sides by 325 to get N by itself on one side.

$$\frac{N}{1} = \frac{325}{25} = 13 \text{ nurses}$$

3. B: The formula for the volume of a cylinder is $\pi r^2 h$, where r is the radius and h is the height. The diameter is twice the radius, so these barrels have a radius of 1 foot. That means each barrel has a volume of:

$$\pi \times 1 \, ft^2 \times 3 \, ft = 3\pi \text{ ft}^3$$

Since there are three of them, the total is:

$$3 \times 3\pi \, ft = 9\pi \text{ ft}^3$$

4. A: The tip is not taxed, so he pays 5% tax only on the $10. To find 5% of $10, calculate $0.05 \times \$10 = \$0.50$. Add up $10 + \$0.50 + \$2$ to get $12.50.

5. A: Taylor's total income is $20,000 + \$10,000 = \$30,000$. 15 percent as a fraction is $\frac{15}{100} = \frac{3}{20}$. So:

$$\frac{3}{20} \times \$30,000 = \frac{\$90,000}{20} = \frac{\$9,000}{2}$$

$$\frac{\$9,000}{2} = \$4,500$$

6. D: Exponential functions can be written in the form: $y = a \times b^x$. The equation for an exponential function can be written given the y-intercept (a) and the growth rate (b). The y-intercept is the output (y) when the input (x) equals zero. It can be thought of as an "original value," or starting point. The value of b is the rate at which the original value increases ($b > 1$) or decreases ($b < 1$). In this scenario, the y-intercept, a, would be $1200, and the

243

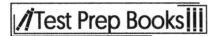

growth rate, b, would be 1.01 (100% of the original value combined with 1% interest, or $100\% + 1\% = 101\% = 1.01$).

7. D: This problem can be solved by using unit conversion. The initial units are miles per minute. The final units need to be feet per second. Converting miles to feet uses the equivalence statement 1 mi = 5,280 ft. Converting minutes to seconds uses the equivalence statement 1 min = 60 s. Setting up the ratios to convert the units is shown in the following equation:

$$\frac{72 \text{ mi}}{90 \text{ min}} \times \frac{1 \text{ min}}{60 \text{ s}} \times \frac{5,280 \text{ ft}}{1 \text{ mi}} = 70.4 \frac{\text{ft}}{\text{s}}$$

The initial units cancel out, and the new units are left.

8. C: To find the drop in value, subtract the new value from the old value. To see what percentage of the initial value this is, divide the difference by the initial value, then multiply by 100.

$$\frac{20,000 - 8,000}{20,000} = 0.6$$

$$(0.60) \times 100 = 60\%$$

9. A: The question only asks how long they owned the house, so ignore the extra details about prices. There are 6 years between May 1, 2010 and May 1, 2016. There are another 4 months between May 1, 2016 and September 1, 2016. Therefore, they owned the house for a total of 6 years and 4 months. Each year has 12 months, so the total number of months is $(6 \times 12) + 4 = 72 + 4 = 76 \ months$.

10. D: The formula for finding the volume of a rectangular prism is $V = l \times w \times h$, where l is the length, w is the width, and h is the height. The volume of the original box is calculated:

$$V = 8 \ in \times 14 \ in \times 4 \ in = 448 \ in^3$$

The volume of the new box is calculated:

$$V = 16 \ in \times 28 \ in \times 8 \ in = 3,584 \ in^3$$

The volume of the new box divided by the volume of the old box equals 8.

11. A: The formula for the area of a circle is $A = \pi r^2$. Here, $r = 9$, so we calculate $A = \pi(9^2) = 81\pi$.

12. D: The slope from this equation is 50, and it is interpreted as the cost per gigabyte used. Since the g-value represents the number of gigabytes and the equation is set equal to the cost in dollars, the slope relates these two values. For every gigabyte used on the phone, the bill goes up 50 dollars.

13. A: The perimeter of a rectangle is $P = 2l + 2w$. We are told $P = 44$, so $2l + 2w = 44$. We are also told that the width is 2 cm less than the length: $w = l - 2$. Substituting this for w in the perimeter equation, we get $2l + 2(l - 2) = 44$, which is Choice A. Although it's not necessary to answer the test question, we could solve the equation to find the length and width. The equation simplifies to $4l - 4 = 44$, or $l = 12$, and since $w = l - 2$, we find $w = 10$.

14. D: For manufacturing costs, there is a linear relationship between the cost to the company and the number produced, with a y-intercept given by the base cost of acquiring the means of production, and a slope given by the cost to produce one unit. In this case, that base cost is $50,000, while the cost per unit is $40. So:

$$y = 40x + 50,000$$

244

15. C: A dollar contains 20 nickels. Therefore, if there are 12 dollars' worth of nickels, there are:

$$12 \times 20 = 240 \text{ nickels}$$

Each nickel weighs 5 grams. Therefore, the weight of the nickels is:

$$240 \times 5 = 1{,}200 \text{ grams}$$

To find the total weight of the filled piggy bank, add the weight of the nickels and the weight of the empty bank:

$$1{,}200 + 1{,}050 = 2{,}250 \text{ grams.}$$

16. C: The range of the entire stem-and-leaf plot is found by subtracting the lowest value from the highest value, as follows:

$$59 - 20 = 39 \text{ cm}$$

All other choices are miscalculations read from the chart.

17. C: To calculate the total greater than 35, the number of measurements above 35 must be totaled; 36, 37, 37, 47, 49, 54, 56, 59 = 8 measurements. Choice *A* is the number of measurements in the 3 categories, Choice *B* is the number in the 4 and 5 categories, and Choice *D* is the number in the 3, 4, and 5 categories.

18. C: In order to calculate the profit, we need to create an equation that models the total income minus the cost of the materials.

$$60 \times \$20 = \$1{,}200 \text{ total income}$$

$60 \div 3 = 20$ sets of materials. $20 \times \$12 = \$240$ cost of materials.

$$\$1{,}200 - \$240 = \$960 \text{ profit}$$

19. A: It can be determined from reading the information given that Jenny, Hector, and Mary scored higher than Sam, so Choice *A* is correct. There is no relation provided between Hector and Mary's scores. Given that Mary could have scored higher or lower than Hector, it cannot be determined if her score is the median, so Choice *B* is incorrect. With the information given, it is possible that Hector scored above 90, so Choice *C* is incorrect. There is no relation given between Hector and Mary's scores. This means that Hector could have scored higher or lower than Mary. So, Choice *D* is incorrect.

20. C: First, find the area of the second house. The area is:

$$A = l \, x \, w = 33 \times 50 = 1{,}650 \text{ square feet}$$

Then, use the area formula to determine what length gives the first house an area of 1,650 square feet. So:

$$1{,}650 = 22 \times l, l = \frac{1{,}650}{22} = 75 \text{ feet}$$

Then, use the formula for perimeter ($A = l + l + w + w$) to get:

$$75 + 75 + 22 + 22 = 194 \text{ feet}$$

21. B: The new price of the purse can be found by first multiplying the original price by 25%, or 0.25. This yields an increase of $32. Taking the original price of $128 and adding the increase in price of $32 yields a new price of $160.

245

22. C: This problem involved setting up an algebraic equation to solve for x, or the number of flower trays Carly purchased. The equation is as follows:

$$6x + 8x = 84$$

So,

$$14x = 84$$

Then divide each side by 14 to solve for x:

$$x = \frac{84}{14} = 6 \text{ trays}$$

Quantitative Comparison

23. C: The equation that produces this series is $2x + 1$. This gives $2(4) + 1 = 9, 2(9) + 1 = 19$, and so on. This means that the value of h in the series is 9, so Quantity A and Quantity B are equal.

24. A: The value of g can be found using the formula for area of a rectangle ($A = l \times w$). So, $56 = g \times 4$, and $g = 14$. This means that Quantity A is greater than Quantity B.

25. B: The first step is to solve for x. For this equation, that is:

$$4x - 12 = -2x$$

$$6x - 12 = 0$$

$$6x = 12$$

$$x = 2$$

The value of x is 2 and Quantity B is 3, so Quantity B is greater.

26. A: The first step here is to solve each of the ratios. The first ratio is all of Jimmy's marbles divided by all of Steve's marbles. This gives:

$$\frac{15}{10} = \frac{3}{2}$$

The second ratio is all of Jimmy's blue marbles divided by all of Steve's green marbles. This gives:

$$\frac{8}{6} = \frac{4}{3}$$

Since $\frac{3}{2}$ is greater than $\frac{4}{3}$, Quantity A is greater.

27. B: First, find the area of both figures. The area of the triangle is:

$$\frac{1}{2}(7) \times 8 = 28 \text{ square inches}$$

The area of the rectangle is $13 \times 8 = 104$ square inches. So, 7 times the area of the triangle would be 196 square inches, and 2 times the area of the rectangle would be 208 square inches. This means that Quantity B is greater.

246

28. A: First, convert the distance that Truck A drove to feet. This is:

$$1,236 \times 3 = 3,708 \text{ feet}$$

This means that Truck A drove further than Truck B. So, Quantity A is greater than Quantity B.

29. D: Either quantity could be greater for given values of x and z. For example, if $x = 7$ and $z = 1$, then Quantity A is 8 and Quantity B is 1. If $x = 10$ and $z = -8$, then Quantity A is 2, and Quantity B is 4.

30. C: The probability of choosing a rough rock is $\frac{4}{16}$. This is equal to $\frac{2}{8}$.

31. D: If Jim is 2 years old, then Bill is 6 years old. Twice Jim's age is 4, so Quantity B is greater. However, if Jim is 20 years old, then Bill is 24. Twice Jim's age is 40, so Quantity A is greater. Thus, the relationship cannot be determined from the given information.

32. D: If Angie has 5 cats, then Janet may have 4 cats. Four more than Janet is 8 cats, so Quantity B would be greater. But if Angie has 10 cats and Janet has 2 cats, then four more cats than Janet is 6, and Quantity A is greater. Thus, there is not enough information to determine which quantity is greater.

33. C: Call Gage's age g and Cam's age c. The sentence above, "Gage is twice as old as Cam," can be written as $2c = g$. Dividing both sides by 2, we find $c = (\frac{1}{2})g$, that is, Cam's age equals half of Gage's age.

34. A: A prime number is a number that only has factors of 1 and itself. Quantity A is the largest prime number less than 35. The number 34 is even, or divisible by 2, so it is not prime. 33 is divisible by 3 and 11, and 32 is even, so neither of those is prime. 31 has factors of only 1 and itself, so it is the largest prime number less than 35. Quantity B is the smallest prime number greater than 25. The next number is 26, which is even. 27 has factors of 3 and 9, while 28 is even. 29 has factors of only 1 and itself; therefore, it is the smallest prime number greater than 25. Comparing these two numbers, 31 and 29, Quantity A is greater. The correct answer is Choice *A* because Quantity A is greater.

35. A: To find a percentage of a number, convert the percentage to a decimal and multiply. Quantity A is $0.28 \times 345 = 96.6$. Quantity B is $(\frac{1}{5}) \times 300 = 300 \div 5 = 60$, so Quantity A is g   reater.

36. C: The angles inside a triangle are supplementary, which means they add up to 180 degrees. The third angle not named in the triangle and the exterior angle z are also supplementary because they add up to a straight line, or 180 degrees. If the unnamed angle is given the value w, then the equations can be written: $x + y + w = 180$ and $w + z = 180$. By the transitive property of equality, the equation can be written:

$$x + y + w = w + z$$

Subtracting w from both sides yields the equation $x + y = z$. Using this equation, Quantity A and Quantity B can be stated as equal. The correct answer is C because Quantity B is equal to Quantity A by the proof given above.

37. A: The circumference of a circle can be found by using the formula $C = 2\pi r$. The radius of this circle is x cm, so its circumference is $C = 2\pi x$. The perimeter of a rectangle is $P = 2l + 2w$, or in this case, $P = 2(x) + 2(5) = 2x +$

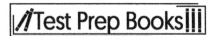

10. We can find when the circumference and perimeter are equal by setting the two expressions equal and solving for x:

$$2\pi x = 2x + 10$$

$$2\pi x - 2x = 10$$

$$(2\pi - 2)x = 10$$

$$x = \frac{10}{2\pi - 2} \approx 2.34$$

So when x is about 2.34 cm, the circumference is equal to the perimeter. When $x > 2.34$, the circumference is greater than the perimeter, and when $x < 2.34$, the perimeter is greater. Since the question doesn't give a value for x, we can't say which is greater.

Mathematics Achievement

1. B: To simplify this inequality, subtract 3 from both sides:

$$3 - 3 - \frac{1}{2}x \geq 2 - 3$$

$$-\frac{1}{2}x \geq -1$$

Then, multiply both sides by −2 (remembering that this flips the direction of the inequality):

$$\left(-\frac{1}{2}x\right)(-2) \geq (-1)(-2)$$

$$x \leq 2.$$

2. B: To expand a squared binomial, it's necessary to use the first, outer, inner, last (FOIL) method.

$$(2x - 4y)^2$$

$$(2x)(2x) + (2x)(-4y) + (-4y)(2x) + (-4y)(-4y)$$

$$4x^2 - 8xy - 8xy + 16y^2$$

$$4x^2 - 16xy + 16y^2$$

3. D: The expression is simplified by collecting like terms. Terms with the same variable and exponent are like terms, and their coefficients can be added.

4. A: $\frac{810}{2,921}$

Multiply across the top and across the bottom.

$$\frac{15 \times 54}{23 \times 127} = \frac{810}{2921}$$

248

This matches Choice A, but we must decide whether it can be reduced. Because the numbers are so large, it may be difficult to tell, so the easiest method may be to look at each of the other answer choices. With Choice B, we can tell that the denominator, 292, is not a factor of 2,921 because $292 \times 10 = 2,920$, not 2,921, so that doesn't work. With Choice C, again, we can see that the denominator, 150, is not a factor of 2,921, because 150 is a multiple of 10 and 2,921 isn't. Finally, in Choice D, the numerator is the same as in our original fraction, but the denominator isn't, so this can't have the same value. The other choices are eliminated, so the answer must be Choice A.

5. A: Finding the product means distributing one polynomial to the other so that each term in the first is multiplied by each term in the second. Then, like terms can be collected. Multiplying the factors yields the expression:

$$20x^3 + 4x^2 + 24x - 40x^2 - 8x - 48$$

Collecting like terms means adding the x^2 terms and adding the x terms. The final answer after simplifying the expression is:

$$20x^3 - 36x^2 + 16x - 48$$

6. B: We can try to solve the equation by factoring the numerator into $(x + 6)(x - 5)$. Since $(x - 5)$ is on the top and bottom, that factor cancels out. This leaves the equation $x + 6 = 11$. Solving the equation gives the answer $x = 5$. When this value is plugged into the equation, it yields a zero in the denominator of the fraction. Since this is undefined, there is no solution.

7. B: The perimeter of a rectangle is the sum of all four sides. Therefore, the answer is:

$$P = 14 + 8\frac{1}{2} + 14 + 8\frac{1}{2}$$

$$14 + 14 + 8 + \frac{1}{2} + 8 + \frac{1}{2} = 45 \text{ inches}$$

8. B: For an ordered pair to be a solution to a system of inequalities, it must make a true statement for both inequalities when substituting its values for x and y. Substituting $(-3, -2)$ into the inequalities produces $(-2) > 2(-3) - 3$ which becomes $-2 > -9$, and $(-2) < -4(-3) + 8$, which becomes $-2 < 20$. Both are true statements.

9. A: Converting a fraction to a percentage takes two steps. First, divide the numerator by the denominator to turn the fraction into a decimal:

$$\frac{2}{9} = 0.2222 \dots$$

The "..." indicates a repeating decimal with an infinite number of 2's.

Now, to convert to a percentage, move the decimal point two places to the right:

$$22.22\%$$

10. A: The volume of a cone is $(\pi r^2 h)$ divided by 3, and $(\pi \times 10^2 \times 12)$, divided by 3, is 400 cm³. Choice B is $10^2 \times 2$. Choice C is incorrect because it is 10×12. Choice D is also incorrect because that is $10^2 + 40$.

11. A: Converting a fraction to a percentage takes two steps. First, divide the numerator by the denominator to turn the fraction into a decimal:

$$\frac{3}{8} = 0.375$$

249

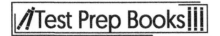

Now, to convert to a percentage, move the decimal point two places to the right:

$$37.5\%$$

12. B: 300 miles in four hours is $\frac{300}{4} = 75$ miles per hour. In 1.5 hours, the car will go 1.5×75 miles, or 112.5 miles.

13. A: Divide the total amount by the number of days:

$$\frac{\$150}{4} = 37.50$$

So, she needs to save an average of $37.50 per day.

14. C: $40N$ would be 4,000% of N. All of the other coefficients are equivalent to $\frac{40}{100}$ or 40%.

15. C: An x-intercept is the point where the graph crosses the x-axis. At this point, the value of y is 0. To determine if an equation has an x-intercept of -2, substitute -2 for x, and calculate the value of y. If the value of -2 for x corresponds with a y-value of 0, then the equation has an x-intercept of -2. The only answer choice that produces this result is Choice C.

$$0 = (-2)^2 + 5(-2) + 6$$

16. A: The total fraction taken up by green and red shirts will be:

$$\frac{1}{3} + \frac{2}{5} = \frac{5}{15} + \frac{6}{15} = \frac{11}{15}$$

The remaining fraction is:

$$1 - \frac{11}{15} = \frac{15}{15} - \frac{11}{15} = \frac{4}{15}$$

17. C: If Shawna has used $\frac{1}{3}$ of the paint, she has $\frac{2}{3}$ remaining. The mixed fraction can be converted because $2\frac{1}{2}$ gallons is the same as $\frac{5}{2}$ gallons. The calculation is:

$$\frac{2}{3} \times \frac{5}{2} = \frac{10}{6} = \frac{5}{3} = 1\frac{2}{3} \text{ gallons}$$

18. D:

$$9x + x - 7 = 16 + 2x \qquad \text{Combine } 9x \text{ and } x.$$

$$10x - 7 = 16 + 2x$$

$$10x - 7 + 7 = 16 + 2x + 7 \qquad \text{Add 7 to both sides to remove } (-7).$$

$$10x = 23 + 2x$$

$$10x - 2x = 23 + 2x - 2x \qquad \text{Subtract } 2x \text{ from both sides to move it to the other side of the equation.}$$

$$8x = 23$$

$$\frac{8x}{8} = \frac{23}{8} \qquad \text{Divide by 8 to get } x \text{ by itself.}$$

$$x = \frac{23}{8}$$

19. A: Parallel lines have the same slope. The slope of the given equation is 3. The slope of Choice C can be seen to be $\frac{1}{3}$ by dividing both sides by 3. The other choices are in standard form $Ax + By = C$, for which the slope is given by $\frac{-A}{B}$. For Choice A, the equation can be written as $6x - 2y = -2$. Therefore, the slope is:

$$\frac{-A}{B} = \frac{-6}{-2} = 3$$

This is the same as the given equation. The slope of Choice B is:

$$\frac{-A}{B} = \frac{-4}{-1} = 4$$

The slope of Choice B is 4. The slope of Choice D is:

$$\frac{-A}{B} = \frac{-2}{-2} = 1$$

The slope of Choice D is 1. Therefore, the only equation with a parallel slope of 3 is $6x - 2y = -2$.

20. B: The origin is (0,0). The slope is given by $\frac{(y^2 - y^1)}{(x^2 - x^1)} = \frac{1 - 0}{2 - 0} = \frac{1}{2}$.

The y-intercept will be 0 since it passes through the origin. Using slope-intercept form, the equation for this line is:

$$y = \frac{1}{2}x$$

21. D: The slope is given by the change in y divided by the change in x. The change in y is $2 - 0 = 2$, and the change in x is $0 - (-4) = 4$. The slope is $\frac{2}{4} = \frac{1}{2}$.

22. D: "Sum" means the result of addition, so "the sum of twice a number and one" can be written as 2x+1. Next, "three times the sum of twice a number and one" would be $3(2x + 1)$. Finally, "six less than three times the sum of twice a number and one" would be $3(2x + 1) - 6$.

23. C: The coordinates of a point are written as an ordered pair (x, y). To determine the x-coordinate, a line is traced directly above or below the point until reaching the x-axis. This step notes the value on the x-axis. In this case, the x-coordinate is -3. To determine the y-coordinate, a line is traced directly to the right or left of the point until reaching the y-axis, which notes the value on the y-axis. In this case, the y-coordinate is 2. Therefore, the current ordered pair is written $(-3, 2)$. To reflect the point over the x-axis, the x-coordinate stays the same, but the y-coordinate becomes -2, since after a refection over the x-axis, the point would be located equivalently far below the x-axis as it is above the x-axis. Since the current y-coordinate is 2, the y-coordinate would become -2.

24. C: Let r be the number of red cans and b be the number of blue cans. One equation is $r + b = 10$. The total price is \$16, and given the prices for each can, the second equation is $1r + 2b = 16$. Multiplying the first equation on both sides by -1 results in $-r - b = -10$. Add this equation to the second equation, leaving $b = 6$. So, she bought 6 *blue* cans. From the first equation, this means $r = 4$; thus, she bought 4 *red* cans.

25. B: To be directly proportional means that $y = kx$. If x is changed from 5 to 20, the value of x is multiplied by 4. Applying the same rule to the y-value, also multiply the value of y by 4. Therefore:

$$y = 12$$

26. D: Solve a linear inequality in a similar way to solving a linear equation. First, start by distributing the -3 on the left side of the inequality.

$$-3x - 12 \geq x + 8$$

Then, add 12 to both sides.

$$-3x \geq x + 20$$

Next, subtract x from both sides.

$$-4x \geq 20$$

Finally, divide both sides of the inequality by -4. Don't forget to flip the inequality sign because you are dividing by a negative number.

$$x \leq -5$$

27. A: First, simplify the larger fraction by separating it into two. First, simplify the larger fractions by separating it into two. When dividing one fraction by another, remember to invert the second fraction and multiply the two as follows:

$$\frac{5}{7} \div \frac{9}{11} = \frac{5}{7} \times \frac{11}{9}$$

The resulting fraction $\frac{55}{63}$ cannot be simplified further, so this is the answer to the problem.

28. D: The slope is given by the change in y divided by the change in x. Specifically, it's:

$$slope = \frac{y_2 - y_1}{x_2 - x_1}$$

The first point is $(-5, -3)$, and the second point is $(0, -1)$. Work from left to right when identifying coordinates. Thus, the point on the left is point 1 $(-5, -3)$ and the point on the right is point 2 $(0, -1)$.

252

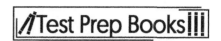

Now we just need to plug those numbers into the equation:

$$slope = \frac{-1-(-3)}{0-(-5)}$$

It can be simplified to:

$$slope = \frac{-1+3}{0+5}$$

$$slope = \frac{2}{5}$$

29. B: The figure is composed of three sides of a square and a semicircle. The sides of the square are simply added:

$$8 \text{ in} + 8 \text{ in} + 8 \text{ in} = 24 \text{ in}$$

The circumference of a circle is found by the equation $C = 2\pi r$. The radius is 4 in, so the circumference of the circle is approximately 25.13 in. Only half of the circle makes up the outer border of the figure (part of the perimeter), and half of 25.13 in is 12.565 in. Therefore, the total perimeter is:

$$24 \text{ in} + 12.565 \text{ in} = 36.565 \text{ in}$$

The other answer choices use the incorrect formula or fail to include all of the necessary sides.

30. B: A rectangle is a specific type of parallelogram. It has 4 right angles. A square is a rhombus that has 4 right angles. Therefore, a square is always a rectangle because it has two sets of parallel lines and 4 right angles.

31. C: The number line below can be labeled with all 4 given numbers.

The number 5 is shown with the open dot. By observing the placement of the dots and their relation to the open dot at 5, the number -1 can be eliminated as an answer because it is the closest. After that, the distance to the other dots can be counted. The distance is shown below with the arcs.

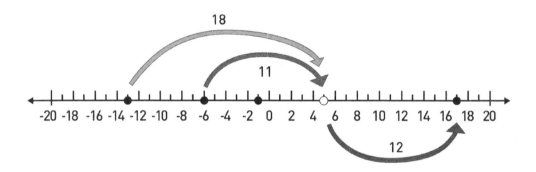

As demonstrated from the arcs showing distance on the number line, the number -13 is furthest from 5 on the number line, at a distance of 18.

32. B: Start by squaring both sides to get $1 + x = 16$. Then, subtract 1 from both sides to get $x = 15$.

33. A: Putting the scores in order from least to greatest, we have 60, 75, 80, and 85, as well as one unknown. The median is 80, so 80 must be the middle data point out of these five. Therefore, the unknown data point must be the fourth or fifth data point, meaning it must be greater than or equal to 80. The only answer that fails to meet this condition is 60.

34. C: The volume of a rectangular prism *is $V = length \times width \times height$*. Substituting the values given in the problem, we find $V = 2 \times 4 \times 6 = 48$.

35. A: The volume of a cylinder is $\pi r^2 h$ and $\pi \times 5^2 \times 10$ is 250π in^3.

36. A: Let the unknown score be x. The average will be:

$$\frac{5 \times 50 + 4 \times 70 + x}{10} = \frac{530 + x}{10} = 55$$

Multiply both sides by 10 to get $530 + x = 550$, or $x = 20$.

37. B: An equilateral triangle has 3 sides of equal length, so if the total perimeter is 18 feet, each side must be 6 feet long. A square with sides of 6 feet will have an area of $6^2 = 36$ square feet.

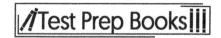
38. A: Operations within the parentheses must be completed first. Division is completed next, and finally, addition. When adding decimals, digits within each place value are added together. Therefore, the expression is evaluated as:

$$(2 \times 20) \div (7 + 1) + (6 \times 0.01) + (4 \times 0.001)$$

$$40 \div 8 + 0.06 + 0.004$$

$$5 + 0.06 + 0.004 = 5.064$$

39. D: To find Denver's total snowfall, 3 must be multiplied by $27\frac{3}{4}$. In order to easily do this, the mixed number should be converted into an improper fraction.

$$27\frac{3}{4} = \frac{27 \times 4 + 3}{4} = \frac{111}{4}$$

Therefore, Denver had approximately $\frac{3 \times 111}{4} = \frac{333}{4}$ inches of snow. The improper fraction can be converted back into a mixed number through division.

$$\frac{333}{4} = 83\frac{1}{4} \text{ inches}$$

40. C: Set up the initial equation.

$$\frac{2x}{5} - 1 = 59$$

Add 1 to both sides.

$$\frac{2x}{5} - 1 + 1 = 59 + 1$$

$$\frac{2x}{5} = 60$$

Multiply both sides by $\frac{5}{2}$.

$$\frac{2x}{5} \times \frac{5}{2} = \frac{60}{1} \times \frac{5}{2}$$

$$x = 150$$

41. C: We can first find the total cost of the hat and jersey, then multiply by 0.5 to apply the 50% off:

$$(32.99 + 64.99) \times 0.5 = 48.99$$

Finally, we calculate the sales tax of 6% (that is, 0.06) and add it to the total:

$$48.99 + (48.99 \times 0.06) = 51.93$$

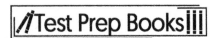

42. D: List the givens.

$$\text{Store coffee} = \frac{\$1.23}{\text{lb}}$$

$$\text{Local roaster's coffee} = \frac{\$1.98}{1.5\ \text{lb}}$$

Calculate the cost for 5 pounds of the store-brand coffee.

$$\frac{\$1.23}{1\ \text{lb}} \times 5\ \text{lb} = \$6.15$$

Calculate the cost for 5 pounds of the local roaster's coffee.

$$\frac{\$1.98}{1.5\ \text{lb}} \times 5\ \text{lb} = \$6.60$$

Subtract to find the difference in price for 5 pounds.

$$\begin{array}{r} \$6.60 \\ -\$6.15 \\ \hline \$0.45 \end{array}$$

43. D: Find how many feet are left after the first 1,800 ft:

$$3{,}125\ \text{ft}$$

$$\underline{-1{,}800\ \text{ft}}$$

$$1{,}325\ \text{ft}$$

At $1 per foot, this part will cost $1,325. Add this to the $2,000 for the first 1,800 ft to get the total cost:

$$\$2{,}000 + \$1{,}325 = \$3{,}325$$

44. D: First, the train's journey in the real world is $3 \times 50 = 150$ miles. On the map, 1 inch corresponds to 10 miles, so there is $\frac{150}{10} = 15$ inches on the map.

45. B: The total trip time is:

$$1 + 3.5 + 0.5 = 5\ \text{hours}$$

The total time driving is:

$$1 + 0.5 = 1.5\ \text{hours}$$

So, the fraction of time spent driving is $\frac{1.5}{5}$ or $\frac{3}{10}$. To convert this to a percentage, multiply the top and bottom by 10 to make the denominator 100. We find $\frac{3}{10} \times \frac{10}{10} = \frac{30}{100}$. Since the denominator is 100, the numerator is our percentage: 30%.

256

46. A: The value went up by:

$$\$165,000 - \$150,000 = \$15,000$$

Out of $150,000, this is:

$$\frac{15,000}{150,000} = \frac{1}{10}$$

If we multiply the top and bottom by 10 to give us a denominator of 100, the result is $\frac{10}{100}$, or 10%.

47. B: The journey will be $5 \times 3 = 15$ miles. A car traveling at 60 miles per hour is traveling at 1 mile per minute. The resulting equation would be:

$$\frac{15 \text{ mi}}{1 \text{ mi/min}} = 15 \text{ min}$$

Therefore, it will take 15 minutes to make the journey.

Reading Comprehension

1. B: This item asks you to determine the purpose of this passage. Choice *B* is the correct answer because the passage is written to inform readers about companies that offer more modern means of transportation. Choice *A* is incorrect because the author does not promote either company in the passage. Choice *C* is incorrect because the author does not try to persuade readers to schedule a ride for their children, and Choice *D* is incorrect because the author only makes a brief statement about conventional methods of transportation in the first sentence.

2. A: This item asks you to determine which statement can be supported based on information that is given in the passage. Choice *A* is the correct answer because the text explains how parents can use DeerHaul to help transport their children when they are unavailable. Choices *B* and *D* are incorrect because the third paragraph explains who can drive for DeerHaul and what safety precautions are taken by the company. Choice *C* is incorrect because the author offers no opinion on which company is the better option.

3. D: Your task here is to use information from the text to determine which detail is correct. The passage explains how payments are made electronically through the app. Choice *A* is incorrect since buses and subways are considered public transportation. Choices *B* and *C* are incorrect because when payments are made and tipping are not discussed in the article.

4. C: In this context, battery is synonymous with series, so the correct answer is *C*. Although a battery can be a cell used to provide power to something, an artillery of guns, or an act of violence, none of these are the meaning that best fits this sentence. Thus, Choices *A, B,* and *D* are incorrect.

5. B: Choice *B* is correct because the most prevalent idea in the passage is the accessibility of transportation. Choice *A* is incorrect because it is a supporting detail. Choices *C* and *D* are introductory sentences for their paragraphs. They do not represent the entire text.

6. A: Choice *A* is correct because both the second and third paragraphs explain a means of private transportation. Choices *B, C,* and *D* are incorrect because the author does not offer an opinion on the best method of transportation or the best company to use.

7. A: Choice *A* is correct because the passage discusses how a department store's advertising project made Rudolph a famous Christmas tradition. Choice *B* is mentioned in the passage as a supporting detail. Choices *C* and *D* are not mentioned in the passage.

8. B: The passage explains that Rudolph leads Santa's team through a blizzard, making him "the most famous reindeer of all", so Choice *B* is the correct answer. The passage does not support the claims made in answers *A*, *C*, or *D*.

9. B: Originally, May was asked to create a promotional coloring book, so Choice *B* is correct. The passage does not support the claims made in choices *A*, *C*, or *D*.

10. D: Your task here is to identify the meaning of the word *misfit*. The word *misfit* means "oddball," so Choice *D* is correct. The words *member, conformist,* and *insider* are all antonyms, or opposites, for the word *misfit,* so Choices *A, B,* and *C* are incorrect.

11. C: This item asks you to identify the author's tone in this passage. The author's tone is informative, so Choice *C* is correct. The author is not humorous, apologetic, or sad in this passage, so Choices *A, B,* and *D* are incorrect.

12. C: Your task here is to determine which type of figurative language the phrase *Rudolph the Red-Nosed Reindeer* represents. Choice *C*, alliteration, is correct. Alliteration is the repetition of a consonant at the beginning of multiple consecutive words. Because no comparison is made in this phrase (simile or metaphor) and the phrase is not an onomatopoeia (a word that is formed by its sound), Choices *A, B,* and *D* are incorrect.

13. A: This item asks you to identify information in the passage. Sentence 7 indicates that as the temperature of water increases, water molecules move rapidly and spread farther apart, so Choice *A* is correct.

14. A: This item asks you to draw a conclusion based on information learned in the text. Choice *A* is correct because as water vapor cools, the water molecules move closer together and move more slowly to form a liquid.

15. A: The question asks which sentence best represents the main idea in the passage. The passage discusses water having the ability to occupy three states of matter, so Choice *A* is the correct answer. Choices *B, C,* and *D* are main ideas for support paragraphs in the passage, so they are incorrect.

16. D: Your task here is to determine the meaning of the word *molecules*. Molecules are tiny units, or particles, of something, so Choice *D* is correct. Choices *A, B,* and *C* are antonyms for the word *molecule,* so they are incorrect.

17. B: This item asks you to identify specific details in the passage. Because steam, also known as *water vapor,* is water in the form of gas, Choice *B* is correct.

18. D: *Conversely* is a word used to mean "the other way around." The words for choices *A, B,* and *C* say the opposite thing and are incorrect.

19. C: This item asks you to determine the main purpose of this passage. The author tells this sad story to illustrate the impact texting while driving can have, not just on the driver, but also on the passengers, so Choice *C* is correct.

20. B: Your task here is to identify the type of figurative language in the passage. Choice *B* is correct because the phrase *screeched like an alley cat* is a simile. A simile is a comparison of two similar things (the sound of the tires and the screech of an alley cat) using the words *like* or *as.* Choice *A* is incorrect because a metaphor does not contain the words *like* or *as.* An alliteration is the repetition of a consonant sound at the beginning of several consecutive words.

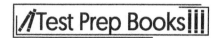

21. A: This item asks you to identify the story's point of view. Choice *A* is correct because the story is told from a first-person point of view. In first-person narratives, the author is a character in the story and uses words such as *I*, *me*, and *we*. Second person, Choice *B*, which is uncommon, includes words such as *you*, *your*, and *yours*. In third person, Choice *C*, narratives, the narrator is not a character in the story and uses words such as *he*, *she*, and *they*. Choice *D*, fourth person, is a made-up choice.

22. A: This task asks you to draw a conclusion based on information provided in the last sentence of the passage. The author says that Ricky, Bobby, and Alyssa never got to see the dancing lights of the ambulances and police cars. Thus, readers can conclude that they didn't survive the accident.

23. B: This task asks you to determine the overall message of this passage. This story serves to highlight the potential consequences of texting and driving to dissuade readers from doing it. This means Choice *B* is the answer.

24. C: This item asks you to examine details from the story. The first paragraph explains in detail how the girls' mothers wanted the day to be fun. Readers can conclude Choice *C* is the correct answer. The story includes no information to indicate *A* or *D* are correct. Choice *B* might be correct, but the text does not provide enough information for that conclusion.

25. C: This item asks you to determine the type of passage. Choice *C*, an obituary, is the correct answer. Obituaries are biographies written to honor someone who has passed away.

26. B: This question asks the meaning of the phrase *in lieu of* in the last paragraph. *In lieu of* means "instead of"; thus, the family is requesting that instead of sending flowers, people donate money to Princess Diana's memorial fund.

27. B: This item asks you to use details in the story to determine what Princess Diana was passionate about. Paragraph three explains her dedication to charity work, so Choice *B* is the correct answer.

28. C: This item asks you to use details in the story to determine a sequence of events. Sentence 3 explains that after school, Princess Diana became a teacher's assistant, so Choice *C* is the correct answer.

29. B: This item asks you to make an inference based on information from the passage. The passage explains that Diana did a great deal of charity work for children in need. The passage also states that the family is asking mourners to donate to the Diana, Princess of Wales Memorial Fund instead of purchasing flowers for the funeral. Readers can safely assume at least some of the donation money will help needy children, so Choice *B* is correct.

30. A: This item asks you to analyze the organization of the passage. Choice *A* is correct because basic information given about Princess Diana's life is followed by current events, such as details about the funeral and where to send donations.

31. C: This item asks you to determine the meaning of a specific phrase in the passage. Idioms are phrases that take on a meaning different from the inherent meaning of the words, like *running the roads*. This means the correct answer is *C*.

32. D: The task here is to draw a conclusion based on information from the text. Throughout the passage, the author speaks of ways Mr. Walter touched the lives of everyone in the town of Vinson, so Choice *D* is correct.

33. B: This item asks you to decide how this passage is categorized. This passage is considered a short story because it has a message, a sequence of events, and characters. Thus, Choice *B* is correct.

34. A: This item asks you to identify details in the passage. Choice *A* is correct because sentence 7 tells readers that Mr. Walter gave out gloves and hats during the winter to children who needed them.

35. B: This item asks you to identify the overall message in this passage. Choice *B* is correct because the author is trying to point out that heroes can be everyday people who consistently do little things in their communities to impact the lives of others.

36. A: This item asks you to identify the type of figurative language used in the phrase *leapt tall buildings in a single bound.* A hyperbole is an exaggeration not meant to be taken literally, so Choice *A* is correct.

Index

Factors, 10, 34, 47, 48, 49, 50, 145, 151, 172, 247, 249
Fallacy, 130
False Analogy, 130
False Dichotomy, 130
Fantasy, 125
Fiction Genres, 124
Figurative Language, 123, 135, 188
Fraction, 30, 31, 34, 35, 42, 43, 45, 49, 50, 51, 54, 55, 56, 57, 58, 59, 61, 98, 111, 112, 206, 230, 232, 249, 250, 252, 255, 256
Fractional Exponents, 60
Function, 49, 130, 152, 153, 218, 222, 230, 243
Fundamental Theorem of Arithmetic, 47
Greatest Common Factor (GCF)
    GCF, 48, 50
Guiding Idea, 216
Improper Fractions, 49
Inference, 117, 119, 122, 259
Inferences, 117, 118, 120
Integers, 42, 43
Intersecting Lines, 90
Introduction, 20, 162, 163
Isosceles Triangle, 76
Joint Frequencies, 65
Lateral Faces, 79, 80
Least Common Multiple (LCM)
    LCM, 48
Line of Symmetry, 91
Line Segment, 74, 75, 90
Logical Fallacy, 130
Logical Relationships, 137
Logos, 138
Main Idea, 9, 115, 116, 117, 118, 131, 132, 133, 142, 143, 164, 186, 212, 213, 237, 239, 258
Mean, 21, 41, 102, 103, 104, 105, 120, 123, 131, 144, 145, 146, 150, 151, 154, 168, 169, 182, 185, 186, 191, 204, 206, 210, 214, 215, 216, 218, 258
Median, 64, 102, 103, 104, 105, 106, 107, 108, 179, 204, 223, 233, 245
Memoir, 127
Message, 116, 124, 130, 133, 134, 157, 240, 242, 259, 260
Metric System, 97
Mixed Numbers, 49
Molecule, 258
    Molecules, 238, 239, 258
Multiples, 47, 48
Multiplication, 24, 25, 32, 33, 34, 36, 37, 38, 52, 207, 208

Narrative, 123
Negative Exponents, 61
Nonfiction, 121, 126, 128
Nouns, 154
Nucleus, 161
Number Line, 23, 42, 43, 45, 46, 59, 60, 70, 99, 100, 108, 110, 173, 233, 253, 254
Numerator, 34, 49, 50, 51, 54, 55, 56, 57, 58, 60, 61, 97, 98, 202, 206
Object, 57, 88, 94, 96, 135, 153, 154, 156, 216, 218
Obtuse Angle, 90, 91, 92
Obtuse Triangle, 76, 91
Odd Numbers, 47
Opinion, 19, 20, 118, 121, 122, 123, 129, 138, 157, 183, 185, 186, 211, 212, 213, 241, 257
Opposite, 34, 38, 43, 59, 61, 62, 77, 83, 87, 119, 120, 146, 152, 161, 210, 212, 213, 218, 258
Order of Magnitude, 62
Ordered Pair, 100, 108, 109, 204, 229, 252
Outline, 121, 162, 163, 164, 216
Overgeneralization, 130
Paragraph, 115, 119, 121, 127, 141, 142, 143, 162, 163, 165, 166, 167, 182, 185, 186, 188, 189, 191, 210, 213, 257, 259
Parallel, 77, 79, 80, 81, 90, 91, 166, 174, 230, 251, 253
Parallelogram, 77, 84, 91, 253
Paraphrasing, 131, 132
Part of Speech, 148
Pathos, 138
PEMDAS, 37, 61, 206, 208
Percentages, 45, 46, 53, 54, 56, 65, 107
Perfect Squares, 40, 62, 63
Perimeter, 81, 216, 227
Perpendicular Lines, 91, 203
Persuasive, 116, 123, 124, 127, 138, 242
Place Value System, 44
Plagiarizing, 119
Poetic Structure, 126
Poetry, 125, 126, 187, 197
Point of View, 136
Points, 20, 64, 71, 80, 81, 90, 99, 100, 101, 102, 103, 105, 106, 107, 108, 110, 111, 116, 117, 119, 130, 149, 162, 164, 166, 204, 211, 212, 218
Polygon, 75, 76, 80, 81, 85, 86, 175, 203
    Polygons, 74, 75, 76
Polyhedrons, 79, 80
Prefix, 146, 147, 215
Prepositions, 154, 157
Prime Factorization, 49

Dear ISEE/SSAT Test Taker,

Thank you for purchasing this study guide for your ISEE/SSAT exam. We hope that we exceeded your expectations.

Our goal in creating this study guide was to cover all of the topics that you will see on the test. We also strove to make our practice questions as similar as possible to what you will encounter on test day. With that being said, if you found something that you feel was not up to your standards, please send us an email and let us know.

We would also like to let you know about another book in our catalog that may interest you.

SSAT Upper

amazon.com/dp/1637755570

We have study guides in a wide variety of fields. If the one you are looking for isn't listed above, then try searching for it on Amazon or send us an email.

Thanks Again and Happy Testing!
Product Development Team
info@studyguideteam.com

FREE Test Taking Tips Video/DVD Offer

To better serve you, we created videos covering test taking tips that we want to give you for FREE. **These videos cover world-class tips that will help you succeed on your test.**

We just ask that you send us feedback about this product. Please let us know what you thought about it—whether good, bad, or indifferent.

To get your **FREE videos**, you can use the QR code below or email freevideos@studyguideteam.com with "Free Videos" in the subject line and the following information in the body of the email:

     a. The title of your product

     b. Your product rating on a scale of 1-5, with 5 being the highest

     c. Your feedback about the product

If you have any questions or concerns, please don't hesitate to contact us at info@studyguideteam.com.

Thank you!

SCAN HERE

Made in the USA
Las Vegas, NV
04 November 2024

11155492R00151